3 1215 00041 9413

PRIVILEGED COMMUNICATION AND THE PRESS

Contributions in Political Science
Series Editor: Bernard K. Johnpoll

The New Left in France: The Unified Socialist Party
Charles Hauss

The Communist Parties of Western Europe: A Comparative Study
R. Neal Tannahill

France's Vietnam Policy: A Study in French-American Relations
Marianna P. Sullivan

The Capitol Press Corps: Newsmen and the Governing of New York State
David Morgan

The McNamara Strategy and the Vietnam War: Program Budgeting in the Pentagon, 1960–1968
Gregory Palmer

On the Edge of Politics: The Roots of Jewish Political Thought in America
William S. Berlin

Water's Edge: Domestic Politics and the Making of American Foreign Policy
Paula Stern

Ideological Coalitions in Congress
Jerrold E. Schneider

Constitutional Language: An Interpretation of Judicial Decision
John Brigham

Marx and the Proletariat: A Study in Social Theory
Timothy McCarthy

Maurice Van Gerpen

PRIVILEGED COMMUNICATION AND THE PRESS

THE CITIZEN'S RIGHT TO KNOW VERSUS THE LAW'S RIGHT TO CONFIDENTIAL NEWS SOURCE EVIDENCE

Contributions in Political Science, Number 19

GREENWOOD PRESS
WESTPORT, CONNECTICUT • LONDON, ENGLAND

Library of Congress Cataloging in Publication Data
Van Gerpen, Maurice.
    Privileged communication and the press.

    (Contributions in political science; no. 19
ISSN 0147-1066)
    Bibliography: p.
    Includes index.
    1. Confidential communications—Press—
United States.   I. Title.   II. Series.
KF8959.P7V3   343'.73'0998   78-55334
ISBN 0-313-20523-X

Library of Congress Catalog Card Number: 78-55334
ISBN: 0-313-20523-X
ISSN: 0147-1066

First published in 1979

Greenwood Press, Inc.
51 Riverside Avenue, Westport, Connecticut 06880

Printed in the United States of America

10 9 8 7 6 5 4 3 2 1

To my wife, Nora, and our children, Kendrick and Lorelei,
who with their patience and understanding
collaborated in this work.

Contents

Preface

This book comes at a time when the issue of privileged communication and the press is as unresolved as ever. Journalists are still vulnerable to compulsory process to reveal sources. Judges and attorneys are uncertain about where to draw the lines on this issue, and decisions in the courts have veered in several directions. The public is confused. State laws attempting to resolve the impasse have only created more controversy over interpretations and qualifications. The effort to establish a constitutional right to refuse to divulge confidences has created more confusion than clarity. Congress has attempted but thus far has failed to produce legislation creating more orderly contours to the problem. Journalists are more divided now over the ultimate remedy than they were some time ago. They have come to fear that statutory remedy may create such a range of exceptions to the privilege as to swallow it.

In spite of this pessimistic account, some progress can be noted. In the past several years many more states have adopted laws intending to clarify the situation. At both state and national levels there is now much greater awareness of what the legislative difficulties are, and a winnowing process has begun. The least acceptable alternatives have been rejected by various sides in the controversy. The Supreme Court of the United States has for the first time confronted the issue at its most abrasive points, and although the ruling falls short of being definitive, it has led to decisions in lower federal courts that are following similar paths in interpreting the Supreme Court's ruling. Thus, for the time being, it appears that the issue has attained a maturity and ripeness that may lead to ways of resolving some of its more important aspects.

If the analysis could be left with the aforementioned comments, the future would be less clouded. Later Court rulings going beyond the subpoena issue to newsroom search and media access to prisons have greatly disturbed the press community.

Acknowledgments

I want to extend my sincerest thanks to those faculty members at the University of California at Santa Barbara who first reviewed this manuscript. C. Herman Pritchett carefully read the chapters as they developed and provided useful suggestions. Stanley E. Anderson was encouraging and helpful. Raghavan Iyer helped with the conclusion and suggested possibilities for the publication of this work.

I also wish to express special thanks to James Bort, Jr., former city editor and presently ombudsman for the *Fresno Bee* of Fresno, California; Jeff Wall, attorney with the firm of Fullerton, Lang, Richert, and Patch, of Fresno; and Max E. Robinson, Fresno County assistant county counsel. They supplied me with the information and materials that enabled me to obtain a firsthand account of a press subpoena case.

PRIVILEGED COMMUNICATION AND THE PRESS

CHAPTER 1

The American Historical Record of Press–Subpoena Confrontations: Inquiries by Legislative, Administrative, and Judicial Officers

THE ISSUE

In a constitutional democracy there are at least two principles that are assumed. One is that the public has the right to know what is happening in the political system. The other is that the public through its prosecutors and defense counselors has the right to everyman's evidence.

In fulfillment of the first principle the press acts to convey political information that in turn enables the public to check its government. Although the press is only one aspect of the check-and-balance system, which includes the separation of powers, a federal system, and party and interest group competition, it has become one of the most controversial elements in this system of accountability in recent years.

It is over the application of the second principle that the debate has been intensified between government and press protagonists. Many spokesmen for the press note that the rules of evidence do not absolutely require everyman's evidence. They observe that various forms of privileged communication have long been legally recognized. Executive, legislative, and judicial privilege shields communications of governmental officials. In the private realm there are many recognized forms of privileged communication between the following: attorney-client, doctor-patient, husband-wife, psychiatrist-subject, fiduciary-client, social worker-recipient, priest-penitent, informer-government, juror-juror, broker-investor, banker-borrower, banker-depositor; there are also trade secrets and the secret ballot.[1] The aforementioned privileges are not universally recognized in all of the states of the United States. Advocates of the press privilege do not want to appeal for recognition as merely another interest seeking equal protection along with other privileged groups. They prefer to view their request for source confidentiality within the context of the public's right to know about corruption or other government wrongdoing that might not otherwise be disclosed without anonymous sources. They believe that government will be less secretive and authoritarian and more open and democratic if journalists are provided greater protection in the area of source disclosure and information flowing therefrom.

On the other hand, opponents of a press privilege believe that evidence of wrongdoing will be kept from the institutions of law enforcement and adjudication, evidence that is necessary to convict the guilty or to exonerate those whose reputations have come under attack. The opponents also believe that privilege such as the one journalists are seeking will be abused and turned into irresponsible gossip.

If newsmen's privilege had never been recognized prior to the debate over the conflicting principles of the public's right to be informed versus the needs of prosecuting and defense attorneys to fulfill their roles, we could begin the debate without an involved historical preview. In like manner, if a Supreme Court decision had emerged that unequivocally elevated the public's right to be informed over the law's right to everyman's evidence or vice versa, this book could be more simply organized.

What in fact happened is that prior to the Surpeme Court's June 29, 1972, decision in *Branzburg*,[2] there had been recognition in various states of just such a right as newsmen were seeking from the Supreme Court that would apply nationally. Some federal judges also affirmed the right.[3] They were overturned by the Supreme Court, which ruled that requiring newsmen to appear and testify before state and federal grand juries does not abridge the freedom of speech and press guaranteed by the First Amendment. But the door was left open to Congress and the state legislatures to continue to address the issue. Justice White declared:

At the federal level, Congress has freedom to determine whether a statutory newsman's privilege is necessary and desirable and to fashion standards and rules as narrow or broad as deemed necessary to address the evil discerned and, equally important, to refashion those rules as experience from time to time may dictate. There is also merit in leaving state legislatures free, within First Amendment limits, to fashion their own standards in light of the conditions and problems with respect to the relations between law enforcement officials and press in their own areas. It goes without saying, of course, that we are powerless to erect any bar to state courts responding in their own way and construing their own constitutions so as to recognize a newsman's privilege, either qualified or absolute.[4]

Following the Court's ruling the issue came under legislative scrutiny. How quickly the legislative effort would gather momentum would depend greatly upon what courts would do with the *Branzburg, Caldwell, Pappas* decision (hereinafter referred to as the *Branzburg* decision). The subpoena challenges that led to the jailing of newsmen during the latter half of 1972 spurred the drafting of shield bills in the Congress and newsmen's privilege hearings in both the Senate and the House of Representatives in February and March 1973.

The legislative effort was revived in 1975.[5] In 1978 a new Court decision on newsroom search[6] led to renewed congressional interest in a press shield statute.[7]

THE FIRST REFUSAL TO DIVULGE CONFIDENCES

The name John Peter Zenger has long been associated with press freedom. In 1734 this courageous journalist dared to criticize a British colonial governor, one William Cosby, in the *New York Weekly Journal*. The principle of truth as a protection against libel charges had not yet been established in American jurisprudence. Fortunately for Zenger, the colonial public was angry with Cosby over what it perceived was his abuse of power.[8]

Zenger was arrested and charged with criminal libel. He spent nine months in jail before his trial. He was represented by a distinguished lawyer, Andrew Hamilton, who appealed to a friendly colonial jury for acquittal on the libel charge. In the colonies the jury was the final check on abuse of executive or judicial power, and the panel was persuaded that the reporter's candid coverage of charges embarrassing to the governor should not be punished. Thus a precedent was set whereby journalists could expose practices of public officials that might be used to hold them accountable to the people.

The concept of a testimonial privilege was not a legal issue at the trial, but the issue was raised in the broader historical setting. While in prison, Zenger refused to name the sources of his stories. The governor during this time was offering a reward of fifty pounds for the identity of the sources that had been used by Zenger.[9] Thus Zenger's silence became part of a trend toward press refusals to reveal sources. In the years that followed, other confrontations with government would continue to bring this issue to the fore.

NEWSMEN PROTECT SOURCES AGAINST LEGISLATIVE INQUIRIES

Benjamin Franklin was another of the early American journalists to be involved in a subpoena controversy that began with a legislative body. In his autobiography he stated:

One of the Pieces in our News-Paper, on some political Point which I have now forgotten, gave Offence to the Assembly. He was taken up, censur'd and imprison'd for a Month by the Speaker's Warrant, I suppose because he would not discover his Author. I too was taken up and examin'd before the Council; but tho' I did not give them any Satisfaction, they contented themselves with admonishing me, and dismiss's me; considering me perhaps as an Apprentice who was bound to keep his Master's Secrets.[10]

Coming after the Revolution and Constitutional Convention, the Bill of Rights spoke in general terms of freedom of the press. There is no evidence that reporter's privilege to protect confidences was a discussion topic when the first ten amendments were drafted and adopted. One could argue that the reference to compulsory process in the Sixth Amendment implied forced disclosure of sources and information.

The next subpoena conflict occurred several decades later and involved conflict-of-interest charges reminiscent of the current Korean lobby pressure in the Ninety-fifth Congress. In January 1857 the *New York Times* used an editorial[11] to criticize lobbying activity in Congress whereby a number of congressmen were being paid as much as $1,500 if they would vote in accordance with the wishes of certain interest groups. As a result of the *Times* coverage, an investigating committee probed the charges. One of the congressmen even began to corroborate the charges. Instead of pursuing his story, the committee sought out the reporter covering the initial press exposé. When this journalist, Simonton, refused to reveal his sources for the information, he was ordered to jail. The House of Representatives voted to uphold the contempt by a vote of 136 to 23. After nineteen days the committee released Simonton for two reasons. First, they doubted that he would reveal his sources. Second, they learned that the charges were true without learning the sources for the news story. The House members involved resigned rather than endure further investigation as with the case of House member Wayne Hayes in 1976.

During the Simonton episode, there was little reference to or support for the journalist privilege. There was still no legislation on the subject, and the common law was opposed to such a concept. Statements of constitutional law would not reach the issue until a century later.

In the twenty years following the 1857 confrontation more than a dozen similar conflicts occurred. The *New York Evening Post* published an article on June 7, 1870, charging that Cuban leaders had spent a great deal of money trying to influence congressional votes over the recognition of the Cuban republic.

Scott Smith, who authored the article, based his account on tips from a confidential informant. He agreed to testify when summoned but refused to identify his informants. There was a threat to expel him from the House reporters' gallery, but upon further examination of the matter the matter was dropped.[12]

One year later, in 1871, a third New York paper, the *New York Tribune,* published an official document relating to a diplomatic matter, the Treaty of Washington, which was being considered by the Senate. Confusion resulted when different standards were established by the executive and legislative branches of the government over classification of the treaty. The secretary of state had already released a summary of the treaty to the press. The President favored the release of the text. But the Senate ruled that it be classified. Two reporters, White and Ramsdell, were subpoenaed by a Senate committee for the purpose of revealing who gave them a copy of the treaty. They refused to comply and were jailed. They rested refusal on the grounds of professional honor. Their editor moved to double their salaries for the time spent in jail.

In commenting on their case, Senator Carpenter was very concerned about the supremacy of law when he declared:

The consequence of this proposition is that the privilege of a newspaper correspondent overrides the Constitution of the United States and the acts of Congress passed in pursuance thereof, which by the Constitution itself are declared to be the supreme law of the land.[13]

The *Tribune* complained that it was not in business to keep the government's secrets, especially in cases in which there was great confusion within the government over whether material should be classified.

Finally, the two were released when the Senate concluded that it did not have the constitutional power to hold them beyond the close of the legislative session. Thus the press again was able, with mixed success, to challenge authority on this question because of uncertainty within officialdom over how to resolve the competing interests.

Conflict of interest and testimonial privilege were in the center of the legislative arena once again in 1894. This was a period rife with criticism of the trusts and the best senators their money could buy. Two newspapers, the *Philadelphia Press* and the *New York Mail and Express,* were now involved in reporting allegations that certain senators had taken bribes from sugar trust lobbyists in exchange for favorable votes on the Wilson-Gorman tariff bill. When summoned, reporters from both papers refused source disclosure before a grand jury and went to jail. The District of Columbia Supreme Court expressed its contempt for the journalists' refusal in these words:

Let it once be established that the editor or correspondent cannot be called upon in any proceeding to disclose the information upon which the publication in his journals are based, and the great barrier against libelous publication is at once stricken down, and the greatest possible temptation created to use the public press as a means of disseminating scandal, thereby tending to lessen, if not destroy its power and usefulness.[14]

When the *San Francisco Examiner* accused California state senators of abuse of office in 1897, two journalists were punished by the California Senate for contempt. The California Supreme Court affirmed the contempt action.[15]

In 1934 another state legislature was to confront the press over the privilege issue. When the *Louisville Courier-Journal* charged corruption in the legislature, a committee ordered disclosure of the names of the sources, and, upon refusal by the reporter, a fine of $25 was imposed.[16]

In 1943 the *Akron Beacon-Journal,* after confidential interviews with marines, reported that because of certain union rules seamen would refuse to unload military supplies on Guadalcanal on a Sunday. The story was widely reported, and a congressional inquiry summoned the city editor, but he refused to name sources. This committee appeared to be the first official body that recognized the refusal to supply source names.[17]

Two years later, a critical press account of medical programs for veterans stirred a House committee into probing for the sources behind the story. The reporter, Albert Deutsch, refused on the grounds of professional ethics and spent eleven days in jail for contempt.[18]

In 1952 the *Providence Journal and Bulletin* referred to upcoming hearings on charges against Senator Joseph McCarthy of Wisconsin. The reporter, Edwar Milne, was summoned to bring his notes and testify. When he refused to appear, the subpoena was withdrawn because the panel expressed its understanding of the newsman's obligation to his sources. Thus for a second time a House committee acknowledged the testimonial privilege.[19]

In 1963 a report on padded payrolls by Jack Anderson led a House committee to ask for names of informants. Anderson has very rigorously refused over the years to reveal confidences, because they were his most vital resource. After much legal maneuvering and constitutional argument with committee members, Anderson was released from further testimony when the committee chairman agreed with Anderson's interpretation of the Constitution. A third legislative acceptance of the press privilege argument was recorded.[20]

A similar result occurred the same year with Scripps-Howard reporter Kantor after he had written an article about the winner of the TFX warplane contract a month before the award was made. After refusing to divulge confidences, he was excused.[21]

On February 23, 1971, a highly controversial CBS News television documentary, "The Selling of the Pentagon," brought cries of anguish from military spokesmen. Vice-President Spiro Agnew referred to the programming and planning of the production as "cut and paste." Representative F. Edward Hebert, chairman of the House Armed Services Committee, filed an official complaint with the Federal Communications Commission, charging that the documentary's producers misleadingly edited film in order to disparage the Pentagon's publicity effort.[22] Representative Harley Staggers threatened to open an inquiry. The

Washington Post also challenged the film's production techniques. Richard Salant, CBS News president, saw the government attack as a Washington witch-hunt reminiscent of the prevailing atmosphere during the Ed Murrow–Joe McCarthy confrontation in 1954. He pictured himself as an "electronic John Peter Zenger."

The House committee asked for transcripts to verify the story's accuracy.[23] Salant thought that the issue was journalistic honesty rather than the presentation of a verbatim transcript. Time would not permit an aired presentation of all the footage. Following the widespread public attention generated by the documentary, it was rebroadcast by CBS on March 23. At the end of the program, critical comments by Vice-President Agnew, Secretary of Defense Laird, and Chairman Hebert were aired. Salant also issued a response to the criticism.[24]

The next act in the drama centered on an April 7 subpoena to CBS president, Frank Stanton, demanding the delivery of "all film, workprints, outtakes, sound-tape recordings, written scripts and/or transcripts" relating to the preparation of 'The Selling of the Pentagon.' The subpoena was issued under the authority of Representative Harley O. Staggers of West Virginia, who was chairman of the Special Subcommittee on Investigations of the House Interstate and Foreign Commerce Committee.

Stanton agreed to provide tapes of the program as it was shown on the air. But he refused to give the subcommittee any of the outtakes. He concluded his statement to the committee by reassuring them that the subpoena had not been taken lightly, but he declared:

We recognize that journalists can make mistakes, that editing involves the exercise of judgment, and that we and other journalists can benefit by criticism. But I respectfully submit that where journalistic judgments are investigated in a Congressional hearing, especially by the Committee with jurisdiction to legislate about broadcast licenses, the official effort to compel evidence about our editing processes has an unconstitutionally chilling effect.[25]

The subcommittee voted to cite CBS for contempt and brought the matter to the House floor. On July 13, 1971, the House voted 226 to 181 to recommit the motion to the committee, thus killing the move to find CBS in contempt of Congress.

In 1972 the *Memphis Commercial Appeal* reported that retarded children were being mistreated at a state hospital.[26] The Tennessee State Senate Committee on General Welfare and Environment began investigating. Although there was already ample evidence of the causes of the abuse, the committee preferred to probe twenty-one-year-old reporter Weiler instead. The committee wanted to stop the adverse publicity. It appeared to be more concerned with staff relations than with child abuse.

After being threatened with jail, Weiler was released from further testimonial obligation, in part because the committee was able to get source information from another reporter. The source, a secretary at the hospital, was suspended from her job.

Out of the welter of the fifteen incidents just related, there were five actual jailings, and one reporter came very close to being jailed. In three of the incidents committees recognized the newsman's privilege. In four of the confrontations the investigating bodies backed down from original subpoena demands early in the proceedings. There were two instances in which contempt was voted. In one case the contempt was not enforced, and in the other case it was reversed soon after it had been voted.

In the Simonton, Weiler, and Anderson incidents the newsmen's sources were definitely unnecessary to a disposition of the cases. In the Smith matter information had already been released by the government to the public, but the effort to seek the press source continued. It is unlikely that source information was even needed in the Smith, White, Ramsdell, Edwards, Shriver, and Lawrence confrontations. A fundamental conflict continues to repeat itself throughout the history of press-subpoena encounters. The government prefers that the public be informed by a governmental version of events and rationale for decisions. The press seeks to keep the door open to an independent appraisal of the situation. Journalists are becoming increasingly reluctant to print official handouts and more insistent on digging into events from an outsider's perspective.

In the instance involving the *New York Evening Post,* expulsion of the reporter from the press gallery would have destroyed his capacity for news gathering. The logical consequence of this action would be to destroy news dissemination of congressional activities by the *Post* for the time being. This newsman's successor would very likely be more cautious, and the ultimate effect would be to make the press less independent.

In the Simonton case the original source publicly charged fraud. He was not investigated, but the media was. The newspaper had only editorialized on the writings of the original source, who was known.

This pattern of investigative behavior creates difficulties for those who argue that press subpoenas are utilized to penetrate the roots of corruption and to uphold the principle that the law has the right to everyman's evidence. If the government consistently applied the information revealed under forced disclosure to a rigorous investigation of governmental wrongdoing, its case against journalist privilege might be easier to sell. The information has frequently not been employed for the correct disposal of litigation, but rather has been used to track down the originator of the embarrassing exposé. One might well question the appropriateness of the argument for the "laws's right to everyman's evidence" by investigators who pursue source disclosure for the purpose of establishing a successful cover-up operation.

NEWSMEN'S PRIVILEGE VERSUS SUBPOENA CHALLENGES BY DEPARTMENTS AND AGENCIES OF THE FEDERAL GOVERNMENT

In 1966, press accounts indicated before official confirmation that the government would expand the soy bean crop. This report benefited speculators. The Agriculture Department wanted to know the sources but respected the journalistic refusal by acknowledging the argument for confidentiality.[27]

In 1971 a syndicated columnist wrote a story that spurred a Federal Trade Commission (FTC) investigation into misleading sales tactics used by magazine publishers. A defense attorney for one of the corporations cited by the FTC tried to subpoena the reporter's notes but was prevented from doing so on the grounds that the material was not germane to the Hearst corporation's defense.[28]

Clearly, the confrontations the press has had with the Congress, state legislatures, and administrative agencies have varied in many respects. Nevertheless, there are some striking similarities, which point toward four general observations.

First, articles that have provoked subpoenas have contained allegations of official corruption or misconduct, or have been stories officials did not want the public to read, for one reason or another.

Second, as we have earlier indicated, legislative bodies and administrative agencies have not investigated the scandals exposed by journalists but have gone after the reporters who brought them to light. The rationale for deposing reporters has often been motivated by vengeance against a reporter or his sources, when instead, the concern should have been directed toward legislative interest in persistent problems.

Third, journalists have rarely revealed their sources.

Fourth, in many cases, the legislative branch and the administrative agencies have been reluctant to take on the more courageous reporters. Public opinion may be a factor, because jail terms for reporters rally defenders to the journalist cause, and the politician or bureaucrat may look like the authoritarian culprit confronting the underdog in defense of principle. It is significant, however, that a reporter's right to withhold information has not been recognized officially. His position has been, and remains, a precarious one, balanced between the whims of often hostile legislators and an outraged public.

NEWSMEN'S PRIVILEGE BATTLES IN COURTROOM AND GRAND JURY PROCEEDINGS

Most of the battles between the government and the press have occurred in courtrooms rather than in congressional or legislative chambers. Unlike Congress, state legislatures, and administrative agencies, the courts have not been reluctant to use their power of punishment of contempt for refusals to reveal subpoenaed information.

In the court struggles treated next, journalist privilege was most often invoked in cases of crime and corruption. The public's right to know about wrongdoing in government is very substantially tied up with the reporter-subpoena issue. Libel suits involving press subpoenas have also generated concern over the issue for almost a hundred years. Unauthorized release of secret information by reporters has been of slightly more recent vintage. Many of the recent court confrontations on privileged information and the press have developed over reporting in the "counterculture" realm of drugs and political dissent.

Crime and Corruption: Does the Press Subpoena Help to Expose Them?

One of Justice White's contentions in *Branzburg* was that the subpoena is essential for compelling testimony that will root out "criminal conduct."[29] How effective has the press subpoena been in exposing corruption? The record is mixed.

In 1897 a man accused of murder admitted to a reporter that he had seen the victim murdered at a particular time and place. The defendant claimed a privilege because of communication with a journalist, but this claim was dismissed with the statement that the request "scarcely merits comment."[30]

Legislators and judges have generally been reluctant to recognize any kind of press privilege in a situation involving testimony about eyewitness accounts of crime. The more serious the crime, the less protection there has been for the communication in question.

In a 1911 case a reporter named Hamilton had written a story about a murder from information passed on by a policeman. Hamilton refused at trial to supply the policeman's name on the grounds that he would lose his job.[31] This claim was rejected, and Hamilton had to pay a fine of $50.

In some cases the courts were very explicit in defending the subpoena as an essential discovery device for unearthing corruption. In 1911, for example, a reporter for the *Jersey Journal* wrote of corruption in a small town. When newsman Grunow refused to name sources, the court answered him as follows:

In effect he pleaded a privilege which finds no countenance in the law. Such an immunity, as claimed by the defendant, would be far reaching in its effect and detrimental to the due administration of justice. To admit of any such privilege would be to shield the real transgressor and permit him to go unwhipped of justice.[32]

The issue of the newsman's privilege has sometimes been contained within another privilege claim. In 1913 the *New York Tribune* published a series of stories about customs frauds. City editor George Burdick, author of the series, was summoned before a grand jury and questioned about the sources of his information. He refused to answer on the ground that his reply might tend to incriminate him. His real purpose was to shield his source of information. Then Burdick was handed a full pardon obtained for him over the signature of President Woodrow Wilson; he refused the pardon and stood silent. The Supreme Court, in an unanimous opinion by Justice McKenna, upheld Burdick's right to refuse the pardon, which implied a crime and consequent disgrace.[33] The decision may be questionable, but the fact remains that Burdick did not talk. Some have argued that the abuse of the Fifth Amendment through this kind of evasion and subterfuge could be avoided by granting a direct newsman's privilege.

Often very embarrassing exposés lead to pressure by local authorities to squelch further comment by the press. In 1929 three reporters for the *Washington Times* reported on speakeasies in Washington, D.C. A grand jury wanted to know who sold them liquor. Their refusal to testify led to their being sentenced to forty-five days in jail. There is no evidence that anything effective was done to deal with the problem.[34]

This incident helped spur the first legislation introduced in Congress to protect reporters from forced disclosure of their sources (see chapter 7).

During the 1930s, several subpoena confrontations revived the drive to establish state legislation protecting journalists.[35] There are fewer recorded cases during the 1940s, however. There were fewer press subpoenas, and reporters were increasing their coverage of corruption. More and more independent reporting was taking place.

In 1948 the *New York World-Telegram* reported on widespread gambling and prostitution in the city of Newburgh, New York. The district attorney claimed that the story was exaggerated.[36] But in order to convince the people of Newburgh, as well as the district attorney, that the allegations were factual, the *Newburgh News* carried stories that included reproductions of "number slips."

The district attorney subpoenaed reporters Charles Leonard and news editor Douglas Clarke to appear before the grand jury. Both refused to divulge the source for the number slips and were sentenced to ten-day jail terms and $100 fines.[37]

Sometimes journalists were protected by judges who shifted the burden of proof to the party seeking the injunction. In 1951 a federal court held that a journalist did not have to reveal information, but only because it was not considered relevant to the matter at hand. After Ethel Rosenberg was convicted of treason, reporter Leonard Lyons wrote a series about death row in the *New York Post*. Lyons stated that Rosenberg's death sentence could be altered if she decided to talk, and Rosenberg tried to force Lyons to reveal his sources for that contention. The court ruled that Lyons did not have to answer the questions, because they were not relevant to the proceedings, but that if they were deemed relevant by the judge, it would be Lyon's duty to testify.[38]

In some instances of criminal reportage journalists went to jail and upon release announced their willingness to do it again if necessary.[39] Indeed, until the late 1950s, newsmen argued for the right to report on criminality on grounds outside the mainstream of constitutional argument.

In the next case, a new argument emerged. It was an interesting case about an allegedly unlawful firing that occurred in Hawaii in 1961. In 1957 newsman Alan Goodfader received confidential information that an employee was going to be fired by the Honolulu Civil Service Commission about a week and a half before she was actually dismissed.[40]

The employee took her case to court, charging that she had been fired unlawfully and sought reinstatement as personnel director.[41] In an attempt to establish a conspiracy to discharge her, the director deposed the reporter (Goodfader), who had appeared with a photographer at the meeting at which the discharge occurred. Goodfader refused to disclose his reasons for bringing the photographer but indicated that he had learned from a confidential source that the director might be discharged. He would not reveal the source.

This case presented the question of whether or not the United States District Court of Hawaii would adopt a newsman's privilege on the basis of the First Amendment. The court discussed the purpose of the amendment as related to the preservation of the rights of the American people to full information concerning the doings and misdoings of public officials, but the majority was not convinced that the privilege was protected by the Constitution. The opinion admitted that forced disclosure might constitute an impairment of freedom of the press but said that such an impairment was subservient to the public interest of compelling the testimony of witnesses.[42] In Margaret Sherwood's view, "The court weighed in the abstract the press's interest in non-disclosure against the necessity of maintaining the court's authority."[43] Put another way, the court labeled the litigant's right to compel testimony a "public" interest and the newsman's interest in nondisclosure a "private" interest.[44]

Despite the court's ruling, Goodfader never revealed his source; nor did he go to jail, because he was not called again to testify.

In 1969, *St. Paul Dispatch* reporter Donald Giese was asked by the defendant's lawyer in a murder trial to reveal his source of information for the articles he had written about the killing. Giese resisted, but the trial court found him in contempt of court and sentenced him to ninety days in jail.[45]

In May 1970 the Indiana Supreme Court affirmed a lower court's decision that included in it a commentary on the scope and application of an Indiana statute granting newsmen immunity from being forced to disclose sources of information before a judicial body.[46] The facts of the case are that Buford Lipps was charged with a robbery during which two police officers and a bartender had been wounded and a holdup man killed. While Lipps was awaiting trial, the wife of one of the gunmen contacted a newspaper reporter. She told the reporter that her husband and Lipps wished to speak to him. At their request, Johnson arranged for an interview to be held in a jury room of the criminal court. During this interview, Lipps confessed to shooting the bartender.

The police were aware of the interview, and during the trial the prosecution called Johnson to testify as to what had transpired. Defense counsel objected, claiming, among other grounds, that the Indiana statute granted Johnson immunity from contempt charges in refusing to disclose his sources of information. The court held that Lipps did not have standing to object under the statute, as it created a right personal to the newsman which only he could invoke.

The first reporter to be jailed after the *Branzburg* decision of June 29, 1972, was Peter Bridge, who covered city hall for the now defunct *Newark Evening News*. Bridge declined to tell a county grand jury unpublished details of an interview with a Newark housing commissioner, Pearl Beatty, who alleged that she had been offered a bribe. Bridge named Beatty in the May 2 article, describing how she was offered $10,000 in return for her vote for a particular candidate seeking the executive directorship of the Newark Housing Authority.[47]

After much legal maneuvering, he was jailed for three weeks in October 1972. The New Jersey courts ruled that the state newsman's privilege law did not protect Bridge because he had already named Beatty, ergo, his source.

Bridge was released when the grand jury disbanded and released its report. That report did not contain indictments, but it was critical of the mayor of Newark and Beatty for making statements to the press about crime in city government.

Bridge later argued in congressional hearings that he had other sources that were confidential and that needed to be protected.[48]

The Bridge accounts were embarrassing to city hall, as were the reports in yet another account of alleged corruption at the county jail in Columbia, South Carolina. In that instance, reporter Hugh Munn interviewed four prisoners in the jail and promised that he would not reveal their names so that they would not have to fear reprisals.[49] In sworn affidavits the prisoners talked about guards propositioning the inmate's wives, with the implication that if the women did not accept the propositions, their husbands would receive tougher treatment. The prisoners also told of beatings and other infractions by prison authorities. This was another instance of rigorous pursuit of the press rather than the evidence. The reporters released the affidavits but it appears that the investigation went no further.

In 1972 two *Los Angeles Times* reporters and their Washington bureau chief were summoned to turn over tapes to a witness aware of Watergate matters, that is, the entry of the Democratic National Committee office in Washington, D.C. The witness was Alfred C. Baldwin III, and Judge Sirica noted that Baldwin was a principal witness in the matter. *Times* reporters turned the tapes over to Bureau Chief John Lawrence as a security measure. Baldwin's interview was possible because of promised confidentiality. Attorneys for the *Times* discussed with Judge Sirica possible chilling effects if the subpoenas were not quashed. Because of refusal to submit the tapes, Lawrence was jailed for contempt of court, but the ruling was stayed by the United States Court of Appeals and Lawrence was free.

Two days later, Baldwin released the *Times* from its pledge of confidentiality and the confrontation ended.[50]

At about the same time another Los Angeles newsman confronted a grand jury over reporting. He reported on a bail bond scandal in which judges were accused of signing blank prisoner release forms and furnishing them to bail bondsmen.

This time the newsman was saved from forced testimony when the grand jury's term ended. Many other journalists were spared over the years by similar convenient expirations.[51]

Some corruption cases have been tied in with civil rights matters, as with the *Balk* case. In December 1972 the Second Circuit Court of Appeals ruled that Alfred Balk, editor of the *Columbia Journalism Review,* did not have to identify a source he used in a 1962 article for the *Saturday Evening Post.* Balk had refused to supply the real name behind the fictitious name of N. Vitchek, who was referred to in the magazine article. This ''Vitchek'' source had provided extensive information about ''blockbusting'' Chicago real estate operators.

Plaintiffs in a civil rights class action in behalf of Chicago blacks had sought an order to compel Balk to name his source for the article so that they could proceed against the real estate operators with the informational ammunition that would prove discrimination.[52] However, the information was requested from Balk in pretrial proceedings, and the plaintiffs had not sought to learn the true identity of ''Vitchek'' except by questioning Balk. The court said that the Supreme Court's ruling in *Branzburg* v. *Hayes* was based on subpoenaed information in criminal proceedings and that there are circumstances at the very least in civil cases in which reporters would not be forced to reveal information.[53]

In the twenty-seven press subpoena cases arising out of reporting on crime and corruption examined in this study, not one judge recognized a press privilege outright. Only in the *Balk* case was it conceded that the *Branzburg* holding did not apply to civil cases or to cases in which plaintiffs had not sought information from alternative sources independent of those shielded by reporters. In seventeen cases the courts clearly rejected a press privilege.

In thirteen cases the reporters went to prison. In six cases they were fined. In one case the issue was avoided because of a Fifth Amendment claim. Loss of employment was judicially recognized in another confrontation but not the privilege itself. In five incidents the question of the relevancy of the information came up without actual recognition of the privilege. In two cases attrition avoided final resolution of the issue one way or the other. In one case the source tried and failed to claim the privilege.

In the vast majority of these cases the courts appeared to be unusually concerned with what was perceived as a challenge to judicial authority. Reporters' sources were pursued at great costs in official time and energy. Alternative source information that would either corroborate or undermine the newsman's assertions or statements was very rarely pressed into service against crime and corruption.

Investigations into wrongdoing that had begun in the heat of publicity often melted away with the disposition of the matter of the newsman's privilege. One was left to wonder about who was most concerned about exposing and fighting crime and corruption.

Libel and Subpoenaing the Press

Judges and legislators have been reluctant to extend an absolute privilege to newsmen in any type of proceeding or case. Litigation over libel has been no exception. The Georgia Supreme Court sustained a trial court's contempt conviction against a publisher.[54] The New Jersey Supreme Court ruled that if the defense was based on "reliability of the source, the newspaper could not refuse to identify the source despite the existence of a state privilege law."[55]

A very famous libel case involving privilege occurred in 1959, when actress Judy Garland brought CBS to a district court for breach of contract and for defamatory statements. The statements, attributed to a CBS executive, were published in Marie Torre's column, "TV-Radio Today," in the January 10, 1957, issue of the *New York Herald Tribune*. Torre concluded with the spokesman's alleged statement: "I don't know, but I wouldn't be surprised if its because she thinks she's terribly fat." Garland claimed that the statements were false and damaging to her reputation: CBS claimed that it had never made the statements or caused them to be published.[56]

Torre insisted that the CBS informant had made such a statement, but she refused to name the person. She was held in contempt but appealed on constitutional grounds, that is, that news flow protected by the First Amendment would be compromised by divulging confidences.[57] She became the first reporter to rely specifically on the First Amendment for the journalist privilege claim.[58]

In 1963 a derogatory article about Orlando Cepeda appeared in *Look* magazine. In the writing of this story, reporter Cohane wished to shield the identity of Giant officials who allegedly made the defamatory statements about Cepeda. Although the case fell under the California "shield law," the court did not extend the law's protection because Cohane was a magazine reporter instead of a newspaper reporter.[59] Many have commented on the absurdity of this distinction.[60]

In a 1969 case, *Alioto* v. *Cowles Communications, Inc.*, the mayor of San Francisco brought a libel action in a federal court for a magazine article accusing him of having Mafia connections.[61] The two reporters who had written the article were not defendants. The plaintiff sought to subpoena the journalists' research, which they delivered to the court after first excising the names of the sources. This degree of compliance was insufficient to satisfy Alioto's counsel, who pressed for disclosure of the newsmen's sources. The transcript of oral arguments reveals that the judge was not impressed with distinctions between the magazine and the reporters, even though the editors of *Look* claimed they had never learned the identity of the confidential sources and the authors were independent contractors.[62]

The judge regarded the magazine and the reporters as being "of the same bolt" and "in the same boat," and he dismissed arguments made on behalf of the journalists that their information was unrelated to the main action of libel. The judge also noted the potential value of the information in corroborating the factual assertions made in the article. Since truth remained an issue in this case, disclosure seemed to him relevant for establishing one of the critical elements of liability. Nevertheless, the judge permitted the journalists to preserve the confidentiality of their sources.

The court may have been influenced by the obvious efforts of the reporters to comply substantially with the plaintiff's wishes short of revealing the identities of their informants, but the key to the holding appears to have been the conviction that contempt should not be enforced against a journalist-witness when the plaintiff may have other means of obtaining the information.

But this was only the first trial. There were three more to follow. The first two trials dealt with questions concerning falsity or defamation in the *Look* articles. The third and fourth articles centered on the issue ot malice.[63] In the final trial federal judge William Schwarzer ruled that the statements in the article were made "with actual malice, i.e., with reckless disregard for their truth,"[64] He awarded a judgment of $350,000 to Alioto.

Marvin Whitmore, president of Cowles, said "We are stunned and saddened by this decision. It represents a further eroding of the protections granted by the First Amendment. We will certainly appeal."

Look spent $700,000 on the case. Contrary to some generalizations about the *New York Times–Sullivan* ruling,[65] it is not impossible for a public official to sue successfully for libel. In the end this case turned not on the testimonial privilege question per se, but rather upon the *Sullivan* ruling.

Nevertheless, because of the interrelatedness of these issues, *Sullivan* had ramifications for the First Amendment. The two competing interests on this issue were the First Amendment reportorial concern about a future chilling effect on news gathering on the one hand, and the right of a libel plaintiff to compel journalist testimony on the other.

In another case involving another mayor and another magazine the issue of libel and the press subpoena flared again. In 1970 *Life* magazine published a critical story entitled "The Mayor, the Mob, and the Lawyer." Mayor Cervantes of St. Louis, Missouri, sued for $12 million in a defamation action. The reporter admitted that some of his informants were from the FBI, but he refused to give names.[66]

Attorneys tried to force revelation of the sources, but the district court ruled for the magazine, saying that those who wrote the story were not acting with reckless disregard for truth or falsity. The Eighth Circuit Court of Appeals upheld the press and cautioned that courts should not routinely grant motions seeking disclosure of news sources "without first inquiring into the substance of a libel allegation."[67]

Thus the key tests in cases involving the confrontation between defamation and testimonial privilege claims are the "heart of the claim" and whether or not "alternative means" have been employed to elicit the relevant information. The exception was *Cepeda,* in which the determining factor was the narrow interpretation of the California shield statute, which was later amended to include magazines.[68]

Journalist Privilege and Secret Information

Judges have not been very tolerant of reporters who divulge information that has been sealed from the public by a court order or that in any way violates grand jury secrecy.[69]

Two cases involving secret information have received considerable coverage. These cases merge the issue of testimonial privilege with the phenomenon of "gag rules," which the media equates with prior censorship. The courts and defendants have countered that assertion by citing *Sheppard v. Maxwell*[70] and the right to a fair trial.

THE FARR CASE The case of William Farr[71] was part of the catalytic process that alarmed the press and encouraged congressional activity in the direction of testimonial privilege legislation during 1972–74. The other, the *Fresno Bee* confrontation[72] with Fresno County Superior Court Judge Denver Peckinpah, is similar to *Farr* in some respects through different in others.

The Charles Manson murder trial involved the press and bench in a dilemma over the handling of secret information. The judge had issued an "order re publicity" prohibiting any attorney, court employee, or witness from publicly divulging any trial testimony.[73]

Reporter William Farr was writing for the *Los Angeles Herald-Examiner* and sought information from a potential witness in the case. In October 1970 Farr received copies of a written statement by the witness, Virginia Graham, and one each from two of the six attorneys in the case.

The trial judge, Charles Older, was told by Graham's attorney that Farr had a copy of her statement. The judge conducted a hearing to determine how Farr had obtained the statement. Farr replied that two of the attorneys had given him the statement, but he refused to give their names.

The *Examiner* published the article on October 9, 1970. Farr had called Judge Older in advance to allow him to prevent the sequestered jury from seeing the headlines.

The October 9 story was headlined, "Liz, Sinatra on Slay List—Tate Witness." The story elaborated the bizarre murders of the Manson cult. The jury did not see the article. Manson and the three women were convicted of murder and the judicial/press confrontation appeared to be over.

But in May 1971 the issue was reopened when Judge Older learned that Farr was no longer a journalist but was a press secretary for the district attorney of Los Angeles County. The judge demanded that he reveal his sources, but Farr refused once more and stated:

Notwithstanding my change of employment, I still feel bound in conscience to the ethics of my profession and my responsibility to my former employer to maintain the same position, to wit: To invoke the provisions of Section 1070 of the Evidence Code (California shield law). To do otherwise in my opinion would be to violate the ethics of my profession, the law of California and my own conscience. To violate my word and that of my former employer would destroy my relationships in my present position, would cause me irrevocable damage in the future and would prevent me from ever obtaining employment with another newspaper, news service or radio or TV station.[74]

Judge Older ruled that the California shield law no longer protected him because he was no longer a reporter.

In December 1971 the California Court of Appeals affirmed the judgment of the lower court. The California Supreme Court denied Farr's appeal, and on November 13, 1972, the United States Supreme Court denied Farr's petition. Judge Older asked Farr once again for his source and when he refused to name it, sentenced him to jail until he answered questions concerning sources.

Farr's first stay in jail was relatively short, four hours. He was released on a writ of habeas corpus contending that Judge Older had lost jurisdiction in the case after the Manson trial. The appeal was rejected and Farr returned to jail for forty-eight days.[75]

He was released by Supreme Court Justice Douglas on January 11, 1973. The California court of appeals now determined whether Farr's disobedience was based upon an "established articulated moral principle."[76] After this hearing Farr was released because the judge was convinced that Farr would not name his source.

The *Farr* case presented certain contrasts with other press subpoena cases.

First, the article did not supply the public with vital information about government corruption.

Second, Farr was criticized by many in the journalistic community. "It seems to us," editorialized the *New Republic*, "that the newspaper erred by rushing into print with a seamy sensational account based on material obtained in contradiction to court order, where the selling of more newspapers was the only public service rendered."[77] The *New York Times* stated that "the sensationalized treatment given to the Manson trial by much of the press reflected little credit on journalism's own record of concern for assuring a fair trial."[78]

Many other members of the press defended Farr. A *Los Angeles Times* editorial typified the dissent:

Farr's imprisonment has less connection with his refusal to betray the confidence of his news source than with two other elements: first, an ugly streak of authoritarianism that is pervading some of the courts and, second, the false free press-fair trial issue that masks an attack on First Amendment protections of press and speech . . . .

Today, as a portent of things to come, William Farr is in jail. His cellmate is the First Amendment. Judge Charles H. Older of the Superior Court of Los Angeles put them both there.[79]

In a third respect the *Farr* case is unusual. The fact that Farr was no longer a reporter provided a loophole whereby the courts could circumvent the California shield law.

Fourth, Farr obtained a "secret" document that was ordered kept secret so as not to compromise the fair-trial rights of defendants.

In spite of these differences the *New York Times* noted that "there is still great damage in the kind of remedy the courts are applying against Mr. Farr. The meanest cases often result in the most embracing and destructive trespasses on basic liberties."[80]

THE FRESNO BEE CASE In October 1974 the Fresno County grand jury conducted proceedings that culminated in the return of felony indictments against a city councilman, a land developer, and a former city planning commissioner. Defense attorneys moved for a court order to seal grand jury testimony. Superior Court Judge Denver Peckinpah issued an order re publicity on November 22, 1974.[81] The court was acting under the authority of the California State Penal Code Section 939.1(b) in ordering that grand jury transcripts be sealed. The judge was responding to defense motions made for the fair trial protection of their clients, city councilman Marc Stefano and land developer Julius Aluisi. Allegedly, the two had conspired with a third man, Norman Bains, to obtain a sewer refund from the city of Fresno. Aluisi reportedly gave Stefano $4,000 and Chief Assistant City Attorney Jim McKelvey said he was offered a bribe by Bains and Aluisi.[82]

Sometime after the court order the *Fresno Bee* allegedly obtained information from the grand jury transcripts directly or indirectly. Two court reporters for the *Bee,* Joe Rosato and William Patterson, contended that they did not get the information from officers of the court subject to the court order.

Stories detailing the contents of the transcripts ran January 12, 13, and 14 in the *Bee*.[83] The paper's managing editor, George Gruner, contended that it was only after a change of venue for Stefano and Aluisi and reassurances of the *Bee*'s attorneys as to legality that the decision was made to run the stories.

The plot thickened when it was discovered that the two court reporters were in possession of what turned out to be a master key that unlocked more than the reporter's offices in the county court house. Any grand jury transcripts left lying on desks of judges or attorneys authorized to have them under the sealing order could be obtained by the use of the master key. There is some question as to whether the reporters were aware of whether they possessed a master key, as mistakes can be made in issuing them.

There was also the possibility that the transcripts could have been picked up for copying during working hours. Testimony indicates that the public defender for Fresno County had a copy of the transcript lying on his desk for several weeks, where it is conceivable that reporters could have reviewed it without illegal entry.[84]

The court contended that the order had been violated by publication of the January stories and proceeded with an investigation that was to be conducted by county counsel in Judge Peckinpah's courtroom. The hearing was to begin January 24, 1975. Testimony was taken from officers of the court to determine whether any of them had violated the court order or knew how the *Bee* had obtained the information on the transcripts. After thirteen witnesses had been interrogated, the court summoned the court reporters for the *Bee,* along with the managing editor, to determine how they had obtained the information for the stories. Eventually, city editor Jim Bort was also called. All of them appeared and answered some of the questions but refused to tell how they had obtained the information, invoking the First Amendment to the United States Constitution and the California "shield" law.[85]

Judge Peckinpah expressed the opinion that the California newsmen's privilege statute interfered with the Court's authority and was therefore unconstitutional. (It is interesting to note that Judge Older in the *Farr* case did not question the constitutionality of the "shield" law but ruled it not applicable to Farr because he was not a reporter at the time.) The *Bee* responded to Peckinpah's argument by challenging the validity of the court investigation by appealing to higher courts on the grounds that the proceeding was inculpatory and therefore defense witnesses were needed as well as cross-examination of all witnesses by defense counsel.[86] The court did not allow the defense to do either. The judge explained that it was not a trial but an investigation and therefore the matter of witnesses and cross-examination was irrelevant in the hearing at hand.

In any event, the central issue of whether the court could conduct an investigation that would lead to the jailing of the newsmen, because of their contempt citations over refusal to answer, was upheld by two levels of appellate courts in California and the United States Supreme Court, although Justice Douglas had stayed the orders below until he was overruled by his colleagues.[87]

In the summer of 1976 Judge Peckinpah retired from the bench. Chief Judge Hollis Best appointed himself to the case. He declared his intention to press for source information. When the Bee Four again refused to divulge sources, he sentenced them to jail for an indefinite term. They were charged with civil contempt as had been the case with Farr.

After spending fifteen days at the Fresno County Prison Farm in September 1976, they appeared in court once again. This time expert testimony was given by fellow journalists Jack Anderson (Washington Merry-Go-Round) and Jack Nelson of the *Los Angeles Times*. These reporters and the Bee Four were attempting to convince the judge that their refusal was based *inter alia* on an articulated moral principle and the likelihood that they would never reveal sources.

At the end of an exhausting day with demonstrators surrounding the court house, Judge Best still clung to the principle that the law has the right to everyman's evidence. Nevertheless, he released the Bee Four. Once again he stressed their infraction but ruled that the fifteen days served would complete the sentence.

Thus it has been demonstrated in these two cases how "gag rules" become entangled in the seamy web of newsmen's privilege.

The *Bee* case demonstrated, first, that shield statutes can be preempted by other state legislation[88] as well as restrictive interpretation over the scope of the law,[89] and, second, that the judicial power of contempt has a potentially chilling effect on reporting. In both the *Farr* and *Bee* cases the courts insisted on blocking interference to their contempt power via the reportorial privilege challenge. The doctrine asserted in *Wood* v. *Georgia* seemed to speak for the judges in those cases: "Courts necessarily must possess the means of punishing for contempt when conduct tends directly to prevent the discharge of their functions including the authority and power . . . to assure litigants a fair trial."[90]

An effort to achieve better protection than journalist privilege statute 1070[91] provides was initiated in California in 1977. Assemblyman Jerry Lewis introduced a measure that would put the issue of reportorial privilege on the referendum ballot and thus freeze such press protection into the state constitution.[92] But media critics urged him to discontinue his effort because they feared that such an approach would be less protective than the First Amendment.[93] This skeptical attitude became increasingly characteristic of press opinion with regard to drafting statutory or constitutional protection. The journalistic fraternity became more and more inclined to believe that press–bench confrontations would more or less continue. This view seemed to be confirmed by United States Supreme Court Chief Justice Warren Burger.[94]

THE INFREQUENT CAPITULATION OF REPORTERS TO SUBPOENA PRESSURES

In the aforementioned press subpoena controversies reporters stood their ground. In rare instances, members of the press have submitted to the court rather than accept punishment for contempt.

In 1914 a city editor in Hawaii printed a story about local government corruption prior to the official release of the information by a grand jury. The editor refused to name his informant in court, claiming privilege as a journalist. The district court denied the claim, and the reporter revealed his source.[95]

Several other cases have been recorded in which newsmen decided to reveal under the threat of imprisonment.[96]

SUMMARY

Thus far it has been demonstrated that the journalist privilege is not generally recognized by legislative bodies, administrative agencies, or the courts.

Once negotiations fail and the momentum of legal proceedings takes over, the journalist very infrequently escapes unscathed. He may escape if the term of the grand jury is about to expire, if the judge believes that the information sought is not relevant, if another source has been found, and if the parties seeking the information are convinced that the reporter will never talk even if that means he will go to jail.

Newsmen are often summoned without serious alternative attempts to procure the information elsewhere. They have been used as an investigative arm of government. Sometimes their investigative function has been the last link in the investigative chain. The investigation into wrongdoing stops when the embarrassment recedes.

Occasionally, newsmen invoke privilege claims that their press brethren believe should give way to countervailing claims. This was true in the *Farr* case. There are journalists who believe that the reporter privilege is generally ill advised. (See chapter 7.)

Rarely do newsmen respond to subpoena or contempt intimidation.

Although that has not prevented many reporters from going to jail, it is likely that a more deferential press would encourage even more subpoenas. In spite of the difficulties, the trend appears to be toward greater independence and increasingly rigorous investigative reporting.

The Press and the Counterculture

THE TURBULENT SETTING AND ITS IMPACT ON RELATIONS BETWEEN THE PRESS AND GOVERNMENT

In the past, government has tended to employ greater restraint in the issuance of subpoenas to newsmen. Any demands authorities made were met, on the whole, with fairly inconspicuous compliance or resistance at the presubpoena stage. The public became aware of the pressure placed on newsmen during relatively infrequent and ordinarily nonpolitical occasions when the newsmen showed up in court and the press covered the incident. The newsman almost always took the contempt citation in order to uphold the principles of his profession, and the public came to accept the barrier to disclosure made possible by journalistic sacrifice.

Recently, however, subpoenas and court orders have been used more frequently. Why did the government find it necessary to employ subpoenas for newsmen's testimony, films, and notes?

First, government was facing social unrest over Vietnam, civil rights issues, and the War on Poverty. In a rush to establish order, efforts were made to cull information from any available sources. Second, subpoenas for journalist film increased with greater television coverage of disorders. Third, the press became more resistant to presubpoena requests for information. As a more hostile relationship developed between the "law and order" emphasis of the Nixon administration and the investigative curiosity of the press, the tension increased. An attitude of resistance to subpoenas gathered journalistic support. It was feared that easy compliance with presubpoena requests would lead to more voracious requests as time went on.

The 1968 Democratic Convention in Chicago only heightened the tension, when reporters covering the counterculture were punished along with the demonstrators. As the press became more exposed to the counterculture's attack on established values, it became increasingly obvious that the administration believed journalists sympathized with the demonstrators.

Vice-President Agnew challenged the media to become more objective. In his view, coverage of the Panthers and the Weathermen factions of the Students for a Democratic Society only aided subversion because coverage translated into credibility for the radical cause. Speeches about racial injustice, foreign policy criticism, drug use, and government deception only used the press against the government. Reporters argued, however, that such reporting helped to create a dialogue whereby establishment and antiestablishment leaders could come to understand each other better.

Attorney General John Mitchell approved the subpoenaing of news media throughout the country. "According to Jack Landau, the Attorney General's former chief information officer, the 'chilling effect' of Agnew's addresses and Mitchell's subpoenas upon the press were psychologically devastating."[1]

The first series of subpoenas was issued in October 1969 to "four Chicago newspapers, NBC News, and *Time, Life* and *Newsweek* magazines which were to produce unedited files, photographs, film, and notebooks of reporters who had covered a four-day disturbance in Chicago by the Weathermen."[2] As the subpoena momentum built to a crescendo, newsmen began to tell the public the ramifications of the unfolding events. Ben Bagdikian, national news editor of the *Washington Post,* declared:

Vice-President Spiro Agnew has graciously assumed the role of editor-in-chief of the country's newspapers. He has sustained a long attack on the news media strengthened by the known hostility of the President toward the media, the subpoena power of the Department of Justice and the licensing discretion of the Federal Communications Commission.[3]

Agnew was concerned about journalistic balance and perspective. He viewed reporting as too independent and aggressive and would have preferred a more deferential attitude from the press. Reporters played up the public's right to know about government from an investigative journalist perspective.

Increasingly, the agonizing behavior of "hard drug" users such as Charles Manson gave further stimulus to defense requests for judicial gag orders proscribing media coverage of counterculture behavior in instances in which accused dissidents were in court.[4]

In the past few years the gag order has occasionally upstaged the press–subpoena issue and is often merged with it. This was true in the *Farr* case in Los Angeles, the Zebra killings news coverage in San Francisco, a judicial order in New Orleans over a rape-murder case, a gag order in the matter of the Gainesville Eight, which involved a demonstration by Vietnam Veterans Against the War, the restraining of comment on the "alphabet" bombings in Los Angeles, and a silence order in Fresno, California, re grand jury investigation into a corruption charge involving a Fresno city councilman.[5] What is especially chilling about the gag issue for journalists of late is the Dickinson doctrine.[6] This doctrine holds that a reporter must, on penalty of being held in criminal contempt of court, obey an order not to publish accounts of open court proceedings, even if that order is ultimately ruled unconstitutional by an appellate court. It raises a vital question: Who is to decide whether or not to publish, and when—the courts or the media? It would certainly appear to discourage any reporter from challenging a judge who issues a gag order even if he believed that it clearly violated the First Amendment. It may effectively dampen a thorough investigation into a pattern of corruption with broad contours going beyond an initial hearing or full trial and is similar to the privilege issue in that the flow of news is affected whether sources become reluctant to talk to reporters or reporters fear comment on matters covered by judicial "news blackout" orders.

SUBPOENA CONFRONTATIONS RESULTING FROM COVERAGE OF COUNTERCULTURE ACTIVITIES

Cases relevant to counterculture activities will be treated in five general subject areas in which journalists and writers have experienced communications difficulties as a result of the subpoena.

The Drug Scene

Investigative reporting on drug abuse has provided the public with heretofore unavailable information about the activities of various elements of the society.

In 1966 Annette Buchanan, managing editor of the *Oregon Daily Emerald,* the student newspaper at the University of Oregon, obtained interviews with seven users of marijuana by promising not to reveal their identities.[7] For purposes of publication they expressed to her their opinions that the use of marijuana is beneficial and that drug laws penalizing it should be changed. After her report of the interviews had been published, the district attorney demanded that she reveal the names of the seven. She refused and was eventually held in contempt of a court order commanding disclosure of the names to a grand jury investigating the use of marijuana on campus. On appeal to the Supreme Court of Oregon she argued that freedom of the press necessarily includes the freedom to gather news.[8] Therefore, since many news stories cannot be obtained unless a reporter is capable of promising anonymity to a confidential source, a judicial order compelling disclosure abridges First Amendment freedoms by placing limitations on the flow of news. She also made the point that her lips were sealed by the Code of Ethics of the American Newspaper Guild, in effect since 1934, which states "Newspapermen shall refuse to reveal confidences or disclose sources of confidential information in court or before judicial or investigating bodies."[9]

The court took a unique tack in refuting the reporter's argument. It reasoned that although the government at times extends to selected representatives of the news media privileges (such as access to war zones and seats on presidential aircraft) not accorded to the general public, these privileges are not necessarily rights conferred by the Constitution solely upon those who can qualify as members of the press.[10] The court noted: "It would be difficult to rationalize a rule that would create special constitutional rights for those possessing credentials as news gatherers which would not conflict with the equal privileges and equal protection concepts found in the Constitution."[11]

What the court's opinion seemed to overlook was the fact that attorneys and their clients, doctors and their patients, and so on, have this privilege without violating the equal protection concepts of the Constitution. The court also struck a balance between the First and Fourteenth Amendments and found the former outweighed by the latter. The court implied that news flow has less constitutional protection than communications between licensed professionals and those they serve.

Three years later, a story on drugs was to create a press-judiciary confrontation that would be driven all the way to the United States Supreme Court for final disposition. In October 1969 Paul Branzburg, a reporter for the *Louisville Courier-Journal,* began researching an article on drug use in Frankfort, Kentucky. Branzburg explained the need for developing a relationship of trust with informants so that their identities would be protected.[12]

Branzburg usually showed his contacts a copy of the Kentucky shield statute, which provides:

No person shall be compelled to disclose in any legal proceeding or trial before any court, or before any grand or petit jury, or before the presiding officer of any tribunal, or his agent or agents, or before the General Assembly, or legislative body, or any committee thereof, or elsewhere, the source of any information procured or obtained by him, and published in a newspaper or by a radio or television broadcasting station by which he is engaged or employed, or with which he is connected.[13]

This assurance seemed to assist Branzburg toward more candid coverage.

One of Branzburg's articles, published November 15, 1969, was very revealing about the drug scene in that area:

The Hash They Make Isn't to Eat

by Paul M. Branzburg

Courier-Journal Staff Writer

Larry, a young Louisville hippie, wiped the sweat off his brow, looked about the stuffy little room and put another pot on a stove over which he had been laboring for hours.

For over a week, he has been proudly tending his pots and pans. But he also had paused frequently to peek out the door in search of "The Man" (police).

Larry and his partner, Jack, are engaged in a wierd business that is a combination of capitalism, chemistry, and criminality.

They are operating a makeshift laboratory in south-central Louisville that may produce them enough hashish, or "hash," a concentrate of marijuana, to net them up to $5000 for three weeks of work.

Larry and Jack were once run-of-the-mill dope dealers, but in the past few months they have expanded operations and become dope manufacturers.

On a sunny afternoon last week, Larry entered his "lab" and began another day of cooking hash. With long-handled pruning shears, he began chopping marijuana stems into a large tub.

"I don't know why I'm letting you do this story." he said quietly. "To make the narcs (narcotics detectives) mad, I guess. That's the main reason." However, Larry and his partner asked for and received a promise that their names would be changed. . . .[14]

After the article appeared, Branzburg was summoned before a grand jury. Source names were sought, but he refused to reveal them and invoked the shield statute in his defense.

Judge Pound ordered Branzburg to answer. The Kentucky Court of Appeals supported Judge Pound. The courts were concerned that Branzburg had been an eyewitness to a crime, and argued therefore that the shield statute did not protect this reporter's claim.[15]

However, one of the judges, Judge Hill, dissented. He believed that the court had misconstrued the statute:

The majority opinion to my mind has adopted a strained and unnecessarily narrow construction of the term "source of any information procured or obtained" used in KRS 421.100. I believe that the phrase "source of any information" is a broad comprehensive one, certainly not a technical phrase.

The majority opinion stands for the proposition that the statute in question does not apply in instances in which a newspaper reporter witnesses the commission of a crime. But the statute does not place any such limitation on the privilege. It certainly would have been no trouble for the Legislature to have provided for an exception to the privilege had it thought one advisable. The statute in question is the expression of public policy by the proper branch of government, the Legislature, after nearly 150 years' experience, and this court has no business interfering with great and fundamental policy questions of our system of government.[16]

Aside from revealing a Holmesian philosophy of judicial restraint, the judge went on to note that the present case did not involve questions of injury to life and limb or property and that the eyewitness issue must turn on a more serious crime than was involved in the *Branzburg* case.

Branzburg continued to report. On January 10, 1971, two more stories on the drug syndrome appeared. Branzburg was subpoenaed again. He appealed to the United States Supreme Court for a writ of certiorari. He argued that a First Amendment privilege should be declared. We shall review his arguments and the Court's ruling in chapter 5.)

A third case dealing with the drug scene occurred later in 1971 when David Lightman of the *Baltimore Evening Sun* wrote about drug activities of young people at Ocean City, Maryland. One of his stories depicted a casual, matter-of-fact acceptance of the drug culture along the Ocean City boardwalk:

A shop near the lower end of the boardwalk wants to be sure its customers are satisfied with the pipes they buy. So salesmen sometimes let them draw some marijuana before they make a purchase.

The shop has pipes for all purposes—combination pipes, with bowls for opium, tea, and hash; adjustable pipes for smoking pot with and without water, buckle pipes, which clip on to one's belt buckle (and are thus easily camouflaged), and others.

Last Friday night, a uniformed Ocean City policeman was standing in another part of the shop. The shopkeeper, her legs stretched out on a waterbed in the next room, tried to explain uses of the various pipes to a customer.

The shopkeeper asked him if he would like to "draw some grass." He pointed to the officer.

"Don't worry about him. We have a lot of cops come in. You know, it's rough for them, most are under 21. We're nice to 'em, so they don't come sniffing around." The customer declined the offer.[17]

Lightman was summoned before a grand jury to give source names. Lightman refused, citing the Maryland shield statute, which was the nation's first such statute and dated back to 1896.[18]

Lightman was found guilty of contempt because the court did not perceive the Maryland shield statute as protecting a reporter in a situation in which he did not establish a confidential relationship (as with the shopkeeper). Because Lightman was only an observer and stranger to the people he observed, he could neither claim the privilege on confidence grounds nor as a newsman. The court also alluded to the eyewitness aspect of the facts:

Where a newsman, by dint of his own investigative efforts, personally observes conduct constituting the commission of criminal activities by persons at a particular location, the newsman, and not the persons observed, is the "source" of the news or information in the sense contemplated by the statute.[19]

The court suggested that if the testimonial privilege was to be broadened to extend beyond the source to the information itself, "it can only be done by the Legislature."[20]

The decision was affirmed by the Maryland Court of Appeals, the state's highest court, on October 17. Lightman was sentenced to thirty days in jail.

The arguments of the court in the Lightman case were almost identical to the Branzburg court's reasoning; if a newsman hears of an event, he can protect his source; but if he sees the event, he becomes the source and has no protection. The court preferred to look at who was protected without looking at what was not protected, namely, news flow.

In November 1972 newspeople for the Brigham Young University's *Daily Universe* printed a story reporting that they had found out through interviews with drug dealers that police were offering protection in return for money. For the next few months, reporter Mike Gygi was repeatedly subpoenaed and harassed, although he was not sent to jail.[21]

Editor Arthur Kunkin and reporter Robert G. Applebaum of the *Los Angeles Free Press* were forced to disclose the confidential source of information about state narcotics undercover agents. The forced disclosure occurred because Kunkin and Applebaum had to defend themselves against charges of receiving stolen property (that is, a list of state narcotics agents given to the newspaper by a source).[22]

The pattern from the five preceding cases is clear. Courts are reluctant to apply a journalist privilege statute when a reporter witnesses a crime. Even if no crime has been witnessed, as in the Buchanan matter, the state shield law does not protect news flow because the court does not wish to provide preferential treatment for a "special class." The judiciary has a tendency to refrain from judicial restraint on the reporter privilege when the drug scene is involved.

Caldwell and Pappas: The Black Panther Party

Earl Caldwell, a black reporter, was assigned by the *New York Times* to cover the San Francisco and Oakland Panthers. It had become apparent that the white reporters in that area could not develop a relationship of trust for candid coverage of Panther activities.[23]

Caldwell had much experience with militant groups. He explained his background:

I was on the balcony with Martin Luther King in 1968, and I saw him die. I saw the blood come out of his neck and stack up around his head. I watched Ralph Abernathy cradle King's head in his arms. I was there, and I looked into King's eyes and watched him die.

Before that I had done my time in the streets. I wasn't just in Newark or Detroit. I was on Blue Hill Avenue in Boston. I was on the west side in Dayton. I was in Cincinnati and Watts and Sacramento and Chicago and a lot of other places where black folks showed their anger and rebelled during the summer of

1967. . . . Out of that summer came Rap Brown. I went across the country with him, and I watched thousands of black folks who were fed up, who were so filled with rage that they, too, were about to explode. Out of all that came the Black Panther party.[24]

In spite of his background Caldwell had difficulty gaining the confidence of the Panthers for many months. They thought he was working with the police. They defined the *New York Times* as establishment and therefore as pro-police.

Eventually, Caldwell was accepted:

I had friends who knew Kathleen Cleaver; she was my first contact with the party. But to make it, you had to be able to deal with the Panthers in the streets, the Panthers whose names you never asked, whose names you never read in the paper. They were the ones who showed me what I needed to know. Late one night in San Francisco they yanked an old couch away from a wall in a cramped apartment, exposing stacks of guns of every sort. I could tell my readers then to take these people seriously, and I did.

I watched the Panthers' breakfast program before other reporters knew it existed. I wrote about it in the *Times*. If I've ever written a page-one story, that was it. The story was all there, but it was buried somewhere in the thickness of the Sunday edition. I told how painstakingly they went about their work, cooking big breakfasts—eggs, bacon, ham, grits, bisquits—they had it all. But they also added politics, in the songs they sang, in the literature they gave to the kids.
. . .

As I became more deeply involved with the Panthers, I began to keep all kinds of files on them. On Panther personalities. On off-the-record conversations. I kept tapes too and I would write my personal reactions to everything involving the Panthers that I covered. At this point they were under attack by police groups across the country. At a time when the party was shutting out reporters, I was closer to it than ever. . . . The party trusted me so much that I did not have to ask permission to bring along a tape recorder.[25]

Caldwell's confidential relationship with the Panthers enabled him to write stories that no one else in the country could have written. The articles informed readers of the *New York Times*—as well as readers of as many as sixty other newspapers—about the Black Panther party and made an enormous contribution to public understanding of a previously unknown phenomenon.

In late 1969, according to Caldwell, the FBI "began to interfere with my work. They wanted to pick by brain. They wanted me to slip about behind my news sources, to act like the double agents I saw on old movie reruns on TV."[26] The FBI began calling Caldwell on a daily basis. *Times* bureau chief Wallace Turner had an assistant in the bureau,

Alma Brackett, take all of Caldwell's calls, but they still kept coming. Between December 23, 1969, and January 12, 1970, FBI agents attempted six times to interview Caldwell, but he refused to see them. Then one day an agent told Brackett that if Caldwell did not come in and talk to them, he would be telling what he knew in court.

In February 1970 Caldwell was summoned by a federal grand jury in San Francisco. His attorneys tried to discover the purpose of the subpoena and explained the delicacy of Caldwell's relationship with the Panthers. There was the fear that Panther knowledge of Caldwell's appearance before a grand jury would end serious reporting on the Panthers.

On March 17 a motion to quash the subpoena led the government to issue another subpoena, but Federal District Judge Zirpoli issued a protective order, which read:

. . . he need not reveal confidential associations that impinge upon the effective exercise of his First Amendment right to gather news for dissemination to the public through the press or other recognized media until such time as a compelling and overriding national interest which cannot be alternatively served has been established to the satisfaction of the Court.[27]

Caldwell now appealed to the Ninth Circuit Court of Appeals because he did not wish to appear at all. Grand jury proceedings are closed to the public, and he did not want to leave the Panthers in doubt over whether he was talking to the grand jury.

On November 16 the Ninth Circuit ruled that Caldwell did not have to appear before the grand jury until the government could demonstrate an overriding interest and lack of an alternative source. The court noted:

If the grand jury may require appellant to make available to it information obtained by him in his capacity as news gatherer, then the grand jury and the Department of Justice have the power to appropriate appellant's investigative efforts to their own behalf—to convert him after the fact into an investigative agent of the Government. The very concept of a free press requires that the news media be accorded a measure of autonomy; that they should be free to pursue their own investigations to their own ends without fear of governmental interference; and that they should be able to protect their investigative processes. To convert news gatherers into Department of Justice investigators is to invade the autonomy of the press by imposing a governmental function upon them. To do so where the result is to diminish their future capacity as news gatherers is destructive of their public function. To accomplish this where it has not been shown to be essential to the grand jury inquiry simply cannot be justified in the public interest.[28]

But the court cautioned that the rule was a narrow one and noted that not all news sources are as sensitive as those involved in Caldwell's reporting. "It is not every reporter who so uniquely enjoys the trust and confidence of his sensitive news sources."

The government appealed the case to the United States Supreme Court, and the Court ruled on it in conjunction with the *Pappas* and the *Branzburg* cases. (The Court's rule and rationale will be covered in chapter 5.)

Pappas also covered the Black Panther party, but his experience with the judicial process was different from that of Caldwell in that he was not as involved with his sources. He worked in a state without a shield law. Massachusetts courts would shape his destiny. Caldwell worked in a nation without a shield law. National courts would control his future and, in the end, that of Pappas too.

Pappas was a newsman for Channel Six in New Bedford, Massachusetts. In July 1970 civil disorders in New Bedford involved this reporter because the Panthers wanted the press to report the disturbances from the Panther view, that is, in their presence and looking out from their headquarters.

Pappas was given an address, but when he arrived in the riot area, the street was barricaded and he turned back. After another request for his presence, he threaded his way through a circuitous route to the headquarters.

When he arrived, there was some confusion over what he would be able to do. Conditions were laid down by the Panthers. He would be free to photograph and report any police raid but everything else such as conversations would be held in confidence. At one point some of the Panthers feared that he was only a spokesman for the police, but he assured them that he would accurately report what he saw.

Pappas was at the headquarters for three hours, made no notes but talked and listened. A police raid did not occur that evening and Pappas kept his promise: He did not write a story about his visit.

But two months later the grand jury summoned him for testimony about the events of that evening. True to his promise he would not discuss the content of any conversation at the headquarters.

Several days later he was to appear again. He filed a motion to quash the subpoena on First Amendment grounds and because he feared that "any future possibilities of obtaining information to be used in my work would be definitely jeopardized, inasmuch as I wouldn't be trusted or couldn't gain anyone's confidence to acquire any information in reporting the news as it is."[29] Furthermore, he felt that complying with the order would place him in personal danger.

On October 17, 1970, the Superior Court ruled that "Pappas does not have any privilege and must respond to the subpoena and testify to such questions as may be put to him by the Grand Jury relating to what he saw and heard, and the identity of any persons he may have seen."[30]

The Supreme Judicial Court of Massachusetts affirmed the lower court ruling in January 1971.[31] The court noted that Massachusetts did not have a shield law[32] and that for the court to create one would be tantamount to judicial legislation.[33]

It is interesting how consistently courts have narrowly construed press shield laws to the point of discovering exceptions that swallow the shield. Where there is no shield law, the courts very seldom create one; but in other statutory circumstances laws have been given broad construction, and in the absence of statutes, common law rules have been created to protect interests. Judicial officers have been reluctant to give meaningful shape to a press testimonial privilege.

Eventually, the *Pappas* case went to the United States Supreme Court along with those of Branzburg and Caldwell. (Chapter 5 covers the Court's reasoning.)

The *Pappas* case presents an example of the "fishing expedition"; i.e. that is, there was no expression by the grand jury of a nexus between criminal investigation and the Pappas visit to the Panther headquarters that night.[34] Pappas asked only for a qualified privilege that would obligate the grand jury to demonstrate a need for journalist testimony that would help in solving crime.

Coverage of Violence

Journalistic coverage of violence by individuals and groups involves the reporter in the most threatening subpoenas. It is one thing to be asked to give testimony on the workings of an organization or give descriptions of the drug scene. On the other hand, when property has been destroyed or life taken, the compelling interest in securing testimony is greater and the reporter often finds that an argument for privileged communication is outweighed by the concerns of prosecutors, judges, and defendants. However, the record is mixed.

In Chicago the defense counsel for nineteen Weathermen asked that reporters be required to testify and produce transcripts of all their reports of activities concerning the Students for a Democratic Society (SDS). The SDS members had been charged with a variety of offenses. Circuit Court Judge Saul Epton ruled that the reporters did not have to comply with the defense attorney's request:

It is true the defendants have a clear right to subpoena individuals who have knowledge of relevant facts. However, the First Amendment is as sacred as the Sixth Amendment, and if the press is to be free, they cannot be disturbed unnecessarily in reporting or gathering materials to report.[35]

Likewise, in *People* v. *Dohrn* the court weighed the interests involved. Here the state of Illinois proceeded against Bernadine Dohrn and other participants in the disturbances at the Chicago convention in August 1968. Numerous subpoenas were served on newsmen in the course of this action. The Circuit Court of Cook County ruled, on a motion to quash the subpoenas, that the evidence sought must be relevant to issues in the principal case; it must be of compelling need for the fair resolution of the principal case. The subpoena may not be used as a discovery device to uncover unspecified information known to the reporter; a standard of probable cause is required as to relevance. The court also noted that there had to be a showing that "the evidence sought is so important that the non-production thereof would cause a miscarriage of justice."[36] Implicit in the "miscarriage of justice" criterion are two concepts—evidence so compellingly needed that, because of the lack of alternative means of acquiring the information, its "nonproduction" would result in grave injustice. Each element must be satisfactorily met; either standing alone would be insufficient for imposing restraints upon the constitutionally protected news-gathering process.[37]

The two cases mentioned previously had salutary results for reporters, but in the *Knops* case, a discussion of which follows, the reporter ran into difficulty even though the court recognized a First Amendment rationale for journalistic privilege.

Mark Knops, editor of the Madison *Kaleidoscope*, asserted his testimonial privilege when he was subpoenaed to appear before a Walworth County grand jury, which had been convened originally on July 1, 1970, to investigate the alleged arson of Old Main Hall on the campus of Wisconsin State University at Whitewater. Less than two months later, following the bombing of Sterling Hall, which contained the Mathematics Research Center on the University of Wisconsin campus, and in which one student was killed, the grand jury began investigating the possibility that a conspiracy to perpetrate the Sterling Hall crime was committed in Walworth County. *Kaleidoscope,* two days after the bombing, printed a front-page story entitled, "The Bombers Tell Why and What Next—Exclusive to *Kaleidoscope.*" Knops was confronted before the grand jury with specific questions as to the identity of the person or persons from whom his information had been obtained. Having refused to answer, the editor was found to be in contempt pursuant to section 295.01(5) of the Wisconsin statutes and sentenced to imprisonment in the county jail for five months and seven days, or until such time as he purged himself by answering the questions.[38]

Knops appeared before the grand jury twice. On the first occasion, he asserted his Fifth Amendment right against self-incrimination, despite the fact that he had been granted immunity. Having been found in contempt, he petitioned the Wisconsin Supreme Court for a writ of habeas corpus, alleging violation of his constitutional right under the First Amendment to refuse to divulge the information sought.

Although accepting Knop's argument in principle and agreeing there is a First Amendment right protecting news flow, the Supreme Court of Wisconsin nevertheless went on to deny Knops protection under that claim. The court held that the "public's need and right to protect itself from physical attack"[39] outweighed its right to receive such information through the media. In comparing the *Caldwell* case in the Ninth Circuit ruling with *Knops,* the court appeared to distinguish them on the grounds of whether the confidential relationship had equal value in the two cases and also on the imminence of the threat to society if testimony could not be ordered.[40]

The *Knops* court pointed out that the grand jury investigation differed considerably from the "fishing expedition" found in Caldwell, and since the "bombers" were still undetected, the need for disclosure was overriding. In *Knops,* unlike *Caldwell,* the loss of the confidential source of information would not deprive the public of information obtainable only through a relationship of trust and confidence with a dissident group; Knops had no such relationship with the "bombers" in the court's opinion.[41] The court stated:

In this case the public was treated . . . to a long polemic on how property destruction and murder were simply necessary steps en route to a higher goal— the restructuring of society.

If the public were faced with a choice between learning the identity of the bombers or reading their justifications for anarchy, it seems safe to assume that the public would choose to learn their identities.[42]

Knops had also argued that the state must demonstrate the lack of an alternative means of acquiring the information so as to protect his First Amendment rights. The court answered that the burden of proof was on Knops to bring in alternative information if he thought it existed.[43] They also noted that the mere fact that the culprits were still at large was conclusive proof that the state did not know who they were.

The *Knops* decision also went briefly to the troublesome question of who is a journalist and concluded that Knops was a journalist but that a privilege did not apply to him.[44]

There has been considerable criticism of the *Knops* ruling, both positive and negative. On the positive side many newspapers editorialized in favor of the decision. It appeared that where in this case an underground editor was seemingly blocking access to information about violent death, bombing, and alleged arson, it would be necessary to take a stand against that kind of journalism. Eleven of the state's thirty-six daily newspapers editorialized on the ruling. Nine expressed approval of the decision, usually on grounds that freedom of the press places an extra burden on a journalist to be responsible to the public interest. Only two papers disapproved. One editorial, criticizing the majority's determination that it was appropriate to curtail free flow of information so that all other freedoms can flourish, wrote, "This has been the eternal cry of totalitarians since man left the caves.[45] A second newspaper found the decision a "legal landmark" because no state supreme court had previously held that the Constitution protects the journalist's confidential sources; but the editorial criticized the majority's application of its rule.

One dissenting opinion in the case stood out sharply. Justice Heffernan pointed out that records of the state and the United States Department of Justice indicated that the knowledge sought by Wisconsin courts concerning the Sterling Hall bombing had already been attained by alternative means.[46] Consequently, had the "compelling need" test alone been applied, the court would have had no alternative but to find the state without a compelling interest in acquiring testimony concerning the identity of the bombers.

One commentator was critical of the ruling's philosophy that it is proper for the state to shift the burden of proof to the newsman on the "alternative source" issue. He elaborated his dissent:

Under this approach, a newsman could avoid both a contempt citation and violation of his oath of secrecy by leading those seeking disclosure to those possessing the same information, but not having newsman status. Would not knowledge of this among sources restrict the amount of information they would supply and, thus, result in an indirect burden upon the free flow of news—an interest the privilege purports to protect?[47]

The same commentator also wondered whether the court was not saying in dicta that the mere bringing of a criminal charge satisfied the state's burden of establishing a "compelling interest." Would the court make a distinction between crimes of violence and those of a less serious nature?[48]

Another critic asserted that it is precisely during times of great unrest that freedom of expression most needs protection, lest community pressure be allowed to snuff out all critical voices.[49]

The *Knops* decision, finally, contains language that the news media may consider the unkindest cut of all. The Wisconsin majority turned the concept of "the public's right to know" against the newsman in holding that he may not keep secret his knowledge of major and specific crimes; ironically, the "public's right to know" has been the rallying cry, slogan, and banner for journalists attacking secrecy in government for the past two decades.[50]

In the end Knops spent several months in jail and continued to refuse to answer the grand jury's questions. The bombing incident remained unsolved.[51]

In response to the holding in *Knops,* the Wisconsin legislature has considered passage of a newsman's privilege statute. The proposed legislation was sharply qualified on the subject of libel and established a test on the disposition of criminal matters that put the burden on the state to demonstrate a "compelling and overriding national interest which cannot be served by an alternative means."[52]

In the *Knops* case the state did not have a shield law, but the court recognized the concept of privilege while denying it to Knops. In another case in New York, which has a shield law, the court held that it did not apply to the case at hand. Edwin A. Goodman, general manager of the New York City radio station WBAI-FM, was jailed in 1972 for relying on the state shield law in refusing to turn over to a grand jury the tapes of telephone conversations made with unidentified prison inmates and broadcast live during the course of a prison rebellion. The court ignored the possibility that the tapes would be used by law enforcement authorities to identify the prisoners through voiceprints, and ruled that the law's protection against disclosure of news sources did not apply. The court also ignored the fact that the statute does not divest the privilege even in cases in which the content of the information has previously been published.[53]

A second case involving the same station further interpreted the New York law[54] to mean that the privilege against disclosure did not apply when the unidentified source was the one who initiated contact with the newsmen, rather than vice versa. Critics of this decision pointed out that the law does not require that the newsman must affirmatively have sought out the source, as opposed to having the source come to him. If the purpose of the law is to encourage sources to furnish information to the press, then it would appear that this decision undermines that intent.

In the second case an announcer for the station had received a call from a person identifying himself only as a member of the "Weather Underground." The anonymous caller took credit for bombing the offices of the New York State Commissioner of Correctional Services, and directed the announcer to an envelope that had been placed in a public telephone booth. An employee of the station retrieved the letter, which was then read over the air. The letter warned that Commissioner Oswald's offices were about to be bombed. Upon calling the police, the appellant was told that the police knew of the bomb threat. The appellant also disseminated the contents of the letter to "all interested news agencies."[55] Later, a bomb exploded in the commissioner's offices in Albany, and although no one was injured, heavy property damage was inflicted.

As part of a grand jury investigation, the district attorney caused a subpoena *duces tecum* to be served upon the appellant, requesting that the radio station produce the letter. The station manager moved to quash the subpoena, but the Albany County Court denied the motion, arguing that the statute did not apply since the radio station had done nothing to obtain the information but had merely acted as a passive recipient. Although the decision was appealed, the appellate court affirmed the trial court's decision, arguing that the New York shield law protects only the identity of those informants who impart information under a "cloak of confidentiality."

Another case involving violence reportage arose out of the Attica prison riots in September 1971. Between September 9 and September 13, prisoners at the New York State Correctional Facility at Attica took control of the prison and held about thirty-eight correctional officers and civilians as hostages. WGR-TV (Buffalo) television reporter Steward Dan and cameramen Roland Barnes, Jay LaMarsh, and Terry Johnson covered the riot.

On September 9 the prisoners asked that a TV camera crew be sent into the prison. Cameraman Johnson and reporter Dan went inside Attica, shot film, and made notes. WGR-TV broadcast a half-hour news special that evening, using Johnson's film, with narration by Dan. On September 10 Dan and cameramen Barnes and LaMarsh took films and interviews inside the prison. Some of the exclusive footage was made available to the major television networks. The WGR-TV reporters and cameramen entered the prison during the next three days, and their efforts provided photographs for *Newsweek, Time,* and *Life.*

On September 13 the prison was beseiged by police and correctional officers, and the state regained control. Forty-three inmates and hostages were killed during the police assault. There were no WGR-TV reporters inside the prison during the attack.

A Wyoming County (New York) special grand jury was convened later to inquire into possible criminal acts by inmates during the riot. The state attorney general served four subpoenas on WGR-TV and its employees.

The first subpoena was handed to news director Sid Hayman. It required "all video tapes and other photographic material in your custody and control which was publicly aired over Channel Two WGR at any time relating to the events at and in the Attica correctional facility between September 9, 1971, to September 13, 1971."[56] WGR-TV stated its intention to comply with the subpoena, since the station felt there was no privilege for publicly broadcast films and tapes. Although a member of the attorney general's staff viewed the films, they were never shown to the grand jury.

The other subpoenas, served on Dan, Barnes, and LaMarsh, directed them to testify before the grand jury on April 26, 1972. LaMarsh's appearance was postponed pending a determination of the issues presented by Dan and Barnes.

Dan and Barnes read the following statement, which they referred to when asked to answer questions about occurrences inside the prison while they were reporting and filming there:

I entered Attica Penitentiary between September 9 and September 13, 1971 in the course of my employment as a newscaster. My sole and only purpose for being there was to gather and disseminate news to the general public. Therefore, as to those matters which occurred inside of the prison during those days, I respectfully decline to answer any questions. I do so as a protected newscaster and professional journalist within the provisions of Section 79-h of the Civil Rights Law and in furtherance of the First Amendment Constitutional rights of freedom of the press and in furtherance of the public's interest in free and untrammeled news reporting.[57]

State Supreme Court Judge Carmen Ball cited the Supreme Court's decision in the *Branzburg* case in denying the constitutional claim. He also ruled that the New York statute did not apply, since the reporters failed to demonstrate that the withheld information was based on confidential communications or sources.

On January 9, 1973, the case was appealed before the appellate division of the state supreme court. Dan and Barnes argued that the state statute did not refer to "confidential information" but protected *all* news and information.

On February 23 an upstate panel of the appellate division of the state supreme court ordered disclosure. The five-judge panel upheld Judge Ball's interpretation of the law, namely, events that they personally observed are not privileged from disclosure.[58]

When it became clear to Dan that the legal appeals had run the gamut and a thirty-day sentence for contempt was to begin July 2, 1973, he decided to go to the grand jury and tell all he knew about Attica. He said he did not think anything would be proved by his serving a jail term.[59]

Journalists are not the only ones who might be faced with subpoenas or go to jail for reporting on the prison scene. Truman Capote served a few days in jail for refusing to disclose the content of his confidential interviews with prisoners.[60]

Like the decision in *WBAI-FM* v. *Proskin, Dan* was a brief and unimaginative decision. The court ignored the statutory language that protects a journalist from having to disclose any news that comes into his possession while engaged in news gathering. The decision does not expound upon why a distinction should be made between what the reporter *hears* and what he *sees*. Also ignored was the fact that had it not been for the confidential relationship with the prisoners, the reporter and his cameraman would not have been permitted into the prison. *Dan* is not a case in which a newsman accidently witnessed events that might be relevant to grand jury investigation. The reporter went into the prison with the intention of discovering the conditions inside the prison, a topic that the grand jury was seeking to explore.

In yet another case on this same theme (confidentiality requirements and prison reporting), a zealous district attorney attempted to subpoena the original manuscript of an article published in the *Village Voice* on the Tombs (New York City house of detention) riot.[61] The article had been signed by its author, who was an inmate and who had since become a defendant in a criminal trial stemming from the riot. The district attorney regarded the article as a form of a confession. The *Village Voice* invoked the protection of the New York shield law on the ground that the content of the manuscript was news that had come into its possession while engaged in news gathering. The first department of the appellate division refused to quash the subpoena, arguing that the newspaper had waived the protection of the statute by printing the entire signed article. Although it noted the publication's claim that the article had been edited, the court said that the burden of proof was on the newspaper to prove this fact, since the person asserting a privilege has the burden of proof.[62] The court then went on to state that, as pointed out by the lower court, the manuscript had not been imparted under a "cloak of confidentiality."[63] The court defined confidentiality as an "understanding, express or implied, that the information or its source will not be disclosed. . . ."[64]

It is questionable whether the legislature or gubernatorial intent in respectively drafting and signing the New York shield legislation is congruent with the judicial interpretation. Governor Rockefeller went on record as favoring a strong shield law.[65]

In a memorandum at the time when the legislation was passing both houses of the legislature, the governor stated: "This measure affords a stronger safeguard of the free channels of news communication than most existing legislation, by protecting newsmen from being compelled to disclose the information they gather, as well as the identity of their informants. . . ."[66]

Courts have tried to distinguish between reporter-source conversations as confidential relationships on the one hand but are reluctant to extend the concept of confidentiality to notes, films, or tapes on the other hand. A St. Louis judge refused a request to quash a subpoena against the *St. Louis Post-Dispatch*. The subpoena sought pictures of a demonstration at Washington University. The court ruled that photographs can be required as evidence before the grand jury. Judge Reagan did not see the issue as involving a reporter's confidences.[67]

In June 1978 a California superior court judge ordered a *Sacramento Union* reporter to give up private notes, tape recordings and transcripts of an interview with a witness in a murder case.[68]

The most recent case concerned with reporting the activities of violence-prone organizations also turned on the issue of whether the reporters had established a confidential relationship. The facts in the

Los Angeles case and radio station KPFK were very similar to the WBAI case in New York. Both station managers in the two cases were told that they had not established confidential relationships and therefore were not protected by the state shield laws in their respective states.

On June 7, 1974, KPFK received a telephone call from an anonymous caller who stated that there was a tape recording and a letter in a rubbish heap behind the Pacifica station. (KPFK is one of several noncommercial radio stations working within the Pacifica Foundation, which has stations in Berkeley, New York, and Houston.) The tape recording and letter were found by station officials, and the material was aired shortly thereafter. The recording and communiqué, which contained a message from the Symbionese Liberation Army (SLA), reaffirmed the group's revolutionary convictions. They denounced the Los Angeles police for the shootout in which six other SLA members died on May 17. The mimeographed letter from the "Weather Underground" claimed responsibility for the May 31 bombing of Attorney General Evelle Younger's Los Angeles office. The voices on the tapes were those of Patricia Hearst and Emily and William Harris.[69]

A few days later, a federal grand jury that was investigating the activities of the SLA and the Weather Underground requested the letter and the tape. Will Lewis, the station manager supplied the letter and copies of the tape but refused to give up the original tape. He cited protection from divulging the initial recording under the California shield law and the First Amendment to the United States Constitution.

Federal authorities argued that the original tape was needed in a fingerprint check that might enable law enforcement officials to track down SLA members. Lewis was offered immunity from a contempt citation if he would answer certain questions before the grand jury and if he would deliver the tape. He responded by arguing that either testifying or giving up the original for possible fingerprinting would turn KPFK into a law enforcement arm, thus endangering the free flow of information from those who would no longer trust the station as a news organization.[70]

Following that statement, United States District Judge A. Andrew Hauk found Lewis in civil contempt and ordered him to prison June 19.[71] He was informed that he could be purged of the contempt by releasing the tape and by appearing before the grand jury. Lewis's attorney, David B. Finkel moved in the Ninth Circuit Court of Appeals for a temporary modification and filed notice of appeal. Judge Shirley M. Hufstedler stayed Hauk's order until July 1 on the subject of answering questions before the federal grand jury but sustained Hauk's order that Lewis provide the original communication to the jury.[72]

Will Lewis spent sixteen days in jail at Terminal Island. On July 5 Justice Douglas ordered him released pending an appeal to the Ninth Circuit court on the contempt conviction.[73]

On July 22 the Ninth Circuit court affirmed the conviction saying that its order would become effective in ten days. This gave Lewis's lawyer time in which to appeal to the United States Supreme Court.[74] Judge Hauk was very upset over the Douglas order. He said that there was no confidential relationship involved, "no confidentiality—none whatever." Justice Douglas argued that because Lewis did not have a criminal record, he should be released on his own recognizance until the high court could consider the substantial First Amendment questions that were involved. Judge Hauk believed that a newsman who receives information in a nonconfidential status has no more First Amendment rights than any other human being.

One month before the Ninth Circuit ruling came down, the Pacifica Foundation president came out with a statement of support for Lewis.[75] But the *Los Angeles Times*, which had given strong support to William Farr in his subpoena fight, now took a critical position in the KPFK matter. In an editorial entitled "Press Freedom—and Responsibility" they admonished Lewis:

Will Lewis, manager of radio station KPFK, was jailed Wednesday for arguing what we think an erroneous interpretation of press freedom.

It is always unfortunate when a constitutional confrontation comes to this. And it seems all the more unfortunate in this case because the position taken by Lewis and the station confuses and corrupts the broad constitutional principle as well as the narrower principle of providing reasonable protection for the confidentiality of news sources. . . .

It seems to us an entirely different matter to argue that this tape and this letter come under such protections. No demand for protection was made by the source. Indeed, the evidence suggests that the source is unknown; the station learned of the whereabouts of the tape through an anonymous telephone call.

Obviously, however, the original tape and the original letter could prove useful to law enforcement officials. That is why we turned over a similar letter as soon as it was received. The press, as every citizen, bears, within the constitutional limits, a responsibility for cooperation with law enforcement agencies.[76]

During the period when the matter was on appeal to the Supreme Court, Lewis stated that he would surrender the original if money was not raised by a certain date. "I don't want to go to jail," he said—"I'm not a martyr."[77]

On August 2 Justice Douglas granted another stay, thus halting execution of the Ninth Circuit Court's order pending resolution of the issues raised by Lewis. Douglas now invited the government to respond with arguments.[78] Otherwise, Lewis would have returned to jail on August 5. The government replied that it would frame a response from the solicitor general's office in a week or two. During the fall of 1974 and early winter of 1975, Lewis was not confined.

On February 14, 1975, the Supreme Court declined to hear an appeal of the contempt conviction.[79] In his arguments before the court KPFK's lawyer opined that the California shield law applies in federal proceedings as spelled out by Congress in a recent revision of the evidentiary rules applicable to federal courts. The government had responded with the "fingerprint argument."

On February 20 Lewis gave to the federal grand jury the original of the tape-recorded message.[80] He had maintained all along that he would give up the tape when he had exhausted all appeals. That ended the dispute over the Hearst tape.[81]

The station continued to fight a second contempt of court citation stemming from its refusal to turn over a communiqué received from an organization called the New World Liberation Front. The group took credit for the bombing of Sheraton hotels in San Francisco and Los Angeles in October 1974. The bombs had caused minor damage.

The Pacifica Foundation has not always been unsuccessful in its refusals to pass on SLA communications. In March 1974 the manager and the news director of Pacifica's Berkeley station KPFA-FM declined to answer questions before an Alameda County grand jury about the source of an SLA communication received and broadcast after the assassination of Oakland school superintendent Marcus Foster. They were sustained by a judge in their claim of protection under the California shield law.[82]

As a result of the Supreme Court's action in the first case, Lewis said that KPFK probably would comply with any future subpoenas from the federal government for material supplied by anonymous sources. He continued: "Anyone who wants to get in touch with us will have to realize that we fought the battle and lost and that we will abide by the law of the land."[83]

Even coverage of demonstrations that do not lead to physical violence can be risky. In 1972 a media photographer took pictures of a busing demonstration in Wilmington, Delaware. The *Wilmington News-Journal* was directed by subpoena to give the pictures to a police sergeant so that he could identify a demonstrator who he claimed had made obscene remarks to him.[84]

The paper tried unsuccessfully to quash the subpoena, and its attorney argued as follows:

Several facts stand out in this effort to subpoena the press.

First, the offense thought to have occurred is a misdemeanor of the mildest kind. (The maximum punishment is a $10 fine and ten days in jail.)

Second, there is no present suspect.

Third, the policeman in question cannot identify the offender but thinks his fellow policeman "might" be able to.

Fourth, the entire matter is a police concern. The Attorney General, at the request of the police, provided legal advice as to what offense might have been committed and issued a subpoena when asked to.

This is, then, a case where the police seek to annex the news media as an investigatory arm in a police inquiry into an offense of the most petty sort. The news-photographer becomes, by his coverage of a news story of public interest, the investigating reporter for the police.[85]

In another demonstration case in 1972 the premises of the *Stanford Daily News* in Palo Alto, California, were searched by police with a warrant seeking photographs to identify demonstrators. As part of the search, police sifted through confidential files. The United States District Court condemned the police action in October and ordered the photographs returned.[86]

In spite of those court actions, enforcement groups continued to press the issue (seventeen state attorneys general, police associations, and prosecuting attorneys).[87] In 1978 the Justice Department asked the Supreme Court of the United States to let police make surprise searches of newspaper offices for evidence in criminal cases. This would bypass the subpoena by going directly to the search warrant. The media was critical of the potential chilling effect this practice could have on news gathering and press information storage.[88]

On May 31, 1978, the Supreme Court in *Zurcher* v. *The Stanford Daily*[89] greatly disappointed major spokesmen for the press.[90] The majority opinion by Justice White ruled that police may conduct surprise searches of news organization premises without obtaining a subpoena, although a search warrant is necessary. White argued that newspapers were not deserving of special constitutional protection where there was "reasonable cause" to believe that evidence of crime existed in the confines of the newsrooms. Subpoenas would impede investigations because it would take law enforcement too long to defeat them. It would be easy to find a "neutral magistrate"[92] who would observe Fourth Amendment guarantees. The press would not and should not be intimidated in any case. If abuse occurred, there would be enough time for dealing with it.

The concurring opinion by Justice Powell hoped that judges would carefully balance the interests of the press against those of law enforcement.[93] He had expressed similar concern in *Branzburg*.[94]

The dissenting opinion by John Paul Stevens emphasized the adverse impact that the ruling would have on not only journalists but all citizens seeking protection under the Fourth Amendment's "search and seizure" clause.[95] He was generally concerned about innocent parties as search targets.

Justice Stewart's dissent reemphasized, as with *Branzburg*[96] the special role of the press:

Perhaps, as a matter of abstract policy, a newspaper office should receive no more protection from unannounced police searches than, say, the office of a doctor or the office of a bank. But we are here to uphold a Constitution. And our Constitution does not explicitly protect the practice of medicine or the business of banking from all abridgment by government. It does explicitly protect the freedom of the press.[97]

Justices Stewart and Marshall were both concerned that the element of surprise, the broad-fishing-expedition aspect that the search allowed, the use of the press as an investigative arm of government, and the destruction of reportorial notes would have a dangerously chilling effect on news sources that would dry up under the new judicial guidelines.

Stewart and other critics of the decision preferred the protection of subpoenas with the possibility of motions to quash,[98] as opposed to the more easily obtainable warrant. The *Los Angeles Times* offered the opinion that:

If this new ruling of the Supreme Court had been in effect a few years ago, the burglary of the psychiatrist's office would not have been necessary. Can it be imagined that a "neutral" magistrate would have denied a warrant to raid the offices of newspapers that were investigating the Watergate conspiracy? Wiretapping is one kind of search, and under the White theory of the Fourth Amendment, the government during the Nixon years would have had no difficulty in obtaining approval to wiretap the telephones of reporters assigned to the Watergate investigation.[99]

But some commentators preferred to look at the issue with a wider focus. Anthony Lewis noted that "at the time the Fourth Amendment was adopted, private papers were generally thought to be immune from seizure altogether. The problem needs deeper consideration by the Court and others, in a context broader than the press."[100]

Nevertheless, the ramifications of Justice White's interpretation of the Fourth Amendment appeared to further dampen the press fraternity's hope that the First Amendment could be applied in protecting confidential news sources. It does not seem unreasonable to argue that unannounced searches that turn into fishing expeditions will greatly discourage news sources from providing information, for fear that their comments will surface on some scrap of paper or tape recording swept up in a gleaning and sifting operation as occurred in the *Stanford* case.

Less than a month after the *Stanford* case the Court delivered a decision on press access to prisons that had a slightly different focus from the Attica and Tombs prison reportage, where the issues turned on the use of subpoenas and matters of confidentiality. Nevertheless, the holding affected the issue of news flow. In *Houchins* v. *KQED*[101] the Court ruled that journalists have no more right to visit prisons than other members of the public and that both press and public may be excluded entirely from prisons.

Has court supervision of the press been very beneficial to the public where reporters have covered violence and the underground scene?

In the three demonstration cases previously discussed, there was hardly a compelling need, an overriding interest, the danger of a miscarriage of justice, and so on, but there did appear to be the use of journalists as investigative agents for the police in one case to preserve the "honor" of a sergeant, in another to sift and "expeditiously fish around" in files to see whether something might turn up. In the last case the police were probably most concerned over embarrassment should the public become too aware of police bribes to drug dealers. In all three cases, whatever chilling effect on news flow resulted from subpoena pressures could hardly be justified by the countervailing benefit to society.

Vietnam Protest

The last category in this chapter revolves around the plight of Samuel L. Popkin, an assistant professor of government at Harvard University who is a student of political movements and social forces in Vietnam.

As a research associate of the Harvard Center for International Affairs, he participated in various seminars on the subject of Vietnam.

On November 21, 1972, he was imprisoned in the federal section of the Norfolk County jail in Dedham, Massachusetts, under a contempt order of the United States District Court for Massachusetts.[102] He had refused to answer several questions before a federal grand jury investigating the publication of the Pentagon Papers. He asserted a right under the First Amendment to refuse to answer questions concerning the identity of confidential sources and the content of his opinions on his Vietnam research. He asked that the government show that the information sought was relevant and required for its investigation.

One week later, the grand jury was discharged at the government's request and he was released from jail. But in early January 1973 Popkin filed a petition for a writ of certiorari asking the Supreme Court to review his case. The petition was denied by the Court in April 1973.

The *Popkin* case is the first on record in American jurisprudence in which the question of a scholar's right to the confidentiality of his sources and data has been raised and decided.[103]

The government seemed particularly concerned in this case about any information Popkin might have that would throw light on who possessed copies of the Pentagon Papers prior to publication. Also implied in these questions were concerns as to whether Popkin had seen the papers prior to publication and whether he had talked with Daniel Ellsberg about the content or existence of the papers prior to publication. In all, Popkin was asked 126 questions by the grand jury. His refusal to answer 7 of them became the subject matter of subsequent litigation.[104] In his appeal of the contempt order of the district court, the Court of Appeals for the First Circuit narrowed the required questions to 3. The court also quoted with approval the government's argument that ''the scholar's privilege is a creature not to be found in the province of jurisprudence.''[105]

Upon Popkin's failure to answer the three questions about persons whom he had interviewed in acquiring knowledge of who had participated in the Pentagon Papers study, he was imprisoned for contempt.

In his next stage of appeal to the Supreme Court he did not argue that a scholar has an absolute right or privilege not to testify before a grand jury concerning the identity of confidential sources and the content of data obtained in confidence in the course of research. He advocated a balancing test to determine whether a witness should be ordered to answer. Such a test would require a showing by the government to the satisfaction of the presiding judge that:

1. the information sought bears a direct relationship to the subject of the investigation; 2. there is probable cause to believe the witness has information that is clearly relevant to a specific violation of law; 3. the government has demonstrated that the information sought cannot be obtained by alternative means less destructive of First Amendment rights; and 4. the government has demonstrated a compelling and overriding interest in the information.[106]

In February 1973 the American Anthropological Asosciation, the American Political Science Association, and the American Sociological Association jointly filed a motion in the Supreme Court for leave to file a brief as amicus curiae in support of Popkin's petition. The brief emphasized that in the past scholars assumed that they were able to assure sources of anonymity because the release of any information gained was deemed to be solely within the scholar's discretion. Recently, that pattern has changed so that judicial bodies are inquiring into the most minute details of the scholar's work and the sources that made it possible. The effect of the subpoenas may be to produce more inhibited research dealing with less controversial topics.[107]

Fellow political scientists produced affidavits in support of Popkin's claim. Karl Deutsch stated:

Efforts to compel scholars to testify before Grand Juries on their professional contacts or sources seem to be something of an innovation, particularly if they are made without specific evidence that the scholar has been a witness to any crime or to any plan to commit a crime. From over thirty years of professional practice, I do not recall any such broad and sweeping efforts to compel scholars to reveal their contacts and sources. . . .[108]

James Q. Wilson, chairman of the Department of Government at Harvard, asserted in his affidavit:

A scholar who knowingly violates the confidence imported to him is guilty of a grave ethical infraction; a society that requires a scholar to violate such a confidence in the absence of any showing that the information sought is directly and materially relevant to a criminal act is guilty of placing an unwarranted burden on free inquiry and academic responsibilities. Either the violation of scholarly ethics or the compulsion of scholarly testimony is likely to result in the withdrawal of cooperation by present and future subjects of research and thus in the placing of serious inhibition on the processes of free inquiry.[109]

Popkin's experience with subpoenas, manacles, chains, and imprisonment[110] was one of many confrontations news gatherers had with the Justice Department in the fall following the *Branzburg* decision. J.

Weidman, president of the Author's League of America, stated in reference to the jailing of Peter Bridge and Samuel Popkin that

> . . . these actions are the first bitter fruits of the Supreme Court's 5–4 decision. . . . The majority's narrow view of the First Amendment has created dangerous weapons with which prosecutors can intimidate individuals who would have previously given valuable information on vital issues, on a confidential basis, to journalists and writers.[111]

After the Justice Department had made its point that it could coerce Popkin's testimony, it dropped the matter.

Thus at a time when frank reporting on the drug culture, the Black Panthers, violent events, and demonstrations is essential for a well-informed public, law enforcement institutions from the Justice Department through state and local prosecutions have been attempting to depose reporters. The privilege issue is complex, and it is recognized that law enforcers sometimes need vital information that they believe only the journalist can supply. However, in their determination to discover or convict criminals, an increasingly disturbing pattern appears to be emerging. There is intimidation of sources who are essential to some investigative reporting that reveals essential public information. Such information can have beneficial by-products, among which are consensus building, which subdues cultural polarization through corrective legislation or resistance to harmful legislation. In addition to the problem of lost information resulting from source fear is the diminished capacity of the police for crime apprehension because some of their most effective investigators (journalists) have lost the very informants that lay bare many criminal schemes.

3 | Privileged Communication and News Dissemination: The Common Law

COMMON LAW ANTECEDENTS OR PRIVILEGED COMMUNICATION IN ENGLAND AND ENGLISH-SPEAKING COUNTRIES

Legally privileged communication is rooted in the Anglo-American system of jurisprudence, but the development of the concept was only very reluctantly accepted. As early as 1562, English judges insisted on the absolute obligation to testify. No exceptions were permitted.[1]

Eventually, two exceptions developed. One was the "Point of Honour." Gentlemen who promised not to divulge one another's confidences insisted that the law protect their private communications. But even this doctrine was abandoned after a time.[2]

A second breach of the testimonial rule developed out of the libel law. An English court refused to order a defendant to reveal the names of his informants. The court noted that such identity was not necessary to dispose of the litigation successfully.[3]

As this rule pertains to the press, it is discriminatory. Publishers are protected from not testifying unless the relevancy test is met. Individual reporters, however, are not similarly protected.[4]

In other parts of the United Kingdom, in Australia, for example, the High Court has generally denied a press privilege.[5] In Canada the same basic precedent has been followed.[6]

In 1975 an appeals court in London upheld a television news agency's defiance of a lower court order to submit untransmitted television film of a disturbance at a pop music festival. In handing down its decision the three-judge appellate panel cited cases arising out of the Watergate scandals and other American cases in which the confidentiality of news sources was involved. The decision also drew contrasts between American and British legal views on press freedom. The appeals court held that newsmen, like other British subjects, have no right to withhold information that would be deemed necessary in a trial. But this did not mean that plaintiffs, defendants, or judges should secure access to newsmen's sources and unpublished material merely for the asking. As Lord Denning, head of the appellate panel, put it:

On the one hand there is the public interest which demands that the course of justice not be impeded by withholding of evidence. On the other hand there is the public interest in seeing that confidences are respected and that newsmen are not hampered by fear of being compelled to disclose all information which comes their way, as in the Watergate case.[7]

The ruling grew out of a suburban court trial in January 1975, in which Nicholas Albery sought damages from police for allegedly beating him during a flare-up of violence at a pop festival. Albery secured an order from trial judge Claude Duveen requiring ITN to submit all of the film it had taken during the three-day event on the chance that it might show a scene of the alleged beating. The station agreed to show the film that it presented on the air but claimed that the "outtakes" were not available. A spokesman for the station said that there was no footage on the beatings anyway.[8]

It appears that the following conclusions can be drawn from the short survey of a few English-speaking common law jurisdictions. Judges are very unlikely to accept any form of "absolute privilege." "Absolute" is taken here to mean that the newsman under his own discretion determines the contours of the privilege regardless of the circumstances within which he procured information and no matter what manner of tribunal summons him to appear. Rather than accepting a per se standard, British Commonwealth courts have responded with some kind of balancing formula on an ad hoc basis. In that regard the British experience is not very unlike the general American approach except that the United States has many more cases and overlapping jurisdictional difficulties than the British and this situation has led to more complicated formulas for resolving the difficulty. Another observation that might be noted is that while the John Peter Zenger and Benjamin Franklin encounters with British courts over the privilege issue did not break new ground in the English common law (see chapter 1), the Watergate scandal apparently did evoke enough concern for judicial notice in the recent TV case in London.

LEGAL SCHOLARS AND RULES OF EVIDENCE

Two names are featured in the common law of evidence, McCormick[9] and Wigmore. John Henry Wigmore, late law professor and dean at Northwestern University, is most frequently associated with the common law of evidence and privileged communication.

Wigmore's approach was to assume that there could be no exceptions to the duty to testify and then to proceed to permit exceptions only when they were fully justified. Wigmore stated his view in this way:

For more than three centuries, it has been recognized as a fundamental maxim that the public . . . has a right to everyman's evidence. When we come to examine the various claims of exception, we start with the primary assumption that there is a general duty to give what testimony one is capable to giving, and that any exemptions which may exist are distinctly exceptional, being so many derogations from a positive general rule.[10]

Wigmore established four conditions, which he argued must be satisfied in order to justify the creation of any privilege against compulsory testimony:

1. The communications must originate in a confidence that they will not be disclosed;
2. This element of confidentiality must be essential to the full and satisfactory maintenance of the relation between the parties;
3. The relation must be one which in the opinion of the community ought to be sedulously fostered;
4. The injury that would inure to the relation by the disclosure of the communications must be greater than the benefit thereby gained for the correct disposal of litigation.[11]

In applying Wigmore's conditions, many courts deny reportorial privilege. They argue, first, that the communication itself is not confidential. It is given to be published for the community; second, that the confidentiality of the communication is not essential to the relationship between the parties; third, that the community has no particular interest in protecting the newsman-confidential-informant relationship for its own sake; and, finally, that there is no injury caused by the disclosure of the communications because the communications are intended to be disclosed; only the source of the information remains undisclosed.

In support of the first argument it could be noted that all other privileges emphasize nonpublication and privacy. It is not their purpose to communicate information to the public, with the exception of the policy informer who is communicating information that will necessarily be passed to prosecutors and district attorneys: It is not directly passed to the public, but rather indirectly through those who administer the criminal justice system.

One might agree that the second argument is sound because informants can very well pass on information that the public and law enforcement personnel should know about and that an informant and an investigative reporter are mutually trying to convey without fear of source name disclosure. It is difficult to prove the extent of a chilling effect if source names are discovered. It can also be pointed out that the relationship among reporters, sources, and prosecutors does not necessarily have to be an adversary one, and many sources may even try to gain publicity through the disclosure of their names.

There is room for discussion as to the validity of the third argument because the "opinion of the community" cannot be determined with exactitude.[12] In support of the fourth argument one must show how important a full and complete portfolio of evidence is for the determination of guilt or innocence, default, extent of damage, and so on. What possible public information benefit will outweigh apprehension of a criminal or a fair assessment of damage?

There are those who argue that Wigmore's conditions can be interpreted to support newsmen's privilege. They note that the newsman only wants to conceal the identity of the source and not the information received therefrom and that the mere identity of the source does not fit the notion of "communication" ascertained in the four conditions. Even if the identity of the informant is part of the communication, Wigmore's conditions would still seem to be satisfied.[13] First, the name was communicated in a confidence that it would not be disclosed. Certainly, not all communications between a journalist and his informants are confidential, but there are those in which a source may fear exposure when he is exposing fraud or corruption. Second, the relationship requires confidentiality because in very many cases the informant would not make public his information unless guaranteed anonymity. Third, the community desires to foster the relationship because of its interest in the free flow of news. People are dependent upon the news media for information. Without access to the press, people would be largely unaware of events occurring throughout the world, nationally, and locally, and citizens would be unable to make reasoned judgments in choosing their elected representatives at all levels of government. The cases during the past several years have awakened some community support: A recent Gallup poll indicated that 57 percent of the public sample surveyed supported a reporters' privilege.[14] Fourth, the injury to the relation and consequent free flow of information, in some instances, outweighs the interest in the correct disposal of litigation. In a grand jury matter there may not even be litigation to dispose of because there might be no indictment and no connection of a newsman to a crime. The issue extends beyond the injury to the reporter and his source. The reporter may lose money, his freedom for a time, his job, and therefore his ability to gather news. The source may suffer the loss of employment and threats or actual physical or mental injuries. Beyond those injuries the public's awareness of the news is impaired. In particular, those who argue that the fourth Wigmore condition should include newsmen place a substantial burden of proof on the prosecution or defense seeking the disclosure, by requiring them to show relevancy to litigation, overriding interest, and assurance that they have exhausted alternative sources, and so on.

In spite of arguments by some scholars that Wigmore's conditions are applicable to newsmen, there is a rather substantial body of literature that interprets the leading cases as establishing a common law trend away from acceptance of the newsman's privilege.[15]

In the garden of evidence the privilege is a tolerated weed. The newsman's privilege is often the weed that is pulled while others maintain some measure of standing within the root system of common law.

COMPARING ESTABLISHED COMMON LAW PRIVILEGES WITH THE JOURNALIST PRIVILEGE

At common law the attorney-client relationship was the only professional relationship that enjoyed a privilege. Originally, this privilege arose in the context of a code of honor, expressed by the maxim that gentlemen should not betray confidences. By the end of the eighteenth century, this theory gave way to the one still used as a justification today, that attorneys should have a privilege in the interests of the administration of justice, since a voluntary pledge of secrecy should not be permitted to obstruct the truth.[16] Most states have embodied the attorney-client privilege in statutes.[17] In the past, grants of privilege have been made by reference to professional groups rather than to the content of the particular communication, resulting in inconsistent treatment. Some professionals have secured absolute privileges for their relationships, whereas others have been partially or totally unsuccessful. Perhaps the political leverage of lawyers is greater than that of other groups trying to influence the content of evidence law. But in spite of that possibility, there is a concern among some of the bar and on the bench that privileges have an adverse effect on the judicial system.[18] It is also evident that even the attorney-client privilege, which is more deeply rooted in the common law than any other privilege and which has the blessing of Wigmore, is itself under attack. A recent case in Arizona involved a taxing authority that sought to pry from a Phoenix attorney, Stephen Silver, the names of two of his clients on whose behalf he sent checks in the amount of $4,190 as "conscience money" representing back taxes plus penalties. The state wanted to prosecute the clients for tax evasion. Arizona contended that the lawyer-client privilege did not apply. It maintained that the privilege relieved an attorney from the obligation of testifying as to what his clients told him but that he is still compelled to reveal their identities. Critics of this stand believe that this is inconsistent because part of what they told him was their names. As a result of this case, the legal profession might identify more closely with the newsmen.[19] Hitherto many lawyers have felt that their privilege has several societal advantages over a journalist privilege, one of which is the fact that the privilege is not held by the lawyer himself but by his client. Thus most states with an attorney-client privilege require the client's consent for divestiture.[20]

Historically, there was no privilege for the physician-patient relationship. The nonexistence of the privilege at common law was first articulated in 1776 by Lord Mansfield in the trial of Elizabeth, Duchess of Kingston. When asked by a witness whether it would be proper to reveal information learned as a physician, Lord Mansfield replied, "To give that information in a court of justice, which by the law of the land he is bound to do, will never be imputed to the physician as any indiscretion whatever."[21]

Jeremy Bentham believed that no privilege should exist except the priest-penitent one, which he saw as necessary, since its abolition would "operate like a penal law, prohibiting confession . . . (and) therefore would be contrary to the law . . . which allows the exercise of the catholic religion."[22] Bentham opposed the attorney-client privilege by asking sarcastically, "Whence all this dread of the Truth?" Wigmore advanced several points in answer to Bentham's criticism, including the "unhealthy moral state" in which the lawyer who "betrays" his client finds himself. He also noted that if the privilege were abolished, the prospective litigant would simply tell his lawyer as little as possible.

All of the nonpress privileges mentioned thus far have been qualified either in statutes or common law rules. The communication to be protected must be in the course of the professional relationship. When a third pair of ears is involved, the privilege is divested if the first two parties were aware of the presence of a third person. In the case of the attorney-client privilege the law forbids the use of the relationship to plot a crime or tort, or to prepare the client's future insulation from prosecution or damage recovery for a crime or tort he is planning to commit.[23] As a general rule, all privileges can be waived. There are some situations that are difficult for the common law to anticipate as to the waiver or dissolution of the privilege. One of these might occur when two clients engage the same attorney on a matter in which they have a common interest.[24]

In his contemplation on the physician-patient relationship Wigmore decided that such a privilege did not meet his four conditions. He is usually cited by writers as being opposed to the privilege. Snubbed by the common law, the physician-patient privilege is a creature of statute.[25]

The first departure from the common law rule was made in New York in 1828 by a statute designed as a public health measure in response to a high incidence of certain diseases. (The journalist privilege does not emerge in a statute until 1896 in Maryland.[26]) Presumably, people were more willing to have physical examinations and treatment when they were protected from disclosure of their condition. At any rate, many states followed New York's initiative.

A survey of state statutes granting a privilege to communications of medical, psychotherapeutic, and social work personnel reveals that the grants of privilege have been anything but consistent. This is certainly true of journalist coverage. Inconsistency is particularly apparent when comparing the privileges of psychiatrists and psychologists. The California Law Revision Commission pointed out that psychiatrists are sometimes covered by the physician-patient privilege, but there are more state statutes that expressly protect psychologists as opposed to psychiatrists. Recognizing that psychoanalysis and psychotherapy are dependent upon the fullest revelation of the most intimate and embarrassing details of the patient's life, and in light of the fact that the commission had received several reliable reports indicating that persons in need of treatment sometimes refused it from psychiatrists because the confidentiality of their communications could not be assured, the commission concluded that psychiatrists should enjoy the same privilege as psychologists.[27]

Of the fifty states and the District of Columbia, twelve do not have a physician-patient privilege.[28] Five states have a separate psychiatrist privilege; four of these do not have a physician privilege.[29] Two states have a privilege encompassing both psychologists and psychiatrists.[30] One state has a combined psychiatrist-psychologist privilege.[31] All but fifteen states and the District of Columbia have a psychologist privilege.[32]

Of the thirty-five states having a psychologist privilege, twenty-three were included in licensing statutes, which set out requirements for obtaining licenses to practice the profession involved. Some commentators have suggested a journalist privilege that would require a very specific and formal definition of who is a newsman in determining whether a privilege should apply. Others call for a sweeping privilege statute and set of common law rules that would define the status of all privileges once and for all.[33] In some states particular kinds of privileges are subsumed under other privilege titles. In sixteen states the scope of the psychologist privilege is determined by the scope of the attorney-client privilege. Of the sixteen states only two do not include the psychologist-client privilege in licensing statutes.[34] In thirteen of the sixteen states there is also a physician or psychiatrist privilege.[35] In only two out of those thirteen states is the physician or psychiatrist privilege also placed on the same basis as the attorney-client privilege.[36] In only five states do psychiatrists and psychologists have similar testimonial privileges.[37] Table 1 presents a state-by-state breakdown of the different kinds of privileged communication permitted.

Social workers, on the other hand, have been less successful in securing legislation. New York provides a privilege for certain certified social workers.[38] Colorado, Michigan, New Jersey, and Oregon provide a privilege for marriage counselors.[39]

The interspousal privilege or husband-wife privilege has a purpose different from that of the journalist privilege. Whereas the journalist privilege is often supported with a communications flow argument, the spousal privilege is seeking privacy from open communications. As with the other privileges discussed thus far, this one is not absolute

Table 1

Privileged Communication Statutes in the Several States Applicable to Physicians, Psychiatrists, and Psychologists

States	Physician-Patient Privilege	Psychiatrist Privilege	Psychologists and Psychiatrists	Psychologist Privilege
Alabama				X
Alaska	X			X
Arizona	X			X
Arkansas	X			X
California	X			X
Colorado	X			X
Connecticut		X		X
Delaware				X
Florida		X		X
Georgia		X		X
Hawaii	X			
Idaho	X			
Illinois	X	X		X
Indiana	X	X		X
Iowa	X			
Kansas	X			X

State			
Kentucky	X		X
Louisiana	X		X
Maine	X		X
Maryland		X	
Massachusetts	X		
Michigan	X		X
Minnesota			X
Mississippi			X
Missouri	X		X
Montana	X		X
Nebraska	X		X
Nevada	X		X
New Hampshire	X		X
New Jersey	X		X
New Mexico	X		X
New York	X		X
North Carolina	X		X
North Dakota	X		X
Ohio			X
Oklahoma			X
Oregon	X		X
Pennsylvania	X		X
South Dakota			X
Utah			X
Virginia	X		X
Washington	X		X
West Virginia	X		X
Wisconsin	X		X
Wyoming	X		X

either. Most business communications between spouses are not considered within the privileged domain,[40] and marital communication in the known presence of third persons is not confidential.

The police-informer privilege has common law protection in that Wigmore emphatically recognizes the need for this privilege with regard to government informers, concluding that "its soundness cannot be questioned."[41] He observes that disclosures from informers are discouraged if informers' identities are disclosed, for they then would be subject to great risks, and that "law enforcement officers often depend on professional informers to furnish them with a flow of information about criminal activities."[42] The Supreme Court has also recognized the need for such a privilege.[43] The Court is of the opinion that the public through its elected and appointed law enforcement officers regularly utilizes informers for the purpose of effective law enforcement and public concern for knowledge of the extent of crime.[44] The privilege recognizes the obligation of citizens to communicate their knowledge of the commission of crimes to law enforcement officials and, by preserving their anonymity, encourages them to perform that obligation.[45] There are many who feel that the journalist privilege is at least as beneficial to society as the government-informer privilege. They believe that Wigmore's statement that "law enforcement officers often depend on professional informers to furnish them with a flow of information about critical activities" should be analogized to the newsman's privilege. Wigmore's concern that informers would be subject to great risks if their identities were revealed equally applies to informants who supply news coverage. In congressional testimony in the House the following statement was entered in the record:

But what of the example of, let us say, the young patrolman with knowledge of widespread corruption in his precinct or department and who, being fearful for his job and possibly for his life, turns to a newspaper reporter to make that corruption known in return for a pledge of anonymity? How many articles have we all read by investigative reporters exposing burglary rings operating in some of our major metropolitan police departments, or large-scale pay-offs reaching even to higher ups in the police department, or into a district attorney's office, or a mayor's office? If we are that patrolman, uncertain of the honesty perhaps not even known to him, to whom does he carry his story, knowing that in safety and anonymity, he can make the existence of this corruption known to the public? I am afraid he does not, in Justice White's antiseptic view, "risk placing his trust in public officials" of whose honesty he may be gravely apprehensive. He goes to the press.[46]

It is rather unlikely that a Serpico could go to a police informer to reveal police corruption. The budget for informers' fees could be controlled by the corrupt officials themselves.

In Senate hearings on reporter privilege United States Senator Schweiker of Pennsylvania expressed the following opinion: "It is ironic that government has no problem allowing the identity of police informers to remain secret, for fear of drying up police information, but refuses to apply this same principle to the media.'"[47]

Vince Blasi, who is generally reluctant to draw analogies among the various kinds of privileges, has this to say of the informer privilege:

> If an analogy is necessary, the privilege (newsman's) would most closely resemble that possessed by police informers. The privilege is justified only when it helps a governmental institution—in the one case the prosecutor, in the other the electorate—obtain the information it needs if it is to fulfill its responsibilities.[48]

Neither the disclosure made by an informer nor that of a news source directly involves a personal right of the one making the disclosure. Rather, with respect to an informer, the privilege has been said to be the government's privilege to withhold the identity of persons providing information concerning a violation of the law. With respect to a news source the privilege belongs ultimately to the public although it is exercised on the public's behalf by the journalist.[49]

Justice Burton stated in upholding the informer's privilege: "The purpose of the privilege is the furtherance and protection of the public interest in effective law enforcement.'"[50] The Court of Appeals for the Second Circuit in *United States* v. *Tucker* stated:

> It has been the experience of law enforcement officers that the prospective informer will usually condition his cooperation on an assurance of anonymity, fearing that if disclosure is made, physical harm or other undesirable consequences may be visited upon him or his family.[51]

It should be observed that even though the Supreme Court upheld a government-informer privilege, it was by no means an absolute privilege. In *Roviaro* the Court noted that Sixth Amendment rights are of sufficient importance to override the government's interest in maintaining the confidentiality of its informants' relationships.[52]

There is only one other privilege that has a basis in the common law. That is the juror-juror privilege.[53] The political vote is confidential, but that is secured under legislation. Trade secrets are likewise secured by statute. Secrets of state are covered by congressional elaboration and through executive orders.

There are other privilege claims that vie for judicial and legislative attention. Some brokers would prefer protection for communications with their investors. The same could be true for bankers and borrowers, bankers and depositors, secretaries and employers, and accountants and their clients. But thus far the common law has not recognized them as privileged relationships requiring a legal shield.

The basic problems encountered in a consideration of all privileges is whether there should be a privilege at all and whether the currently proposed privilege should have as much or more standing than those already recognized. In formulating the alternative for new approaches to remedy the present confused state of the law, three choices emerge: (1) abolish all privileges; (2) continue to provide for privileges in particular relationships but reject others; or (3) provide a set of privileged communications rules of common law for judicial recognition that is applicable to a wide spectrum of relationships. Abolishing privileges is a very straightforward but impractical method of approaching the subject. Well-entrenched privileges are relatively permanent. Maintaining the status quo is confusing because of the differences among the many state and federal jurisdictions. The third alternative requires a conference approach in formulating rules of evidence that will apply to judicial administration.[54]

One of the broad umbrellas that could cover several professional-informant privileges is the enterprise of *research*. Under a research doctrine, a court would be justified in finding a communication privileged when the same communication would have been privileged if it had been made to a member of a traditionally protected relationship and if there is social justification for protecting the nontraditional relationship. Thus a social worker counseling on marital problems could receive the same privilege as an attorney offering such advice. As Paul Nejelski notes:

Certain areas of research fall within the protected scope of already privileged professions and similar research, by whomever performed, deserves equal protection. A lawyer in the course of his traditional duties might need to conduct empirical research . . . .

By applying the *functional overlap doctrine* a court would not be creating a new privilege, but rather would merely be extending protection to cover a new type of professional engaging in a form of communication already privileged.[55]

News reporting and research obviously have many similarities. Whether Paul Branzburg, with a law degree from Harvard and a master's degree from Columbia, is working as a researcher or as a reporter in describing drug usage and subcultures in Kentucky may be a distinction without a practical difference.

The research angle might avoid some of the analogizing that has often been detrimental to the outsider seeking privileged sanctuary while protecting the insider who already enjoys it. Vince Blasi states:

> I think the analogies to the professional privilege of clergy, doctors, and lawyers are different. These privileges are safeguarding privacy in a sense of sensitivity. You are trying to encourage a very close personal ongoing relationship. It is a feeling that it is indecent to intrude. Here it is not the case (i.e. Newsman's Privilege). Newsmen are not that close to their sources. They have to keep a distance. It is not like a professional family adviser counseling. I think that the tendency to analogize with those privileges is misplaced. . . . Historically these privileges have emerged when a particular group seeks professional recognition. In a sense it is a status symbol.[56]

The same point was made by Benno Schmidt of the Columbia Law School when he said that he believed that legislators or judges should "decide on the desirability of a journalist's privilege by looking at the situation with respect to journalists and not by attempting to reason analogically to doctors, priests, and lawyers and patients."[57]

Although there are those who apply analogies for excluding those not yet covered by privilege, there are some newsmen who have tried to show analogies so that they might be covered. In referring to the government-informer privilege, they point out that neither the disclosure made by a government informer nor that of a news source directly involves a personal right of the one making the disclosure. Thus far the courts have not seen fit to consider this analogy compelling enough to include newsmen under a common law protection on a case-by-case approach. Nor has this been the case with the general-rules approach to which we now give our attention.

RULES AND GUIDELINES ADVISING JUDICIAL OFFICERS IN THE MATTER OF PRIVILEGE

Four attempts to establish common legal parameters that can be used by judicial personnel to bring order to a chaotic landscape of conflicting cases are: (1) the Attorney General's Guidelines, (2) the Federal Rules of Criminal Procedure, (3) the American Bar Association (Report of the Committee on Improvements in the Law of Evidence), and (4) the Federal Rules of Evidence.

The Attorney General's Guidelines, known officially as United States Department of Justice Memorandum No. 692, contains five sections.[58] The first section expresses the philosophy that even though the First and Sixth Amendment rights are frequently in conflict, there should be a careful weighing of interests that will guarantee First Amendment protection as often as possible. The second section attempts to ensure newsmen that they are not to be viewed as "an investigative arm of government" and that alternative sources will be sought first. The third section emphasizes negotiations antecedent to subpoena. The fourth section emphasizes that if negotiations fail, the subpoena will have to come from the attorney general himself, and if that is not the case, the subpoena will be quashed. The fifth section is examined verbatim:

Fifth: In requesting the Attorney General's authorization for a subpoena, the following principles will apply:

A. There should be sufficient reason to believe that a crime has occurred, from disclosures by non-press sources. The Department does not approve of utilizing the press as a spring board for investigations.

B. There should be sufficient reason to believe that the information sought is essential to a successful investigation—particularly with reference to directly establishing guilt or innocence. The subpoena should not be used to obtain peripheral, non-essential or speculative information.

C. The Government should have unsuccessfuly attempted to obtain the information from alternative non-press sources.

D. Authorization requests for subpoenas should normally be limited to the verification of published information and to such surrounding circumstances as relate to the accuracy of the published information.

E. Great caution should be observed in requesting subpoena authorization by the Attorney General for unpublished information, or where an orthodox First Amendment defense is raised or where a serious claim of confidentiality is alleged.

F. Even subpoena authorization requests for publicly disclosed information should be treated with care because, for example, cameramen have recently been subjected to harassment on the grounds that their photographs will become available to the government.

G. In any event, subpoenas should, wherever possible, be directed at material information regarding a limited subject matter, should cover a reasonably limited period of time, and should avoid requiring production of a large volume of unpublished material. They should give reasonable and timely notice of the demand for documents.

There are those who feel that subpoena guidelines, whether created by agreement between law enforcement agencies and the media, or imposed by judicial control over the subpoena power, are more appropriate for the protection of the newsman than is a blanket absolute right to conceal information.[59] The adequacy of the guidelines in preventing abuse of prosecutorial power, however, has been seriously questioned. First, it is suggested that loopholes in the guidelines render any meaningful protection illusory; the guidelines give little indication of the factors that are to be weighed in determining whether to subpoena a reporter. More important, critics say, the guidelines can be discarded if "emergencies and other unusual situations" should develop.[60] Second, the negotiations implicit in the guidelines involve a bargaining process in which the weak will be pressured into divulging information whereas the media giants will not.[61] Finally, since administrative guidelines may be changed by the stroke of a pen, a vital aspect of freedom of the press is dependent upon the "political machinations within the Justice Department."[62]

But David Gordon of the Medill School of Journalism at Northwestern University has noted:

. . . since the issuance of the *Attorney General's Guidelines* covering subpoenas to newsmen in 1970, only 28 subpoenas have been issued at the request of federal prosecutors, and 26 of these were requested by the newsmen involved, who were willing to testify but preferred to do so only after a subpoena was issued. In only two of the 28 cases was there a confrontation with the newsmen. Prior to the guidelines, the Justice Department was issuing about a dozen subpoenas a month, and confrontations were not uncommon. . . .

The effect of the guidelines is borne out by recent privilege cases. Two-thirds of the dozen reported cases since Branzburg originated on the state level, involving both grand juries and trial proceedings. Six of those 12 cases also arose in shield law states, indicating that the courts have not been totally willing to follow legislative directions, or that the directions are ambiguous. But this may not be a crucial distinction, because the courts seem to be moving toward the same general guidelines whether shield laws govern or not.[63]

Those guidelines appear to be that the First Amendment must be balanced against the competing needs of the judicial system and that grand jury and other criminal proceedings are to weigh more heavily in the balance than civil proceedings.

In the Federal Rules of Criminal Procedure the rule that is applicable to journalist privilege is Rule 53, which provides "the taking of photographs in the court room during the progress of judicial proceedings . . . shall not be permitted by the court."[64] Some courts have interpreted the consequences of Rule 53 to mean that the Supreme Court rejected by implication any news-gathering privilege even before the *Branzburg* holding of a later date.[65] In an analysis of newsmen's privilege legislation before the Ninety-third Congress in hearings as of February 15, 1973, Arthur Hanson, speaking for the American Newspaper Publishers Association, stated: "Federal criminal cases are governed by the Federal Rules of Criminal Procedure and no state reporter's privilege is recognized. . . . This means that a Federal grand jury is always free to investigate without the shackles of state newsman's privilege legislation.[66]

In 1938 the American Bar Association (ABA) adopted the recommendation of its Committee on Improvements in the Law of Evidence, supporting the adoption of statutes comparable to the North Carolina physician-patient privilege, which provides that the judge may require disclosure when it is deemed necessary for the proper administration of justice. The ABA proposal was designed to limit what some attorneys saw as an absolute physician-patient privilege in some states. To date, only two other states have adopted this form of statute. The committee also recommended that legislatures refuse to create any new privileges for other occupations, specifically mentioning social workers, but newsmen were not referred to at all.

The Supreme Court promulgated the Federal Rules of Evidence on November 20, 1972, and reported them to Congress February 5, 1973, with an effective date of July 1 of that year. They did not actually go into effect in July because they ran into opposition from Congress. Many in Congress preferred to reshape them into codes rather than accept them as guidelines from the Supreme Court. The rules make no provision for a newsman-source confidential relationship, but they confirm the inviolability of the lawyer-client relationship.[67] The article on privilege provides coverage only for those communications that are already well rooted in the common law. Those concerning the psychotherapist-patient, husband-wife, clergyman, political vote, trade secrets, and states secrets come under the coverage of Article V, but privileges such as the general doctor-patient privilege and the privilege for accountants have been eliminated because the majority of the justices on the Court felt that they were unwarranted limitations on truth seeking. As Chief Justice Burger observed: "Whatever their (the privileges') origin, these exceptions to the demand for every man's evidence are not lightly created nor expansively construed, for they are in derogation of the search for truth.''[68]

There are also those who believe that privileges are sought merely as status symbols.[69] Justice Douglas thought that approval of the proposed Rules of Evidence exceeded the authority of the Court to set procedural rules, since the rules of evidence contain numerous provisions that appear to be *substantive* rather than *procedural*. "Douglas was also reluctant to give the imprimatur of the Supreme Court to a set of rules that has its greatest impact at the trial level, an area with which he felt the Supreme Court was not intimately familiar.''[70] He preferred to leave the adoption of such rules to the Congress. In summary, he believed that the evidentiary rules were too restrictive and had the effect of undermining those shields already established in so many states. Most particularly, since the proposed rules did not recognize the newsman's privilege of nondisclosure in any federal judicial proceeding, the rules substantially alter prior decisional law.[71]

In the Congress there were those who accepted Douglas's interpretation. The leaders of the drive to prolong consideration of the rules included Representative Holtzman in the House and Senator Sam Ervin in the Senate.[72] Representative Holtzman said that her bill was designed to "restore Congressional prerogative and not put Congress in the demeaning position of accepting rules that neither house would agree with." After much testimony and controversy, the House rejected the more restrictive and conservative draft from the Supreme Court, with its emphasis on the guidelines established by Wigmore and McCormick. They sought to replace it with the following language:

Except as otherwise required by the Constitution of the United States or provided by Act of Congress or in rules prescribed by the Supreme Court pursuant to statutory authority, the privilege of a witness, person, government, State, or political subdivision thereof shall be governed by the principles of the common law as they may be interpreted by the courts of the United States in the light of reason and experience. However, in civil actions and proceedings, with respect to an element of a claim or defense as to which State law supplies the rule of decision, the privilege of a witness, person, government, State, or political subdivision thereof shall be determined *in accordance with State Law*. (Italics mine)[73]

By this statement the House had adopted a stopgap, incremental, common law developmental approach to evidence law. That may not have been the intention of some House members who supported the measure, for many of them were hoping for sweeping changes in the direction of recognizing a journalist privilege and this approach would only appear to interfere with that goal. On the other hand, it would also prevent what they feared most, a uniform standard that would be too restrictive on reporters by failing even to mention them in the rules. As for nonfederal issues, the House constructed its amendment on principles underlying *Erie Railroad Co* v. *Tompkins*.[74] It supported its position by contending that no federal interest is strong enough to justify departure from state policy, that state policy should not be frustrated by the accident of diversity jurisdiction, and that a contrary position would encourage forum shopping.

Those who were critical of the legislative approach emphasized that the Supreme Court has the power to make rules of evidence. They also felt that this power includes the power to elaborate rules of privilege that can supersede state rules of privilege, even in diversity cases. They reemphasized the dictum that the basic rule of evidence is relevancy. A privilege works to keep relevant and otherwise admissible evidence from the trier of facts. It alters the normal mode of proof in a trial by denying the trier information he would otherwise have before him in determining the facts.

Dissenters from congressional action also emphasized that the correct way of interpreting the *Erie* rule would be to recognize that the federal courts are to apply state "substantive law" and federal "procedural law."[75] Because privileges have an impact on modes of proof in federal courts, it is possible that state law could interfere with the appropriate performance of the federal courts' functions. But in spite of all this concern, it appears that state law privileges are applicable in diversity cases but are without effect in other federal cases, such as criminal cases. Yet privileges have the greatest impact in criminal cases. Thus reactions to the fallout from the *Erie* doctrine may not be as great a threat as critics of privilege feared. On the other hand, privilege advocates can take heart from the fact that *Erie* sought to limit the creation of a general federal common law,[75] which in this situation would appear to be much more restrictive than the laws of over half of the states.

On March 19, 1973, the Senate approved H.R. 4958, which included Article V on privileges, and it was signed into law by the President, March 30, 1973, as Public Law No. 93-12, 87 Stat. 9.

WHAT IS THE PROPER BALANCE BETWEEN THE PUBLIC'S RIGHT TO KNOW AND THE LAW'S RIGHT TO EVERYMAN'S EVIDENCE?

Judges have ordinarily rejected the absolute or per se approach and have proceeded with an ad hoc case-by-case method in determining the need for reporter's testimony.

Short of First Amendment claims, the press has presented the following arguments for withholding testimony:

THE CODE OF ETHICS THEORY. Reporters faced with a demand to disclose have frequently refused on the basis that it would be unethical, but the courts have considered this contention over ethics to be overruled by legal considerations. In three often cited cases the canons of the American Newspaper Guild with regard to confidential pledges have yielded to compulsory disclosure.[77]

FORFEITURE-OF-ESTATE THEORY. In 1911 a reporter for the *Augusta Herald* refused to tell the Board of Police Commissioners of Augusta what member of the police department had given him information about a certain murder. The reporter was fined and imprisoned for contempt. Before the Supreme Court of Georgia he argued that to answer the question would "cause him the forfeiture of an estate, to wit, it would cause him to lose his means of earning a livelihood." The court rejected the argument.[78]

EMPLOYER'S REGULATIONS. Related to the foregoing argument is the assertion that the rules of the employer forbid the assertion that the rules of the employer forbid the disclosure of the name of the informant. The courts have also rejected this contention. In *People ex rel. Phelps* v. *Fancher,* a newspaper editor called as a witness before a grand jury refused to disclose the name of the author of an article on the ground that to do so would be to violate a regulation of the newspaper. The court stated: "As the law now is, and has for ages existed no court could possibly hold that a witness could legally refuse to give the name of the author of an alleged libel, for the reason that the rules of a public journal forbade it."[79]

SHIFTING THE BURDEN OF PROOF. Reporters believe that they would fare much better if the relevancy of testimony could be laid out in advance of subpoena by the law enforcement and adjudication authorities who would answer certain preliminary questions. Is there a strong likelihood that a crime has been committed? Is it likely that the reporter has useful information gained in confidence that could throw light on the wrongdoing? Could the information be obtained elsewhere? By and large, the courts have been reluctant to shift the burden in this direction.

The press has not been as convincing before judges as have prosecutors and defense counsel. The attorney's arguments supporting the doctrine of the law's right to everyman's evidence have fallen into the following code-worded tests.

REASONABLE LIKELIHOOD TEST. One state court has suggested that compulsory revelation of informants or confidential information might raise problems, but it proceeded to hold that disclosure of a newsman's information and sources is appropriate when there is a "reasonable likelihood" that the information will be relevant to the judicial subject of inquiry. The test aims to eliminate "fishing expeditions" but is directed at the well-informed administration of justice.[80] It would appear that this test could be restricted or expanded depending upon the judge who interprets it.

HEART-OF-THE-MATTER TEST. The opinion in *Garland* vs. *Torre* held that Judy Garland, who was suing for libel, needed the name of the CBS executive who had insulted her so that she could proceed against the network. The court reasoned that because the action would be defeated if the informer's identity were not revealed, "the paramount public interest in the fair administration of justice" outweighed the potential injury to the free flow of news.[81] A variant of the heart-of-the-matter test has been proposed by the Justice Department guidelines for the issuance of federal investigatory subpoenas. The guidelines emphasize that the information sought should go to the main concern and point of the investigation[82] and that reasonable efforts should be made to get the information from nonpress sources if at all possible.

MISCARRIAGE OF JUSTICE. A test requiring disclosure by a newsman only when a miscarriage of justice would otherwise result appears to be a stricter standard for the parties seeking disclosure than the heart-of-the-matter test. In *People* v. *Dohrn* the burden of proof was shifted somewhat more to the prosecution by the standards requiring proof that alternative means have been exhausted, that there is reason to believe that the newsman is essential to the final solution and that if his cooperation is not forthcoming there will be a "miscarriage of justice." Individual judges would determine how narrow or broad this standard would be.

COMPELLING NEED. The federal district court that first dealt with the *Caldwell* case in the Ninth Circuit granted a protective order stating that Caldwell was not required to testify about matters transmitted to him in confidence until such time as a "compelling and overriding national interest which cannot be alternatively served has been established to the satisfaction of the court."[83] Although the court did not set actual guidelines as to what would constitute such a showing, it referred to those standards formulated in *People* v. *Dohrn* as possible criteria for a state showing of "compelling need." The Ninth Circuit did not indicate whether "compelling need" has a meaning different from the phrase a "compelling and overriding national interest," although the concurring opinion suggested that no distinction was intended.[84]

Newsmen have become increasingly disenchanted with the balancing approach because of the vagueness of the tests and the dependence upon judicial whim. Instead of using common law step-by-step negotiations, they have sought a First Amendment privilege that they have been hoping will eliminate the uncertainties and extend more absolute coverage. In spite of press complaints, it appears that the past several tests referred to previously are moving in the direction of shifting the burden of proof to the government. Apparently, the press does not see the shift as arriving quickly enough or more importantly, as being basic or absolute enough. One arena in particular where they have sought immunity more than any other is the grand jury.

COMMON LAW AND THE GRAND JURY

The most significant journalist privilege cases have involved confrontations with grand juries, namely, the *Branzburg, Caldwell, Pappas, Lightman,* and *Buchanan* cases. It is important that we try to gauge what impact this paticular institution in the common law has had and is likely to have for the press in the future.

The grand jury was created by Henry II in 1166. Originally, it was employed by the Crown as the accusatory arm of the criminal process.[85] Usually a group of men formed in a particular locality was employed to accuse others of a crime; but after the Norman Conquest, this group evolved into a civil jury of general inquiry to obtain information useful to the Crown. Thus the original purpose of the grand jury was not to protect the unjustly accused. The goal, rather, was to centralize and extend both the power and authority of the king in order to ensure that crime against the state would be reported and dealt with. As the population of the British Isles grew, it became impossible for the grand jury to report on crimes on the basis of the members' own first- or secondhand knowledge. It became more and more dependent upon the magistrates to produce evidence. At the same time the Crown assumed a more active role in prosecuting crime.

In 1681 a grand jury refused to return an indictment desired by Charles. From that time on its reputation as a body independent of the king took on a different image, that of a popular instrument guarding the common law from unnecessary incursions by the state. Starting with the case of the Earl of Shaftsbury in that same year, grand jury deliberations were carried out in secret so that the king could not intimidate jurors by observing them at work.

In America the grand jury was particularly useful in checking the king's representatives. Grand juries were used to protest against abuses in government and make known the wishes of the people. They acted as arms of the local assemblies.[86] Critics of the grand jury system worried about laymen on the panel with their unsophisticated judgments and ignorance of legal rules. Jeremy Bentham referred to them as "star chambers" and "secret inquisitions." Thomas Jefferson charged that by 1791 the Federalists had already transformed grand juries "from a legal to a political engine" by inviting them "to become inquisitors on the freedom of speech."[87] England finally abolished the grand jury in 1933.[88]

But the grand jury survived in America. It was used to ferret out corruption in government. Crusading prosecutors such as Thomas Dewey used the system to reveal wrongdoing.[89] But in many states the grand jury was falling from grace. Some states abolished the institution altogether, whereas others turned to the filing of an information by the prosecutor before a magistrate as an alternative to the grand jury. The Supreme Court upheld the use of an information in *Hurtado* v. *California*[90] and the practice has spread ever since.

Today, the grand jury is used in only about half the states. But many of the more populous states with the highest crime rates, such as New York and California, still rely on the grand jury.

The use of federal grand juries is still adhered to because of the promise of the Fifth Amendment. It also survives because many have seen it as a primary defense against hasty, malicious, and oppressive prosecution. As the Supreme Court has noted:

It serves the invaluable function in our society of standing between the accuser and the accused, whether the latter be an individual, minority group, or other, to determine whether a charge is founded upon reason or was dictated by an intimidating power or by malice and personal ill will.[91]

But Melvin Antell has said that: "It simply is not true that the grand jury system protects the individual from oppression; indeed it has a far greater potential as an instrument of oppression."[92]

Grand juries provide few procedural safeguards for the accused and witnesses. When it deliberates and when it investigates, the grand jury sits in secret. Witnesses subpoenaed to testify before a grand jury have no right to notice of the scope and nature of the crimes being investigated, nor whether they are themselves under investigation. A witness has no right to confront or to cross-examine other witnesses who testify against him. And a witness before a grand jury has no right to counsel in the grand jury room. A subpoenaed witness must attend and appear before the grand jury wherever it is sitting. This requirement frequently causes witnesses great inconvenience and expense. In a federal conspiracy case the grand jury could meet in any part of the country. If indictments are issued, they typically charge vague offenses under broad conspiracy statutes. Often no indictments are issued.[93] As the Supreme Court has pointed out:

It is a grand inquest, a body with powers of investigation and inquisition, the scope of whose inquiries is not to be limited narrowly by questions of propriety or forecasts of the probable result of the investigation . . . a grand jury investigation may be triggered by tips, rumors, evidence professed by the prosecutor, or the personal knowledge of the grand jurors.[94]

And according to Justice Stewart, the grand jury is "in effect, immune from judicial supervision." It can be convened by a prosecutor "on virtually any pretext" and "with no serious law enforcement purpose."[95]

The methods used by the grand jury have been defended by some who note that secrecy in the proceedings is necessary because grand jurors will speak more freely and truthfully if they do not have to worry about public reactions. The innocent accused, who is charged by complaint before the grand jury but exonerated by its refusal to indict, should be protected from compulsory disclosure of the fact that he has been groundlessly accused.[96]

Nevertheless, there are newsmen who are quite anxious about grand jury investigations into "radical" activities that they have been covering. The grand jury is using its secrecy to investigate "radicals," while shielding the operation of the Department of Justice and its Internal

Security Division (ISD). Under the direction of Robert Mardian the ISD launched thirteen federal grand jury investigations of three politically active groups—the New Left, the Catholic Left, and the antiwar intellectuals. A subdivision of the ISD, the Special Litigation Section, with Guy Goodwin as head prosecutor, used these investigations to uncover information and, in a few cases, to indict people like Leslie Bacon, Phillip and Daniel Berrigan, and Daniel Ellsberg.[97]

Charles E. Goodell, a target of verbal criticism by former Vice-President Spiro Agnew, had this to say of the political use of the grand jury:

In my opinion, the inquisitions are intended to punish and inhibit protected expression and political activity and to break down the private and professional relationships of academic liberals and of political activists. This must be a matter of concern for all of us. The power to compel testimony behind closed doors of grand jury rooms belongs to whatever political faction wins control of our institutions of government. Today the targets are liberals and radicals—tomorrow's victims may be the Daughters of the American Revolution or the Veterans of Foreign Wars.[98]

And it appears that the Nixon administration granted broad authority to the FBI for the purpose of employing grand juries that would act as an arm of a national police force.[99]

As a result of the broad power grants, questioning often produces ever more dramatic and classical definitions of the "fishing expedition." An example from a Tucson grand jury proceeding in the fall of 1971 follows:

Describe for the grand jury every occasion during the year 1970 when you have been in contact with, attended meetings which were conducted by, or attended by, or been any place when any individual spoke whom you knew to be associated with or affiliated with Students for a Democratic Society, the Weathermen, the Communist Party or any other organization advocating revolutionary overthrow of the United States, describing for the grand jury when these incidents occurred, where they occurred, who was present and what was said by all persons there and what you did at the time you were in these meetings, groups, associations or conversations.[100]

The same prosecutor, Guy Goodwin, asked a series of questions of Leslie Bacon during grand jury proceedings in Seattle:

What did you do or where did you go in Santa Barbara?
Who were the people you saw, visited with, or stayed with in Santa Barbara?

Do you remember the names of the people you traveled to Santa Barbara with?

What were the conversations in the car during the 56-hour drive?[101]

It has been suggested that the grand jury system be abolished, but some would prefer a bill of rights for grand juries. Ironically, news leaks from secret grand jury hearings during Watergate have sparked interest in judicial reform. Two congressmen, Charles B. Randolph (D-New York) and Bob Eckhardt (D-Texas), have filed what could be characterized as a "Bill of Rights" for grand juries. The highlights of the proposed changes are as follows:

1. Allow a seven-day lapse between the serving of a subpoena and appearance of a witness. 2. Permit counsel to be present and witnesses to receive a copy of his transcript. 3. Require a ten-day notice for a contempt hearing—eliminating what has been described as "witnesses being subpoenaed in the morning, immunized by noon and jailed for contempt by evening." 4. Reduce the maximum civil contempt sentence from eighteen months to six months. 5. Prohibit introduction of evidence obtained in violation of an individual's constitutional rights.[102]

Finally, it has been charged that selection methods tend to result in uniformly middle-aged, middle-class, and white grand juries.[103] Such juries would probably not be very understanding of journalists who cover dissent, and they would probably not restrain a prosecutor who wades in with tough questions about "radical" activities. F. Lee Bailey has referred to the modern grand jury as a "flock of sheep led by the prosecutor across the meadows to the finding he wants."[104] In a colloquy before a Senate subcommittee studying journalist privilege, Senator Sam Ervin of North Carolina indicated his concern about the prosecutor's dominion over the grand jurors. He noted that "We still have in my State a grand jury system whereby no one is allowed in the rooms but the witnesses."[105] In all other states the prosecutor is allowed. However, in the state of Michigan the witness is permitted a refusal to testify on grounds of self-incrimination even though immunity has been granted if the witness fears prosecution by a federal panel.[106] The problem has by no means been resolved by the Supreme Court in the two decisions it has handed down on the subject.[107] Each case stands on its own merits, and each judge is left to make the final decision. Thus there are no definite protections for the witness facing this situation.

The press has been understandably anxious about grand juries that will not give notice of whether a crime has been committed and whether the deposed journalist has any connection to it, as in the *Pappas* case. (See chapter 2.) They are also concerned over the effect that *in camera* proceedings will have on the imaginations of their sources, who cannot know whether confidences have been betrayed. (See *Caldwell,* chapter 2.) Because the grand jury has so often subpoenaed reporters such as Branzburg, Lightman, and Buchanan, who were reporting on the counterculture, some legal scholars have recommended a method whereby reportage on dissent might be protected. Vince Blasi has advocated an approach:

Grand jury proceedings present a special case. They fall somewhere between purely investigative proceedings and those that are essentially adjudicative in nature. Particularly when the prosecutor has proposed that a named individual be indicted, the grand jury proceeding has many of the attributes of an adjudicative hearing. I am of the opinion, nonetheless, that all grand jury proceedings should be classified as non-adjudicative such that professional disseminators are privileged against having to give evidence if their capacity to provide information to the public would thereby be harmed.[108]

Blasi goes on to point out that he arrived at this conclusion because of the informality of the proceedings and the paucity of procedural due process guarantees.[109]

SUMMARY

Journalists have become increasingly impatient with common law methods of achieving protection from subpoenas. They have gradually turned from evidentiary research to constitutional questions. During House hearings on reporter privilege, Congressman Mezvinsky of Iowa, who serves on the Constitutional Rights Subcommittee, stated: "I was very intrigued by the argument which says we are getting involved in evidence. Aren't we really talking about a constitutional right that comes right out of the First Amendment?"[110]

Common law methods place a high premium on testimony and a somewhat lower premium on news gathering. The problem is viewed as an institutional and occupational question rather than one of a communications process. Viewed from a common law perspective, newsmen are sometimes seen as trying to "arrive" by acquiring the "status benefits" of the already established social elite professionals. But then they "spit in the soup" by reporting on dissent that is often embarrassing to the established professionals who are in a position to assist newsmen in acquiring the privilege but who feel reluctant to encourage "license" and "gossip." The dialogue on this topic may have become more politicized than some students of evidence and privilege are prepared to admit. On the other hand, evidentiary experts may be alert to what they perceive as a danger to judicial investigations and trials should newsmen be equipped to harbor knowledge about illegal activities.

4

Privileged Communication and News Dissemination: The First Amendment

When newsmen became disenchanted with common law arguments for privileged communication they began to turn toward a constitutional rationale. Many journalists could point to successes achieved under common law balancing formulas, but others found it too difficult to resist subpoenas that they believed were being employed too frequently and too broadly. The press became increasingly convinced that the burden should be on the government to demonstrate a need for testimony rather than the all-too-common practice of requiring the reporter to show cause why he should not appear, reveal confidences, and produce records.

THE SCOPE OF THE CONSTITUTIONAL ARGUMENT

The Fifth Amendment has provided privileged sanctuary for reluctant witnesses; but, for a newsman, immunity from prosecution or advance pardon does not protect a source or confidential information.[1] In a recent court-press encounter a judge suggested that reporters rely on the Fifth Amendment rather than a state shield statute or the First Amendment. The reporters refused to utilize that procedure because they feared immunity and forced testimony would reveal sources and information.[2] They also preferred the neutral status of observers rather than that of participants bearing a presumption of guilt. The Fifth Amendment does not appear to be a practical means for resolving the disputes over the subpoena issue.

The equal protection clause of the Fourteenth Amendment was employed in *State* v. *Buchanan* to deny journalists constitutional protection.[3] The argument turned on the inappropriateness of special treatment for the press. On the other hand, it could be argued that the First Amendment should take precedence over any Fourteenth Amendment right, since the United States Supreme Court has never invoked the equal protection clause of the Constitution when the alleged discriminatory act was protected by another clause of the Constitution.[4] The clearest illustration of this is the absolute application of the Fifth Amendment right against self-incrimination, which clearly carves out special protection for a limited group.[5]

Source confidentiality relates to privacy and the Fourth Amendment.[6] Fulfillment of the right of privacy is at the root of privileges for doctors, lawyers, and ministers. But the newsman is asserting a public right and cannot claim the protection of the Fourth Amendment.

The Sixth Amendment[7] provides a defendant with the protection of compulsory process, which can be invoked to elicit journalist testimony. If the newsman is before a grand jury, he cannot claim Sixth Amendment protection of counsel because American courts have consistently held that the scope of a criminal prosecution, for purposes of the Sixth Amendment's guarantee of counsel, does not encompass the grand jury proceeding.[8]

The section of the Constitution most germane to the journalist's concern for uninhibited communication is the First Amendment.[9] This amendment, coupled with the interpretation of the Fourteenth Amendment, which makes it applicable to the states,[10] is the basis for discussion over the scope of the constitutional argument for a press privilege.

INITIAL EFFORTS AT ESTABLISHING A CONSTITUTIONAL PRIVILEGE FOR JOURNALISTS

Garland v. *Torre* in 1958 was the first journalist privilege case based on the First Amendment constitutional argument, to wit, that compelling news reporters to disclose confidences would block the flow of news from news sources to news media and therefore diminish the flow of news to the public.[11] Justice Stewart, then sitting on the Second Circuit, rejected this contention. He accepted the hypothesis that forced disclosure might entail an encroachment on press freedom, but reasoned that since freedom of the press is not absolute, the question to be determined was "whether the interest to be served by compelling the testimony of the witness in the present case justifies some impairment of the First Amendment freedom."[12] He concluded that freedom of the press had to give way to the "paramount public interest in the fair administration of justice."[13]

In 1961, the constitutional claim was again invoked. In *In re Goodfader,*[14] the plaintiff, who was seeking damages from the Civil Service Commission of the City of Honolulu for wrongful ouster from her job, sought to force a newsman to reveal the source of his information that the commission had been contemplating the ouster. Refusing to comply with the court order to disclose his source, the newsman claimed that the court order was an unconstitutional abridgment of freedom of the press, since the interest served by compelling disclosure did not justify any impairment of press freedom. On appeal the Supreme Court of Hawaii recognized that the First Amendment freedoms were to be given broad scope and that the forced disclosure may constitute an impairment of freedom of the press, but concluded that "such an impairment may not be considered of a degree sufficient to outweigh the necessity of maintaining the court's fundamental authority to compel attendance of witnesses and to exact their testimony. . . . "[15]

In 1968 in *State* v. *Buchanan*[16] the Oregon Supreme Court also rejected the constitutional privilege. The editor of a campus newspaper who had published an interview with seven unnamed drug users was subpoenaed by the local district attorney to appear before the grand jury. She refused to reveal the names of the drug users and was cited for contempt. On appeal she argued that freedom of the press necessarily includes freedom to gather the news and that since certain news stories cannot be obtained unless the reporter can promise anonymity to a confidential informer, forced disclosure abridges a protected freedom. The court rejected this contention on the grounds that the newsman has no constitutional right to information which is not accessible to the public generally and that to give the newsman such "special privileges" would conflict with the equal protection clause of the Federal Constitution.[17]

Although the courts brusquely dismissed a common law privilege, as the *Buchanan* court did in the constitutional context, the *Torre* and *Goodfader* courts made some attempt to analyze the claims asserted. Reluctantly willing to assume that forced disclosure may hinder the flow of news and hence constitute an impairment of freedom of the press, these courts nevertheless arrived at the same conclusion reached by previous courts: Any rights or interests the newsman may have must give way to his duty to testify. They applied balancing tests, but their tests have been criticized. Margaret Sherwood noted:

In the *Torre* case the newswoman Torre's interest was never weighed against the litigant Garland's actual needs and interests; rather, the general press interest in the availability of news was weighed against some general lofty interest in the administration of justice. *Goodfader,* while beginning with a statement that in the area of first amendment rights a balancing of the interests must be undertaken, never went on to explore those interests.[18]

She was especially critical of the way in which the courts labeled the litigant's right to compelled testimony a "public" interest and the newsman's interest in nondisclosure a "private" one.[19] The *Goodfader* court had stated: "The *private* or *individual* interest involved (journalist), must, in each case, be weighed in balance against the *public* interest affected[20] (fair administration of justice).

THE FIRST AMENDMENT'S GOAL OF SECURING AN INFORMED CITIZENRY VIA A FREE PRESS

The First Amendment was drafted for a public and governmental purpose that finds its direction through informed discussion and fearless inquiry. In the words of Alexander Meiklejohn:

The First Amendment does not protect a "freedom to speak." It protects the freedom of those activities of thought and communication by which we "govern." It is concerned, not with a private right, but with a public power, a governmental responsibility. In the specific language of the Constitution, the governing activities of the people appear only in terms of casting a ballot. But in the deeper meaning of the Constitution, voting is merely the external expression of a wide and diverse number of activities by means of which citizens attempt to meet the responsibilities of making judgments, which that freedom to govern lays upon them.[21]

Since the government asserts a broad societal interest in obtaining "everyman's evidence," it is important to set forth those larger values that underlie the journalist's claim. It can be argued that it is not a private right that is at stake but public information that is absolutely essential to self-government. As James Madison explains:

Knowledge will forever govern ignorance. And a people who mean to be their own governors, must arm themselves with the power knowledge gives. A popular government without popular information or the means of acquiring it, is but a prologue to a farce or a tragedy, or perhaps both.[22]

A particularly bold defense of the press as a preferred public representative of the body politic checking the excesses of governmental abuses of power comes from Thomas Jefferson, who was nettled by the "chilling effect" of the Alien and Sedition laws:

The way to prevent these irregular interpositions of the people is to give them full information of their affairs through the channels of the public papers, and to contrive that those papers should penetrate the whole mass of the people. The basis of our government being the opinion of the people, the very first object should be to keep that right; and were it left to me to decide whether we should have a government without newspapers, or newspapers without a government, I should not hesitate a moment to prefer the latter.[23]

From the time of Madison and Jefferson, it has been axiomatic that the guarantees of the First Amendment, particularly the safeguard of a free press, were intended to ensure an informed citizenry, better able to govern itself. This understanding was manifest in *Grosjean* v. *American Press Co.*,[24] in which, in invalidating a special tax on newspapers, the Court noted that any inhibition on the press is of fundamental magnitude and "goes to the heart of the natural right of the members of an organized society, united for their common good, to impart and acquire information about their common interests."[25]

In *Thornhill* v. *Alabama*[26] the Court advised: "Freedom of discussion, if it would fulfill its historic function in this nation, must embrace all issues about which information is needed or appropriate to enable the members of our society to cope with the exigencies of their period."[27]

Associated Press v. *United States* emphasized that the First Amendment "rests on the assumption that the widest possible dissemination of information from diverse and antagonistic sources is essential to the welfare of the public, and that a free press is a condition of a free society."[28]

In *Estes* v. *Texas* the Court noted that "The free press has been a mighty catalyst in awakening public interest in governmental affairs, exposing corruption among public officers and employees. . . . ''[29] And the primary purpose of the First Amendment according to *Red Lion Broadcasting Co.* v. *FCC* is toward "producing an informed public capable of conducting its own affairs.''[30]

This understanding was eloquently summed up by Justice Black, in what proved to be his final opinion:

In the First Amendment the Founding Fathers gave the free press the protection it must have to fulfill its essential role in our democracy. The press was to serve the governed, not the governors. The Government's power to censor the press was abolished so that the press would remain forever free to censure the Government. The press was protected so that it could bare the secrets of government and inform the people. Only a free and restrained press can effectively expose deception in government.[31]

Thomas I. Emerson has argued that First Amendment protection of freedom of expression is essential for individual self-fulfillment, for seeking the truth, for securing participation by citizens in decision making and as a method of maintaining the balance between stability and change.[32] He argues that suppression of discussion makes rational judgment impossible and may lead ultimately to change in more violent and radical forms.[33]

Thus there is substantial support for the assumption that the interest served by the First Amendment is more public than private. It is a mistake to frame the question in terms of society's interest in law enforcement and adjudication as over and against a private or "special interest" known as the press. The press is a vehicle for freedom of expression, which is an individual *and* public *right* and, as Meiklejohn adds, *power*.[34] In order to be fair, the adversary relationship surrounding the journalist privilege question should not be depicted with the public on one side and a special interest on the other. The cards are stacked when the "public's right to know" is pitted against government. Likewise, they are stacked when it is "society's right to everyman's evidence" versus reporters. On both sides there is a public interest, that is, the public's right to a free flow of communications about current affairs versus the public's right to testimony that is essential to secure defendant's rights and aid prosecutors and legislators in their search for the truth. Stated in this fashion the dilemma is more difficult, but the question appears less politicized by such restatement.

THE RELATIONSHIP BETWEEN CONFIDENTIAL INFORMATION AND THE FULFILLMENT OF THE FIRST AMENDMENT'S PUBLIC INFORMATION FUNCTION

In the preceding section it was established that there is considerable support for protecting news dissemination under the First Amendment. Certainly, in the publication process the acquisition of news is as important as dissemination; therefore, it should be equally entitled to protection.

There is no specific indication in writings of the times whether the framers and backers of the Bill of Rights intended freedom of the press to include news gathering.[35]

Logically, however, the right to *gather* news is the opposite side of the same constitutional coin, for without the former, the right to disseminate would be meaningless.[36]

It is settled that the First Amendment encompasses "the right to receive information and ideas."[37] However, the right to gather news is not absolute. In *Estes* v. *Texas*,[38] the Court held that the trial court erred in not barring television transmission of the courtroom proceedings. The question is whether an analogy can properly be drawn between barring reporters from the courtroom to assure fair trials and compelling them to reveal their confidential sources and information to assure fair trials.

Another basis for creating protection for news gathering against compelled disclosure rests upon the emerging notion of a right to express opinions anonymously. In *Talley* v. *California*,[39] the Court struck down a city ordinance forbidding the public distribution of handbills unless they bore the name and address of the author, on the ground that where unorthodox or dissident views are expressed, a requirement of identification would chill free expression. Sherman argued that the *Talley* interpretation should be extended to protect an anonymous informant when he seeks to convey news through handbills.[40]

The Court has also recognized the right of the recipient of printed matter to remain anonymous. In *Lamont* v. *Postmaster General*,[41] the Court held that the Post Office could not compromise the anonymity of recipients of "communist propaganda" by requiring them to request in writing that the material be delivered to them.[42]

Indeed, political anonymity has had a long and noble history:

Anonymous pamphlets, leaflets, brochures and even books have played an important role in the progress of mankind. Persecuted groups and sects from time to time throughout history have been able to criticize oppressive practices and laws either anonymously or not at all.[43]

Policy-making officials who speak to newsmen "off the record," "not for attribution," or in "backgrounders" in order to advance or criticize a particular government program, political radicals who come to trust a newsman and reveal their ideologies, policies, or activities to him, or members of the counterculture engaged in criminal activity and who proselytize the removal of criminal sanctions from that activity— all those individuals are attempting to communicate their ideas to the public in an anonymous fashion because they fear adverse personal repercussions through open communications. In the case of government officials the anonymity or "leak," as it is more commonly known, serves a somewhat different purpose that transcends personal security. As Meg Greenfield notes, "the fact is that for years government officials, including those who howl loudest about "leaks," have been freely trading information that is designated secret in return for a certain consideration in its handling by the press."[44]

It appears that this transactional relationship has utility. Officials cannot be expected to help the press report intelligently if every frank disclosure is going to cause them trouble as a result of their names being disclosed.

Occasionally, a contrary view of the necessity for this confidential relationship is expressed by journalists. Lewis Lapham, who reported for the *San Francisco Examiner,* had this to say of the privilege:

The argument assumes that the protected source of information works to the advantage of the press and so assists the free circulation of the news. My own experience supports an exactly opposite conclusion. The protection of an informed source works to the advantage of the source, inhibiting the circulation of any news that does not enhance the self-importance of the man circulating it. More often than not the reporter who agrees to deal in protected information transforms himself into a press agent. . . . If bureaucrats and politicians were deprived of the convenience of speaking off the record, they might learn to speak in plain words.[45]

However, surveys of the press indicate that a substantial number of newspaper stories are based on information that could only be secured through confidential informer-reporter relationships. Erwin D. Canham, editor in chief of the *Christian Science Monitor,* estimates that 33 to 50 percent of that newspaper's major stories involve confidential sources, and the *Wall Street Journal* states that 15 percent of its articles are based on information from confidential informants. The managing editor of the *San Francisco Chronicle* noted that a very substantial number of stories arise from confidential information.[46] In a survey taken in 1969, twenty-seven out of thirty-two newspapers surveyed reported publishing stories stemming from confidential information.[47]

In his empirical study of journalist privilege Vince Blasi finds that confidential sources are closely linked to the verification function and that investigative reporters rely more heavily than do most newsmen on confidential sources.[48]

This was especially true in *Caldwell,* and the Court of Appeals for the Ninth Circuit recognized the value of the confidential relationship in news gathering:

. . . confidential relationships of this sort are commonly developed and main-tained by professional journalists, and are indispensable to their work of gather-ing, analyzing and publishing the news. . . . compelled disclosure of informa-tion received by a journalist within the scope of such confidential relationships jeopardizes those relationships and thereby impairs the journalist's ability to gather, analyze and publish the news. . . . [49]

The opinion of the Ninth Circuit is grounded in affidavits from work-ing reporters who testified of their own knowledge to the role played in their profession by confidential sources and information. Walter Cron-kite states:

In doing my work, I (and those who assist me) depend constantly on informa-tion, ideas, leads and opinions received in confidence. Such material is essential in digging out newsworthy facts and, equally important, in assessing the impor-tance and analyzing the significance of public events. Without such materials, I would be able to do little more than broadcast press releases and public state-ments.[50]

The professional literature of journalism bears ample witness to the pervasiveness of confidential relationships between reporters and their sources, to their importance and the importance of safeguarding their integrity, and to the sheer volume of news that is derived from them.

The point recurs elsewhere, particularly in memoirs of journalists, with varying illustrations.[51]

Books addressed to the profession rather than emanting from it are equally clear in emphasizing the necessity of preserving the confidential relationship between reporters and their informants. Typical of the teachings in these works is the admonition of C. MacDougall that:

The reporter who didn't live up to this code (of non-disclosure of confidential material) would find himself without "pipelines," and his effectiveness would be reduced greatly. Experience proves that the person with whom the reporter "plays ball" on one occasion is likely to supply the tip which leads to a better story on another.[52]

Or, as Hugh C. Sherwood has written:

This brings up the one rule that can be flatly and unequivocally stated in regard to off-the-record interviews. Once you have agreed to interview someone on this basis, keep your word—you will probably never get another interview from the person if you don't.[53]

The sum of it all, as the *amicus* brief for the Columbia Broadcasting System in the Supreme Judicial Court of Massachusetts pointed out, is that reporters are able to get much indispensable information only on the understanding that confidence may be reposed in them because they can and will keep confidences. Such indispensable information comes in confidence from officeholders fearful of superiors, from businessmen fearful of competitors, from informers operating at the edge of the law who are in danger of reprisal from criminal associates, from people afraid of the law and of the government, sometimes rightly afraid, but as often from an excess of caution and from people in all fields anxious not to incur censure for unorthodox or unpopular views, whether their views would be considered unorthodox and be unpopular in the community at large or merely in their own group or subculture. The assurance of confidentiality elicits valuable background information in important diplomatic and labor negotiations and in many similar situations in which disclosure would adversely affect the informant's bargaining position. Public figures of all kinds, including government officials, political candidates, corporate officers, labor leaders, movie stars, and baseball heroes, who will speak in public only in carefully guarded words, achieve a more informative candor in private communications.

There is substantial testimonial support for the social value of communications flowing from confidential relationships, but is there evidence that supports the theory that sources will dry up or that a chilling effect will be the result if sources and reporters do not have constitutional protection of confidences?

THE CHILLING EFFECT: CAN THE FIRST AMENDMENT ACT AS A BUFFER AGAINST IT?

The chilling effect, a concept that is frequently employed by the United States Supreme Court in First Amendment cases, was first articulated in 1952 in *Wieman* v. *Updegraff*,[54] which set forth the potential harm to First Amendment activity threatened by an overly broad loyalty oath required of Oklahoma professors:

Such unwarranted inhibition upon the free spirit of teachers affects not only those who, like the appellants, are immediately before the court. It has an unmistakable tendency to *chill* that free play of the spirit which all teachers ought especially to cultivate and practice; it makes for caution and timidity in their associations by potential teachers.[55]

The courts have become increasingly more aware of the chill factor,[56] and they have analogized their concern for loyalty oaths to the journalist privilege question.

In *Gibson* v. *Florida Legislative Investigation Committee,* Justice Douglas stated: "If the press and its readers were subject to the harassment of . . . subpoenas, government would indeed hold a club over speech and over the press."[57]

In 1970 an Illinois court commented:

The indiscriminate serving of such subpoenas necessarily has a chilling effect upon the operation and functioning of media in the City of Chicago. . . . Members of the media necessarily become conscious in their news gathering activities of a potential later questioning concerning their conduct and the contents of their stories in relation to what was published and what was not published. In sum, the necessary consequences of indiscriminate subpoenaing could result in the evils inherent in self-censorship.[58]

Students of journalist privilege have found mixed reactions that were often hard to measure tangibly. As Blasi has noted:

From my interviewing and from our qualitative survey it appears that the subpoena spate of the past two years has interfered with reporting efforts in a variety of ways. The most significant effects that subpoenas have on news-gathering are of a highly personal, and relatively unmeasurable, nature. One is the professionally incapacitating worry and hassle to which the reporter is subjected.[59]

He has also pointed out that the drying up of sources can result from any number of factors other than the fear of subpoenas. The source may be dissatisfied with the reporter's coverage. Tactical decisions may be made by sources to lower their profile. If a source believes that it is not possible to manipulate the media, he or she may stop communications.[60]

In another broad observation by a managing editor, A. M. Rosenthal of the *New York Times*, we get another view: "We fear that the wells of information are drying up, that we are not hearing all we should, and that, therefore, the public is not hearing either. You always know when the phone rings, but you never know when it might have rung and was silent.[61]

A number of newspaper editors have given their estimates of what they believe is happening to sources as a result of the denial of the journalist privilege. Steve Rogers, metropolitan editor of the *Miami Herald*, has expressed the belief that sources are not drying up.[62] Gordon Pates, managing editor of the *San Francisco Chronicle*, was not sure. Mark R. Arnold of the *National Observer* thought that it was too early to tell. Jack Anderson thought that his sources trusted him and therefore would not be concerned with the government's policies one way or the other. Rod Van Every, city editor for the *Milwaukee Journal*, thought that sources had great confidence in the paper and the ultimate defense of civil disobedience by reporters. Kenneth Smart, managing editor of the Dallas *Times Herald*, said that its staff did not sense a chill. Ralph Otwell, managing editor of the *Chicago Sun-Times*, states that the subpoena threat was not as great because they had been consistently aggressive in going to court in getting subpoenas quashed and had been relatively successful with the courts in that area. But Rosenthal of the *New York Times* thought that many editors were simply looking at the surface. He believed that it was difficult to tell who was being "elbowed out . . . people with something to reveal but not powerful enough to reveal it with their name tags on.'"[63]

Another way to analyze the chill factor is to go beyond an examination of source intimidation to the question of whether newspapers stay away from controversies because of the costs of responding to subpoenas.

Los Angeles Times editor William F. Thomas noted that in the past few years his newspaper has spent more than $200,000 in resisting some thirty subpoenas and the threat of more than fifty others. He went on to say that both newspapers and their sources are becoming "gun-shy."[64] He also noted that potential sources in Los Angeles have specifically cited the danger of subpoenas in refusing to provide information.[65]

The large newspaper can at least fight off subpoenas because of its substantial legal defense funds, but the small paper has much greater difficulty. Of the 62 million and more subscribers to daily newspapers, 48 percent get their information from newspapers having a circulation of less than 100,000. Also, 1,244 daily newspapers have fewer than 25,000 subscribers. That is more than 70 percent of the nation's daily newspapers.[66] A small-town editor commented on his problems this way:

If a reporter at the *Times* (Los Angeles) had a problem—and the number of them has been escalating at an alarming rate in recent years—an attorney was close at hand. For the Speidel newspapers there is no lawyer standing by.

We have to consider the high cost of seeking legal advice and, occasionally, as much as I hate to admit it, we have to shy away from the story. It is for that reason that the expense entailed by my appearance here today makes economic sense to me.[67]

Thus far we have dealt with testimonials in which the media representatives preferred to make general observations about the chilling effect without citing concrete examples. Here are some illustrations of stories that dried up as a result of subpoena pressures.

Columbia Broadcasting Company wanted to interview a "cheating" welfare mother in Atlanta for a network White Paper on public assistance. Producer Ike Kleinerman agreed to disguise her voice and appearance. But the woman, fearing prosecution, demanded a pledge that the network not divulge her name if subpoenaed to do so. Kleinerman called the CBS legal counsel in New York and was told the network could not guarantee to protect the woman's identity. The interview was canceled.[68]

The Oakland Black Caucus, an organization representing major black groups in the Oakland area, refused to cooperate with the American Broadcasting Company in the filming of a documentary on the Black Panthers when ABC admitted it was unable to provide an assurance that its newsmen would remain silent in the face of possible government subpoenas.[69]

When a *New York Times* reporter was required to testify before the House Committee on Internal Security investigating militant activities, militant groups thereafter refused to talk with either him or other *Times* reporters, asserting that those newsmen could not be trusted with confidential information.[70] A Los Angeles *Newsweek* correspondent who had previously maintained good relations with the Panthers was refused an interview until *Newsweek* agreed to contest judicially any subpoenas the correspondent received; but by the time this agreement was secured, the subject of the interview had left Los Angeles.[71]

In another reporter affidavit Min S. Yee noted:

In February, 1970, I was assigned by *Newsweek* Magazine to write a story concerning the "RED GUARDS" in Chinatown, San Francisco. I was refused interviews on that occasion, and further refused permission to take photographs, because of the expressed fear that my notes and films would be subpoenaed. As a result of these refusals, we were forced to publish, from our files, a year-old photograph of a "RED GUARD" leader. Although a number of the "RED GUARDS" personally consider reporters to be objective and uniquely in a position to communicate fairly "RED GUARDS' " grievances and philosophy to the public at large, some have told me that they feel they have no assurance that our negatives and files will not be turned over to the FBI. As a result, no "RED GUARD" leaders will today consent to interviews or photographs.[72]

Yee went on to describe another incident, in which he had traveled to Cuba to interview members of the Venceremos Brigade. He was subjected to abusive and threatening language at the Brigade camp in Cuba. One remark was, "You take my picture and you're dead. What if pig Mitchell sticks a gun in your stomach and says 'Give me the film,' you're going to hand it over, right?"[73]

There are also situations in which the story was published but the source was exposed and suffered. In one case there were charges that inmates of a Tennessee mental institution were being mistreated. The stories gave rise to an investigation and demands for the identity of the source. The source was disclosed, and the result was that the source of the information, a secretary at the hospital, was fired.[74]

Because some scholars perform many of the same communicative functions as the press, they often find that they need confidential information for their research. There is widespread concern among academicians that if scholars' sources of information are effectively constrained, the public will be deprived of the possibility of learning more of the truth than official sources choose to reveal.[75]

Scholars are particularly concerned about the way in which the chilling effect discourages controversial study. Leonard Rodberg has stated that his own experience and the experiences of other scholars who have been subpoenaed by the same grand jury cause him to hesitate to include in his writing information about which he would anticipate future questioning regarding his sources.[76]

It is clear that journalists are not in agreement about the extent of the chilling effect, but there are enough cases of inhibiting effects on record to address the next question: How can the First Amendment be interpreted to minimize these inhibitions?

One of the characteristics of the law of the First Amendment has been the Court's resourcefulness in cushioning clashes between First Amendment values and competing interests. The Court's interest has been as much with process, with accommodations that take a procedural form, as with the making of ultimate choices between contending interests. Faced with tensions, the Court as often as not has attempted to ease rather than finally to resolve them.[77] A whole series of defensive procedural entrenchments lies between the First Amendment and interests adverse to it.

In *United States* v. *Rumely*,[78] the secretary of an organization that sold books "of a particular political tendentiousness" refused to disclose to a congressional committee the names of persons who bought in bulk for further distribution. The Court upheld the refusal to answer by construing the House resolution that created the investigative committee as inapplicable, thus in effect holding that before it could in this fashion affect the exercise of First Amendment rights, Congress would have to write the charters of its investigative committees in extraordinarily explicit language, beyond what is normally required. This was also the approach of *Watkins* v. *United States*.[79]

The method of *Rumely* and *Watkins* is closely related to the *overbreadth doctrine*.[80] The overbreadth doctrine requires that interests conflicting with the First Amendment be vindicated, if at all, by statutes, ordinances, or other regulations that are precise, narrow, closely drafted, and so designed as to make the least possible inroad on the First Amendment.[81]

What the overbreadth doctrine seeks to guard against is a predicted chilling effect on the exchange of ideas and the freedom of association. The overbreadth cases shade into the group of decisions demanding, as it is variously phrased, a "compelling,"[82] "paramount,"[83] "strong,"[84] interest, in whose behalf alone any infringement of First Amendment values will be allowed. Among the relevant decisions are *Gibson* v. *Florida Legislative Investigation Committee*,[85] *DeGregory* v. *New Hampshire Attorney General*,[86] *Bates* v. *Little Rock*,[87] *NAACP* v. *Alabama*[88] and *Shelton* v. *Tucker*.[89]

In *Gibson*, a legislative committee investigating Communist activities sought to inquire into NAACP membership lists. The Court held that the president of the Miami branch of the NAACP had no obligation to produce his lists of membership. Inquiry into activities of Communists was assumed to be a legitimate governmental interest, but it had not been demonstrated that these lists bore "a crucial relation"[90] to that interest.

In *DeGregory*, a state investigator asked questions about subversive activities going back several years before the date of the investigation. The Court held that the witness could not be made to answer. There was no showing of "overriding and compelling state interest," such as "would warrant intrusion into the realm of political and associational privacy protected by the First Amendment."[91]

Bates v. *Little Rock* was an attempt to obtain a list of contributors to the NAACP as a purported aid in the collection of local license taxes. Here the Court said that "the municipalities have failed to demonstrate a controlling justification for the deterrence of free association which compulsory disclosure of the membership lists would cause."[92]

In *NAACP* v. *Alabama*, the state sought to obtain NAACP membership lists in order to determine whether that organization was conducting intrastate business contrary to the provisions of the Alabama foreign corporation statutes. The Court noted in language almost directly applicable to journalist privilege cases that the fact that Alabama had taken "no direct action to restrict the right of petitioner's members to associate freely, does not end inquiry into the effect of the production order."[93] In the domain of the "indispensable liberties" guaranteed by the First Amendment, the Court went on, an abridgement of rights, "even though unintended, may inevitably follow from varied forms of governmental action."[94] Alabama, the Court held, had "fallen short of showing a controlling justification for the deterrent effect on the free enjoyment of the right to associate which disclosure of membership lists is likely to have."[95]

In addition to requiring the government to show a legitimate governmental interest in the information sought, there are two other requirements that are being demanded. One is a showing by the government of probable cause to believe that a crime has been committed and that a reporter has information specifically relevant to the crime. The other standard requires that the government seek to obtain the information from sources who are not reporters.

In sum, the argument for the First Amendment right is predicated on a right to information, literature, and knowledge. In all of the cases just discussed, the countervailing government interest is, on analysis, revealed as slight, and in the case of press privilege it may well be self-defeating. As the amicus brief for the National Broadcasting Company put it:

For what does it avail to force information out of a reporter because that seems the easiest way to get it, when the price to be paid is the future unavailability of similar information, not only to the public at large, but to government investigators themselves?[96]

As the sun began to set on the decade of the 1970s, the press confidentiality issue shaded from subpoena pressures to newsroom searches. Some journalists feared that the chilling effects of these premise searches would be greater than subpoena confrontations.

UNANSWERED QUESTIONS THAT OVERSHADOW A FIRST AMENDMENT APPLICATION

The overbreadth doctrine has inspired the three-pronged test that requires the government to show probable cause that the journalist has information that is relevant to a specific charge of crime, that the government has sought the information through alternative means, and that there is a compelling need for the reporter's information. This formula does not answer all the questions that will ultimately have to be addressed within the purview of First Amendment considerations.

There are at least four unsolved and troublesome questions that remain: (1) Who is a reporter? (2) What information is protected? (3) Which relationships are protected? (4) In which governmental forums should the protection apply?

There has been much discussion of the press, reporters, and the news. But who is a reporter? If everyone is a reporter of events and news, anyone could claim a privilege not to testify on the grounds that any information sought by judicial authorities is privileged under the public's right to know. This practice would blur the special role the press plays as a conduit for news events. Would everyone be given a press pass? Could anyone attend "backgrounders"? Does the First Amendment establish a privileged sanctuary for the press by mentioning only *that* particular communications institution in its reference to freedoms of expression? Was the word "press" meant to refer to a process of print communication by anyone as opposed to a community of journalists known as *the press?* Is it fair to establish the privilege on the basis of minimum numbers of subscribers and frequency of publication? Are authors of books (who often function as journalists) protected?

What information or communications are protected by the First Amendment? Should a privilege apply to information already published? Can a privilege extend when a journalist has been a participant in criminal activity? What is meant by a participant? Can a privilege apply to information gathered by a journalist in a nonprofessional capacity? Can a line be drawn between on-duty and off-duty activity for reporters who observe news?

What relationships are protected? Must they be confidential relationships? How is confidentiality to be defined?

In which judicial forums does the protection apply? Should there be any greater reluctance to apply the privilege to court trials as opposed to grand jury proceedings, legislative investigations, or administrative agency inquiries?

No attempt is made to answer these questions in this chapter. They are noted because an affirmative declaration of First Amendment protection for journalist privilege is not dispositive of the problems confronting the issue. Those problems must be faced eventually.

The *Branzburg,* *Caldwell,* and *Pappas* Cases: Rejection of a First Amendment Rationale for Newsmen's Privilege

| On June 29, 1972, the Supreme Court finally resolved the question that had remained unsettled for fourteen years.[1] It ruled that journalists do *not* have a First Amendment right to withhold the identity of confidential sources or information from a grand jury. Five justices joined in the majority and four dissented. Justice Byron White, author of the majority opinion, wrote:

Fair and effective law enforcement aimed at providing security for the person and property of the individual is a fundamental function of government, and the grand jury plays an important, constitutionally mandated role in this process. On the records now before us, we perceive no basis for holding that the public interest in law enforcement and in ensuring effective grand jury proceedings is insufficient to override the consequential, but uncertain, burden on news gathering which is said to result from insisting that reporters, like other citizens, respond to relevant questions put to them in the course of a valid grand jury investigation of criminal trial.[2] |

By a five-to-four vote, the Supreme Court generally rejected the newsmen's argument. Besides White, Justices Burger, Blackmun, and Rehnquist also rejected it. These four rejected the three conditions that were requested by the journalists, namely, that the government had to show that (1) there was probable cause to believe that the newsman had information about a specific probable crime; (2) the requested information could not be obtained by alternative means; and (3) there was a compelling and overriding governmental interest in obtaining the information.

In a brief concurring opinion, Justice Powell appeared to vote against the journalist claim to First Amendment protection from grand jury subpoenas, but his position seemed to leave the door open to a different result in some future case. Justice Douglas dissented, maintaining that reporters are completely exempt from mandatory grand jury appearance or testimony. Douglas's dissent was based largely on his absolutist conception of First Amendment rights. Justices Brennan, Stewart, and Marshall found the newsmen's three requirements to be the appropriate standard.

This decision joins the rather scattered landscape of fragmented decisions, so familiar in the area of obscenity holdings,[3] in which there is no majority bloc that expresses a single rationale defining the extent or philosophy of the ruling majority. This general condition creates uncertainty about the status of the law and in this particular case creates doubt over the meaning of the First Amendment.

The *Branzburg* holding is fragmented in four ways. Two of the fragments are absolute arguments. One is somewhat uncertain: The remaining segment accepts the journalist's balancing test.

In reaching its decision, the Court applied a per se balancing test[4] in which the two competing interests are law enforcement and news gathering. Law enforcement prevails altogether over news gathering in the White formula. The three-condition or three-pronged test that was previously elaborated is an ad hoc balancing formula and was rejected.[5] Four justices (White, Burger, Blackmun, Rehnquist) took what appears to be an absolute rather than a balancing position, namely, that there is *no* First Amendment protection for a journalist wishing to resist a subpoena requiring disclosure of confidential sources before a grand jury.

Justice Powell, however, seemed reluctant to join that "majority." He could not quite accept the three-pronged test, nor did he want to say that the newsmen "are without constitutional rights with respect to the gathering of news or in safeguarding their sources.'"[6] Justices Brennan, Stewart, and Marshall accepted ad hoc balancing, which is all the media had requested. Justice Douglas took the media to task for not asking for absolute protection. Thus the four-way split is *four–one–three–one,* that is, two versions of absolutist views and two versions of ad hoc balancing. The split is five–four if one accepts the ruling majority of five as freeing grand jury deliberations from the constraints of press motions. Put another way six justices formally rejected the journalist balancing test. Three favored it. Viewed as a decision over an absolute privilege for the journalist, the vote is eight to one against such a privilege.

It is Justice Powell's unique stand on the issue coupled with his "swing position" on the vote that undermines finality and permanence for the *Branzburg* opinion. The Powell opinion was also to be studied carefully for clues that might reveal the inner meanings of the decision.

OPINION OF THE COURT

Another difficulty with the decision is the approach of Justice White, who discusses numerous arguments, but no single argument or group of arguments is isolated as being determinative of the ultimate issue. The disposition of the four cases being reviewed is summary in form and is prefaced with the remark that the results follow from what has been said.[7] Since the implications vary according to the weight attached to each of the various arguments posited, the White opinion invites conflicting interpretations.[8]

One of the greatest complications of *Branzburg* v. *Hayes*[9] involves the *four* separate cases of *three* different reporters, arising out of separate factual contexts that merge into a single issue and ruling that does not do equal justice to the three men.

In the first matter a writ of certiorari in No. 70-85[10] brought before the Court two judgments of the Kentucky Court of Appeals, both involving Paul Branzburg. The first judgment denied a petition for prohibition and mandamus against a trial court order that Branzburg appear before a Jefferson County grand jury and identify certain individuals he had seen possessing marijuana and making hashish. The second judgment rejected Branzburg's petition to quash a summons directing his appearance before a Franklin County grand jury investigating narcotics violations.[11]

The writ of certiorari in No. 70-94 initiated a Supreme Court review of *In re Pappas,*[12] wherein the Supreme Judicial Court of Massachusetts upheld the denial of a newsman's motion to quash a summons requiring his presence before a grand jury that was apparently investigating Black Panther involvement in a prior civil disturbance.

The writ of certiorari in No. 70-57[13] involved *Caldwell* v. *United States,*[14] a decision of the Ninth Circuit Court of Appeals that had inspired much hope among proponents of a newsman's privilege by reversing the contempt citation of a reporter who refused to appear before a federal grand jury despite the existence of a protective order limiting the permissible range of questioning.[15]

The Branzburg matter was clearly a situation in which a reporter had been an eyewitness to a crime. This is the case that most neatly fits the White formula that "only where news sources themselves are implicated in crime or possess information relevant to the grand jury's task need they or the reporter be concerned about grand jury subpoenas."[16]

The Pappas involvement with crime appeared to be another matter. The case did not involve the commission of a crime during the critical period of Pappas's visit to Panther headquarters, or at least Pappas did not so report as had Branzburg. The prosecutor had no proof of the commission of a crime during that time. The record was silent on the relationship, if any, between activities in the Panther headquarters and the Bristol County grand jury's investigation.[17] This case is the closest of the four matters to what could be designated a "fishing expedition." The Bristol grand jury wanted to know more about the Panthers through revelations flowing from journalist testimony. Pappas answered questions concerning activities outside the headquarters but did not divulge what was discussed in confidence within.

After Caldwell was first subpoenaed to appear before the grand jury, the government did attempt to show the purpose of the grand jury's investigation and how Caldwell related to it. But the government was vague. It stated that "other grand juries"[18] had investigated the Panthers and implied that it was time for another round. No facts were adduced to establish a connection between Caldwell and crime. It was true that Panther David Hilliard had stated:

We are special. We advocate the very direct overthrow of the Government by way of force and violence. By picking up guns and moving against it because we recognize it as being oppressive and in recognizing that we know that the only solution is armed struggle.[19]

But Hilliard had already been indicted before Caldwell was subpoenaed. Caldwell was not sought for questioning at those grand jury deliberations. Although it is a fact that Hilliard's statement, "We will kill Richard Nixon,"[20] related to threats against the President that are the subject of 18 U.S.C. 1751, there is no connection to Caldwell because that matter was already disposed of without him. Perhaps the government thought that Caldwell would tell them about Panther weapons caches. They must have known that Caldwell was afraid to approach the grand jury because of the effect that such an appearance would have on his sources and their future uselessness to him and law enforcement as a result of Caldwell's acceptance.

Because of Justice White's heavy emphasis on crime it would appear that the holding has more direct application to Paul Branzburg than to Earl Caldwell and even less application to Paul Pappas. Branzburg was an eyewitness to a crime by his own admission. Caldwell was not willing to acknowledge that he had ever witnessed a crime in the matter involving his sources. The grand jury wanted to probe such a possibility. In the Pappas case the grand jury did not even suggest that Pappas was a probable witness to crime but that he might throw light on the operations of the Panthers.

Apparently, Justice White intended a more expansive reading of his statement that "only where news sources themselves are implicated in crime or possess information relevant to the grand jury's task need they or the reporter be concerned about grand jury subpoenas."[21]

The emphasis is not only on sources and reporters who are implicated in crime or who possess information of crime, but it is the possession of *"information relevant to the grand jury's task."* [22]

If it is the grand jury's task to establish a link between source and/or reporter on the one hand, to a specific criminal act on the other hand, it would appear that Caldwell and Pappas are barely within reach of an investigation confined to those boundaries.

If instead *task* is defined more broadly as the acquisition of information concerning a perusal of Panther events, life style, and philosophy, a different result follows, and they clearly fall within reach of such an investigation.

That Justice White intended the broader interpretation seems obvious because Branzburg, Caldwell, and Pappas saw their arguments rejected with equal force. It is also clear that the quote from the *Blair* holding leaves little doubt about the majority opinion's philosophy that the grand jury's powers should be very broad and unimpeded by counterclaims. Justice White selected this passage from *Blair:*

It is a grand inquest, a body with powers of investigation and inquisition, the scope of whose inquiries is not to be limited narrowly by *questions of propriety* or forecasts of the probable result of the investigation, or by doubts whether any particular individual will be found properly subject to an accusation of crime.[23]

In another passage of the majority opinion there is an attempt to soften the blow when it is stated that ''No attempt is made to require the press to publish its sources of information or indiscriminately to disclose them on request.''[24] But this must be read against the rejection of the three-pronged test and the insertion from the *Blair* opinion.

Efforts at interpreting the White opinion are dominated by the fact that the grand jury system came in for praise and no criticism before the ruling justices. Contrary to the opinion of some that grand juries have become increasingly politicized, arbitrary, and abusive of individual liberties,[25] the majority holding emphasized that the ''grand jury plays an important role in fair and effective law enforcement in the over-whelming majority of the States.''[26]

But the fact also remains that a word of caution about grand jury abuse concluded the opinion. Some newsmen could take comfort from a section of the last paragraph of the White argument, which stated:

Official harassment of the press undertaken not for purposes of law enforcement but to disrupt a reporter's relationship with his news sources would have no justification. Grand juries are subject to judicial control and subpoenas to motions to quash. We do not expect courts will forget that grand juries must operate within the limits of the First Amendment as well as the Fifth.[27]

This statement appears to be an effort to distinguish valid grand jury investigations from fishing expeditions.

On another issue Justice White opened an old wound when he drew a card-stacked comparison between the journalist's task vis-à-vis crime and the law enforcement interest regarding crime: ''Thus, we cannot seriously entertain the notion that the First Amendment protects a newsman's agreement to conceal the criminal conduct of his source, or evidence thereof, on the theory that it is better to write about crime than to do something about it.''[28]

White is suggesting that writing about crime may expand the public's general awareness of crime simultaneous with law enforcement's lack of specific factual awareness to solve the crime. It is assumed that the reporter can often supply the missing link in the chain of evidence by revealing his source and/or information. The statement also implies that frustration may be the result of tension between a well-informed community anxious to see the crime solved and law enforcement powerless to complete the task because of an obstreperous reporter.

In these days of credibility gaps we are urged in the majority opinion to trust "the authorities characteristically charged with the duty to protect the public interest. . . . "[29]

There should be no special treatment for the press. "The First Amendment does not guarantee special access for the press."[30] Therefore, they have no special immunity from testifying before a grand jury.

Justice White attempts to dispel the arguments over chilling effects and the drying up of information by stating that "the evidence fails to demonstrate that there would be a significant constriction of the flow of news to the public if this Court reaffirms the prior common law and constitutional rule regarding the testimonial obligations of newsmen."[31] He notes that the press has operated without constitutional protection for press informants from the beginning of our country and that the press "has flourished."[32]

White expresses the belief that the police-informer privilege is necessary because its central purpose is law enforcement. The decision to unmask an informer is in "public rather than private hands"[33] as would be the case with the journalist claim.

Justice White is particularly concerned over the problems of application for journalist privilege. He states:

Sooner or later, it would be necessary to define those categories of newsmen who qualified for the privilege, a questionable procedure in light of the traditional doctrine that liberty of the press is the right of the lonely pamphleteer who uses carbon paper or a mimeograph just as much as of the large metropolitan. . . . [34]

Although the opinion notes that there is an absolute obligation for reporters to testify before the grand jury, it expresses the view that a conditional or qualified privilege would not really protect sources anyway.

If newsman's confidential sources are as sensitive as they are claimed to be, the prospect of being unmasked whenever a judge determines the situation justifies it is hardly a satisfactory solution to the problem. For them, it would appear that only an absolute privilege would suffice.[35]

In another reference to source protection the majority ruling noted that the privilege claimed

. . . is that of the reporter, not the informant, and that if the authorities independently identify the informant, neither his own reluctance to testify nor the objection of the newsman would shield him from grand jury inquiry, whatever the impact on the flow of news or on his future usefulness as a secret source of information.[36]

Perhaps it was because the majority anticipated vociferous reactions or because the privilege problem is thorny and difficult to solve by applying judicial formulas: Whatever the reason, Justice White felt it necessary to emphasize that "Congress has freedom to determine whether a statutory newsman's privilege is necessary and desirable and to fashion standards and rules as narrow or broad as deemed necessary. . . . "[37] He also mentioned that the states should "fashion their own standards,"[38] thus leaving the impression that a federal law should not be preemptive on the states.

DISSENTING VIEWS

The majority opinion set forth several positions that the dissenters questioned: (1) They took issue with the absoluteness of the holding, and (2) with the operation of what they feared would be an unrestricted grand jury; (3) they disapproved of the manner in which the discussion of crime was used to dispose of the issue; (4) there was objection to the charge that writing about crime is separate from doing something about it; (5) Justice White's reluctance to recognize a special and protected role for the press and newsgathering was rebutted; and (6) the dissenters were critical of the opinion's assertion that there is not enough evidence of a constriction of news flow to warrant setting aside common law privilege rules.

Justice Stewart challenged the absoluteness of the holding by noting that "the longstanding rule making every person's evidence available to the grand jury is not absolute. The rule has been limited by the Fifth Amendment, the Fourth Amendment, and the evidentiary privileges of the common law."[39]

Justice Douglas responded to the majority's absolute position by presenting his own absolute perspective as viewed from the opposite end of the spectrum of this issue: "It is my view that there is no 'compelling need' that can be shown which qualifies the reporter's immunity from appearing or testifying before a grand jury, unless the reporter himself is implicated in a crime."[40]

But the word "implicated" can be read with a very broad construction to include the observance of crime, awareness of an intermittent series of criminal incidents, and acquaintance with criminals. So broadened, it could conceivably approach a meaning that even Justice White could accept. Such is the irony and poverty of language on this complicated issue.

Nevertheless, it is difficult to question Justice Douglas's intent when he stated his view that "all of the 'balancing' was done by those who wrote the Bill of Rights,"[41] and admonishing the *New York Times* by stating his view of the First Amendment: "By casting the First Amendment in absolute terms, they repudiated the timid, watered-down, emasculated versions of the First Amendment which both the government and the *New York Times* advanced in the case.'"[42]

Whereas Douglas believed that the First Amendment always takes priority over law enforcement, the majority apparently believed the latter always prevailed over the former.[43]

Commentators in support of the Douglas position carried his reasoning to the conclusion that evidentiary rules should not take priority over the First Amendment. As Susan Steiner Sher has noted:

. . . the fifth amendment privilege against self-incrimination takes priority over the evidentiary rule that one must tell all he knows. Instead of defining a newsman's privilege as an exception to the common law presumption, one should start with a constitutional presumption of a privilege based on the first amendment interest in the free flow of information, and the government must then try to justify an exception to the constitutional privilege based on the common law rule.[44]

The Court is not bereft of precedents in which limits have been placed on investigative bodies having extensive powers. Justice Douglas has noted that "congressional committees have broad powers but they are subject to restraints of the First Amendment.'"[45] And according to Justice Stewart:

We have long recognized the value of the role played by legislative investigations, for the power of Congress to conduct investigations is broad. Similarly, the associational rights of private individuals, which have been the prime focus of our First Amendment decisions in the investigative sphere, are hardly more important than the First Amendment rights of mass circulation newspapers and electronic media to disseminate ideas and information, and of the general public to receive them. Moreover, the vices of vagueness and overbreadth which legislative investigations may manifest are also exhibited by grand jury inquiries, since grand jury investigations are not limited in scope to specific criminal acts.[46]

There are at least two reasons why the holding should not be portrayed as too absolutist. First, Justice White's opinion heavily stresses the criminal aspects of investigations and leaves the inference that he would not be averse to some control over more general investigations that are not confined to specific criminal acts. Second, Justice Powell's statement about "the limited nature"[47] of the holding acts as a buffer to an absolute interpretation. He further stated: "The Court does not hold that newsmen, subpoenaed to testify before a grand jury, are without constitutional rights with respect to the gathering of news or in safeguarding their sources."[48]

But troublesome questions remain. Will it not be very difficult to quash any grand jury subpoena without the protective checks of the three-pronged test? Are the constitutional rights referred to previously only Fifth Amendment rights? Justice Powell did say that "the courts will be available to newsmen under circumstances where legitimate First Amendment interests require protection."[49] Branzburg, Caldwell, and Pappas did not apparently present legitimate First Amendment interests according to Powell, and that leaves much doubt as to what interests would pass constitutional muster.

If Justice Powell had accepted the Stewart–*New York Times* three-pronged test, the dramatic effect of the announced ruling would have been a less resounding NO to the press and it would have had a different psychological impact on the press and civil libertarians. But would the post-*Branzburg* rulings in federal district and circuit courts have been markedly different as a result of a reversed five-to-four voting order in which Justice White's position became the minority, with Justice Stewart writing the opinion of the Court as Justice Powell reluctantly concurred with the three-pronged test? Acting as a linch pin to such a ruling, Justice Powell would probably sow as much confusion about reporters' futures by concurring in this result as opposed to the actual concurrence in the case at hand. Although the psychological climate would be better, it might be somewhat deceptive regarding a reporter's real opportunities and restrictions. Some reporters only want to know whether they have the privilege or not.

Had the result been different by one vote they could have cried betrayal when the government was upheld over the reporter after a balancing consideration. The other way around there is a sigh of relief when some newsmen are protected, although the debate continues over whether the decision opened the floodgates to additional subpoenas.

If a shift by Powell is difficult to assay as to consequences, such is not the case with Justice Rehnquist, who in the opinion of one commentator[50] should not have voted on a newsmen's privilege issue. Rehnquist's activities and associations with the Department of Justice, which was the prosecuting agency and wrote the government's brief in the *Caldwell* case, led to doubt by some that he could be impartial. As an attorney with the department, he was closely connected with the government's side of the problem. As head of the Office of Legal Counsel—as the man whom Nixon called his lawyer's lawyer—Rehnquist was in a high-level position in the Department of Justice and had a hand in formulating many important policies. One of those policies was the department's policy of subpoenaing newsmen. Both the Office of Legal Counsel, and Rehnquist personally, participated in the drawing up of the Attorney General's Guidelines. Later, at the conference on media problems, Rehnquist represented the department's position. Thus Velvel argued he should not have participated in the *Branzburg* case because of "his recent association as a lawyer with one side of the controversy. . . . "[51]

If one of the five majority judges had not participated, there would have been a tie in the Supreme Court and the decision in the court below would have continued in operation. In the *Caldwell* case, this would have benefited the newsmen, who won below, but it would have been disadvantageous to the newsmen in the *Pappas* and *Branzburg* cases, in which the reporters lost in the court below. As far as the Supreme Court was concerned, however, the question of a newsman's privilege would have been left for resolution in a later case.

The absoluteness of the holding touched off a second concern in the minds of the dissenters, namely, the unrestricted power of the grand jury. Justice Stewart noted that "The uncertainty arises, of course, because the judiciary had traditionally imposed virtually no limitations on the grand jury's broad investigatory powers."[52]

Stewart indicated his disagreement with previous Court approval of broad grand jury powers and urged a balance between the competing interests of law enforcement and legislation. "Surely the function of the grand jury to aid in the enforcement of the law is no more important than the function of the legislature, and its committees, to make the law."[53]

Justice Douglas was most concerned about the grand jury's abridgement of freedom of expression. He was concerned that "fishing expeditions" would too menacingly inquire into belief systems and life styles as a means of intimidating future dissent. He was concerned that barriers to "exposing for the sake of exposure"[54] without demonstrating a valid governmental purpose were falling with the instant decision.

Under previous decisions that protected organizations and individuals from ''unwarranted'' or ''unnecessary'' disclosure,[55] it should not be difficult to extend the analogy to Caldwell's desire to withhold the names of ''members'' of his circle of informers. He noted:

Under these precedents there is no doubt that Caldwell could not be brought before the grand jury for the sole purpose of exposing his political beliefs. Yet today the Court effectively permits that result under the guise of allowing an attempt to elicit from him ''factual information.''[56]

Concerned that ''Even the most trustworthy reporter may not be able to withstand relentless badgering before a grand jury,''[57] he referred to the charge by Donner and Cerruti:

The secrecy of the grand jury's proceedings and the possibility of a jail sentence for contempt so intimidate the witness that he may be led into answering questions which pry into his personal life and associations and which, in the bargain, are frequently immaterial and vague. Alone and faced by either hostile or apathetic grand juries, the witness is frequently undone by his experience. Life in a relatively open society makes him especially vulnerable to a secret appearance before a body that is considering criminal charges. And the very body toward which he could once look for protection has become a weapon of the prosecution.[58]

A third concern of the dissenters is the manner in which the discussion of crime is used to justify broad investigation. Justice Stewart observed that the broad grand jury investigation is ''not limited in scope to specific criminal acts.''[59] He challenged the usefulness or truthfulness of Justice White's promise to journalists and sources that they need not worry if they themselves are not implicated in crime.

The crux of the Court's rejection of any newsman's privilege is its observation that only ''where news sources themselves are implicated in crime or possess information relevant to the grand jury's task need they or the reporter be concerned about grand jury subpoenas.'' But this is a most misleading construct. For it is obviously not true that the only persons about whom reporters will be forced to testify will be those ''confidential informants involved in actual criminal conduct: and those having ''information suggesting illegal conduct by others.''[60]

There was a fourth objection over the statement by Justice White that the Court ''cannot seriously entertain the notion that the First Amendment protects a newsman's agreement to conceal the criminal conduct of his source, or evidence thereof, on the theory that it is *better to write about crime than to do something about it.*''[61] The dissenters tried to show that writing about crime and doing something about it are not mutually exclusive. Governments should be able to combat crime without relying on a reporter's testimony. More instances of crime will come to the attention of law enforcement agencies if reporters are not forced to divulge.

Congressman Bell of California has argued:

I would maintain that "to write about crime" is "to do something about it." Bringing criminal conduct to light in the press alerts law enforcement officials to the existence of crime of which they would have remained unaware *but for* the work of the reporter and the cooperation of his confidential sources. And news reports on crime also rouse the public to demand more effective law enforcement from and within agencies of the government which are at times complacent and/or corrupt. The Supreme Court has created a dichotomy between "writing" and "doing" which simply does not exist.[62]

But, of course, no one was arguing that it is better to write about crime than to do something about it. What was being argued was that the protection of confidential sources will enable the press to discover and bring out more information about crime and chicanery and will thereby better enable the government "to do something about it." The dissenters felt that the government should act by using methods other than issuing subpoenas to newsmen.

The fifth dissenting objection turned on Justice White's refusal to accept the view that the press is immune from grand jury subpoenas because of a constitutionally mandated and uniquely protected role to disseminate news. Justice Douglas emphasized that "The press has a preferred position in our constitutional scheme not to enable it to make money, not to set newsmen apart as a favored class, but to bring fulfillment to the public's right to know."[63]

Justice Stewart commented on the especially vulnerable but essential gathering and disseminating process performed by the press by quoting from *Sweezy* v. *New Hampshire*.

It is particularly important that the exercise of the power of compulsory process be carefully circumscribed when the investigative process tends to impinge upon such highly sensitive areas as freedom of speech or press, freedom of political association, and freedom of communication of ideas.[64]

Another part of the fifth objection is the displeasure with the majority's use of the "equal protection" argument as a means of denying the media privilege. Justice White stated that the Court refuses to create a privilege for newsmen that "other citizens do not enjoy."[65] Finally, the

Court asserted that the press has "no constitutional right of special access to information not available to the public generally."[66]

The answers to the equal protection argument are, first, that reporters *are* in a special class, as also are attorneys and priests. The Court has never held that the attorney-client, priest-penitent, or other testimonial privileges deny equal protection, and the Court should not hold such with regard to newsmen.[67]

A second answer is that the privilege is not for reporters but for the public. According to David Marcello, "Numerous Supreme Court opinions attest to the fact that First Amendment rights are not private rights of the appellants so much as they are rights of the general public."[68] The news gatherers therefore should be "privileged" from testifying not because of their own private interests but because of their role as guardians of a free press. Dissenters charged that the Supreme Court confused the question of *who* would be granted a privilege by arguing against "constitutional protection for press informants"[69] and "a virtually impenetrable constitutional shield . . . to protect a private system of informers operated by the Press."[70] It has been argued that the fact that informers would personally benefit from a privilege of reporters, which itself is only incidental to the "true beneficiaries of such a privilege: the public."[71]

A third argument under the fifth objection noted by Sher is that "even if it is granted that the privilege is for the benefit of news gatherers, there is still no denial of equal protection, because news gatherers are protected by the first amendment."[72]

The sixth dissenting objection turns on the question of whether news dissemination is affected by subpoena pressures. The majority opinion expressed the view that there is insufficient empirical evidence demonstrating a constriction on news flow. Justice Stewart replied:

But we have never before demanded that First Amendment rights rest on elaborate empirical studies demonstrating beyond any conceivable doubt that deterrent effects exist: we have never before required proof of the exact number of people potentially affected by governmental action, who would actually be dissuaded from engaging in First Amendment activity.[73]

Justice White cited Blasi's empirical study,[74] which discussed *inter alia* inhibition of news flow as a result of grand jury subpoena pressure. In an opinion footnote White stated:

Professor Blasi's survey found that slightly more than half of the 975 reporters questioned said that they relied on regular confidential sources for at least 10%

of their stories. Of this group of reporters, only 8% were able to say with some certainty that their professional functioning had been adversely affected by the threat of subpoena; another 11% were not certain whether or not they had been adversely affected.[75]

What Justice White does not mention is that the quantitative aspect of the Blasi evidence is only the surface of the data. Blasi then went on to point out that "investigative reporters rely more heavily than do most newsmen on confidential sources."[76] The most important stories in recent years have often been those based on confidential relationships. Investigative reporters make up only a small fraction of all reporters, but they often write the most relevant and informative articles. Also unmentioned by White is Blasi's substantial evidence to demonstrate that subpoena fear hampers reporting by greatly increasing the time it takes to get a story.[77] He also noted that "newsmen who pay little attention to verification and interpretation . . . tend to be relatively unaffected by the subpoena threat. . . . "[78] Also left out of the majority opinion footnote was the statement from the qualitative side of the study, to wit:

The reporters most hindered by the possibility of being subpoenaed are those who seek a composite picture, who check and cross-check their information with numerous sources (particularly sources who are not officially designated "spokesmen," and who are relatively inexperienced and cautious about dealing with the press), and who keep extensive files and tapes for future verification reference and for trend stories.[79]

Blasi said essentially that the thorough reporter is penalized by a system that maximizes subpoena restraints.

The majority opinion indicated an interest in surveying media opinion, but their sample was only a small slice of the Blasi study and it could be argued that it was not a perfectly contextual slice. Another way to measure journalist opinion about constriction of news flow is to ask reporters whether they believe that they have enough legal protection. Blasi continued:

I was surprised by the number of reporters in the quantitative survey who were willing to say that the best of the qualified privileges offered them on the questionnaire was not enough . . . . A majority (167–50.3%) of the 332 reporters who have been entrusted with confidential information from dissident groups expressed the belief that a stronger privilege is needed. . . . *Nothing,* in the opinion of every reporter with whom I discussed the matter, would be more damaging to source relationships than a Supreme Court reversal of the Ninth Circuit's Caldwell holding.[80]

Finally, Blasi stated in his conclusion to the study that "the adverse impact of the subpoena threat has been primarily in 'poisoning the atmosphere' so as to make insightful, interpretive reporting more difficult. . . . "[81] One would hardly expect him to say that after looking only at the majority opinion's selection from his study. Blasi's own position with regard to grand jury subpoenas was spelled out in a statement made before the Senate Subcommittee on Constitutional Rights where he made clear that an *"unqualified privilege* against grand jury subpoenas is appropriate."[82] This is a stronger position than Stewart took. Blasi made a distinction between adjudicative proceedings, in which he thought newsmen were obligated to give testimony, and nonadjudicative proceedings, in which newsmen should be immune from subpoenas.[83]

In the other study cited by the majority on the topic of constriction of news flow, namely, that of Guest and Stanzler,[84] a mixed impression was left in the opinion's characterization of the study. Some newspaper editors claimed that confidential sources were very significant to news gathering, whereas others said they were inconsequential.

But the authors of the study had come to a definite conclusion that was not reported in the opinion of the Court. The title of their work was not even included in Justice White's footnote.[85] It read: "The Constitutional Argument for Newsmen Concealing Their Sources."[86] The title revealed the authors' position on the issue, but one would never know that from the opinion. Although the article does not purport to center on proofs of "sources drying up" or the "chilling effect," it referred to examples such as the *Atlanta Constitution's* exposé based on information received from a doctor who asked to remain anonymous, about the peddling of narcotics inside the Georgia state prison.[87] In this case the grand jury exerted pressure that finally led the doctor to save the reporter from contempt punishment by revealing himself as the source. The grand jury then adjourned with investigating the prison and without even calling the doctor. Guest and Stanzler used this incident to demonstrate the degree of pressure that can be applied to the will and conscience of a source and the lack of investigative follow-up once the source was made available. One conclusion that might be drawn is that the investigators were more concerned with who put out the embarrassing information that reflects unfavorably on the law enforcement establishment rather than how to get at the root of the problem by completing the investigation.

After assuming that news flow is not seriously constricted by grand jury subpoenas, Justice White stated: "From the beginnings of our country the press has operated without constitutional protection for press informants, and the press has flourished."[88]

Whether the press has flourished is hard to measure of course: flourished in comparison to what? Perhaps it might have flourished more with a press privilege all along. It might also be noted that until recently there has been no de facto recognition of such a privilege on several grounds, only one of which has been the First Amendment argument. It should also be observed that subpoena pressures have been greater in recent years as compared with the entire sweep of United States press history to which White referred. Perhaps the press has continued to flourish as well as it has for the reason stated by one of the majority opinion's authorities, Guest and Stanzler: "If newsmen were not willing to face incarceration in such circumstances it is clear that sources would dry up and the free flow of news would be seriously reduced."[89]

The dissenting justices were convinced that news flow would be affected by subpoenas. Justice Stewart opined:

The error in the Court's absolute rejection of First Amendment interests in these cases seems to me to be most profound. For in the name of advancing the administration of justice, the Court's decision, I think, will only impair the achievement of that goal. . . . the newsman will not only cease to be a useful grand jury witness; he will cease to investigate and publish information about issues of public import. . . . interests protected by the First Amendment are not antagonistic to the administration of justice.[90]

Justice Douglas saw the same general result and noted that if a reporter "can be summoned to testify in secret before a grand jury, his source will dry up."[91] He also believed that if the Court ruling becomes settled law, the reporter's main function "will be to pass on to the public the press releases which the various departments of government issue."[92] In yet another reference he noted:

Today's decision is more than a clog upon news gathering. It is a signal to publishers and editors that they should exercise caution on how they use whatever information they can obtain. Without immunity they may be summoned to account for their criticism. Entrenched officers have been quick to crash their powers down upon unfriendly commentators.[93]

One of the best rebuttals to Justice White's insistence on empirical evidence as a prelude to privilege came from Justice Stewart:

We cannot await an unequivocal—and therefore unattainable—imprimatur from empirical studies. . . . Empirical studies, after all, can only provide facts. It is the duty of courts to give legal significance to facts; and it is the special duty of this Court to understand the constitutional significance of facts. We must often proceed in a state of less than perfect knowledge, either because the facts are murky or the methodology used in obtaining the facts is open to question. It is then that we must look to the Constitution for the values that inform our presumptions. And the importance to our society of the full flow of information to the public has buttressed this Court's historic presumption in favor of First Amendment values.[94]

BRANZBURG AFTERMATH

What was to be the fate of the journalistic profession after the *Branzburg* decision? We have already discussed several of the cases that were decided after the ruling and which for various reasons, generally unrelated to First Amendment considerations, denied the privilege in every case.[95] (See chapter 2 re: Lightman [1972], Bridge [1972], McGowan [1972], Dan and Barnes [1973], Popkin [1973] and Lewis [1975]. For more extended coverage of the *Bridge* case see chapter 1.)[96]

There have been several post-*Branzburg* cases in which the reporter has been protected from disclosing confidential sources. In *Brown* v. *Commonwealth*,[97] for example, the Supreme Court of Virginia recognized a qualified First Amendment privilege. In that case, a criminal defendant had subpoenaed a newsman to give testimony. The court did not feel that the testimony sought was essential to a fair trial and upheld the privilege claim.

In *State* v. *St. Peter*,[98] the Vermont Supreme Court noted Justice Powell's reference to some measure of protection for journalists and formulated its own two-pronged rule: Before compelling a newsman to answer, the court said, there must be no other adequately available source of information, and the information sought must be relevant to the issue of guilt or innocence. In this case, as in *Brown* v. *Commonwealth*,[99] a criminal defendant was seeking to obtain by subpoena the testimony of a newsman.

In December 1972 the Second Circuit Court of Appeals ruled that Alfred Balk did not have to identify a source he used in an article.[100] Plaintiffs in a civil rights class action suit sought the subpoena. The court held that petitioners could obtain the information elsewhere. Thus, in effect, the Stewart–*New York Times* alternative-means test was being applied only a few months after the *Branzburg* ruling. The court reasoned that since a reporter does not have an absolute right under the First Amendment not to disclose his sources, whether he can be forced to disclose confidential sources must depend on a balancing of interests of "the freedom of the press and the public's right to know" against the interests to be served by compelling the testimony of the witness.[101] (For more extensive coverage of the facts of the *Balk* case see chapter 1.) The court also noted that the *Branzburg* case did not control the result in the *Baker* suit because *Branzburg* was narrowly limited to the newsmen's privilege in criminal matters and, more specifically, grand jury investigations. Since the *Baker* case was a civil suit with no such "criminal overtones," the *Branzburg* ruling was of only "tangential relevance" to Baker.[102]

In *Democratic National Committee* v. *McCord*[103] the District Court for the District of Columbia granted a motion to quash ten subpoenas issued by the Committee for the Re-election of the President against newsmen for the *New York Times,* the *Washington Post,* the *Washington Star-News,* and *Time* magazine. The committee for the Re-election of the President was seeking to discover a wide range of notes, documents, photographs, and tapes for use in its defense and counterclaim to a civil action brought by the Democratic National Committee based on claims arising from the Watergate break-in and espionage activities.

The district court's treatment of the newsmen's claimed constitutional privilege in the *McCord* case is similar to that of the Second Circuit in the *Baker* case. In the face of contentions by the newsmen for both absolute and qualified newsmen's privilege, the court, citing the *Garland* case,[104] found that the Committee for the Re-election of the President had not demonstrated that the testimony and materials sought went to the "heart of the claim." As in both *Garland* and *Baker,* the newsmen were not parties to the suit for which the information was sought. *McCord,* like *Baker,* distinguished *Branzburg* on the ground that the Supreme Court had concerned itself only with criminal matters, particularly grand jury investigations.

However, the *McCord* court noted that a "chilling effect" might result from enforcement of these particular subpoenas "where, as here, strong allegations have been made of corruption within the highest circles of government."[105] In addition, since a specific claim for an absolute privilege had been forwarded, the court analyzed the claim more thoroughly than did the *Baker* court, explicitly and emphatically rejecting the contention: "It is of critical importance in these cases to note and bear in mind that the main purpose of the judicial system—a search for the truth—must be flexible in order to accommodate itself to the needs of our times and the needs of an individual case.''[106]

Both cases above apply the ''heart of the claim'' test, which its critics note is vague and uncertain of application. One commentator stated:

In a ''heart of the claim'' jurisdiction, the costs of silence, and their determination, are uncertain. The uncertainty stems from the very nature of the ''heart of the claim'' test: it is essentially an ad hoc determination in which presence or absence of the privilege is dependent on the ''necessity'' of the confidential information in the course of the lawsuit. Necessity, in turn, depends upon a showing of relevance and unavailability from independent sources.[107]

In sum, the trend is toward protecting the reporter over a civil litigant who must show that the information sought is central to his claim, and criminal defendants must show relevance to the issue of guilt or innocence before journalists can be compelled to testify.

But in a libel case in November 1977, the Idaho Supreme Court observed that there was no journalist privilege protection against public officials who sue reporters for libel. The official does not have to demonstrate specifically that the information is necessary to the lawsuit, according to this ruling.[108] Furthermore, the Supreme Court of the United States refused to review the case.

The facts are that a police officer was responding to press criticism that he overreacted in shooting a suspect. Reporter Jay Shelledy contended that agent Michael Caldero of the Idaho Bureau of Narcotics and Organized Crime shot Dale Johnson, who did not know he was being pursued by police. Johnson thought instead that ''hippy'' ruffians were attacking him. Caldero and his partner were disguised as ''hippies.'' Shelledy claimed that a confidential ''police expert'' passed the information about the police brutality and shooting that led to the story.

Shelledy was sentenced to thirty days in the Latah County jail.[109] The news media feared that if this case were to begin a new judicial trend, reporters would face more and more nuisance libel suits.

Some commentators have expressed the view that the *Branzburg* decision is very tentative and that it will still take some time to establish settled principles of law in its aftermath.[110] Others are quite apprehensive and pessimistic about what they view as further erosions of press freedom.[111]

In order to put the journalist privilege into proper perspective following *Branzburg,* it might be helpful to select cognate questions and rulings that affect the status of the reporter privilege. The ''gag rule'' is such an issue both because it involves inhibitions on press comment while a trial is in progress and because it has been a part of the process leading to privilege confrontations. The *order re publicity* not only "chills": It "freezes" press comment. When newsmen write about events close to the subject matter under order, they may find themselves in contempt and try to fight back by invoking the media privilege as in the *Farr* and *Fresno Bee* cases in California.[112]

Another companion issue that potentially affects newsmen as witnesses before a grand jury came to a head in the case of *Bursey* v. *United States*.[113] As already indicated, the grand jury's power has been broad and has only been deterred by the Fifth Amendment, common law and statutory privileges. In the *Bursey* case the United States Court of Appeals for the Ninth Circuit expanded Fifth Amendment rights by restricting the ability of grand juries to compel testimony by means of a federal transactional immunity statute. The court also recognized the right of witnesses to refuse to answer questions infringing on First Amendment freedoms.

On December 10, 1969, Sherrie Bursey and Joyce Presley, members of the Black Panther Party and staff workers for the Black Panther newspaper, were summoned to testify before a federal grand jury. The grand jury was investigating the possibility that certain statements in a speech made by David Hilliard, chief of staff of the Black Panther Party, and published in the Black Panther newspaper, constituted threats against the President prohibited by federal law[114] (a reminder that Caldwell was also to be questioned about Hilliard by the FBI). The witnesses answered a few questions, but declined to answer others concerning the publication of the speech and the *internal operations of the paper,* basing their refusals on the First and Fifth Amendments.

The major premise on which the *Bursey* court relied in concluding that the First Amendment applied to grand jury proceedings was that there is no justification for applying the amendment less rigorously to a grand jury investigation than to other governmental activity. In considering the press rights the court focused on the administrative aspects of the news medium—editorial responsibility, distribution, and financing. It stated that absent a showing of criminal intent in publishing material, no news organization would be forced to divulge information concerning these administrative operations to a grand jury. The holding appeared to be limited to internal operations only. The aspect of the First Amendment involved was freedom of association rather than the newsman's privilege question of press and the public's right to know.

The *Bursey* holding can be viewed as being congruent with the *Branzburg* decision, although it limited its thrust. In *Branzburg* the Court denied that freedom of the press exempts a newsman from appearing before a grand jury or from answering questions about his news sources. Although the exact scope of the Supreme Court's holding remains unclear, it seems unlikely that press rights alone would justify withholding the information about the Black Panther Party sought in the *Bursey* case. In contrast, details about the operation of the internal mechanisms of a news medium represent a clearly distinct type of information. But by the very fact that the *Bursey* decision limits the power of the grand jury to compel testimony in this particular area, it acts as yet another check among a gathering number of deterrents and restraints against overly broad investigations.

It is impossible to forecast how far the courts will go toward limiting grand jury activities. One commentator is of the opinion that recent decisions have at least marked the beginning of the end of the grand jury's unrestricted investigative power. The *Bursey* decision appears to be one of the steps in this direction. The final disposition of the *Bursey* case occurred a few months after the *Branzburg* holding when a government request for rehearing was denied on October 5, 1972.[115]

Thus the discussion has been confined to judicial reactions to the *Branzburg* holding. Following the decision, several additional states enacted newsmen's shield statutes, and both houses of Congress held hearings on the possibilities of a federal journalist privilege law.

6

The Legislative Effort Regarding News Dissemination and Privileged Communication: State Shield Laws

Whenever the press has been convinced that courts are not taking their interests seriously enough, one of their means of redress has been through statutory remedy. This has sometimes been in the form of closing loopholes where legislation already exists. Where there is no legislation, it often appears following an unpleasant showdown between the press and antagonists employing compulsory process.

This chapter surveys state legislation that was passed with the intention of rectifying some of the difficulties that prosecutors, defendants, courts, and law enforcement personnel were getting entangled in as they dealt with reporters.

CHRONOLOGICAL DEVELOPMENT

At present there are twenty-six states with newsmen's privilege laws.[1]

In addition to the states that presently have a reporter's privilege statute in effect, eight other state legislatures have shown unsuccessful efforts to pass similar legislation in recent sessions.[2] Florida house bill 2794 died in committee in 1972. In Idaho, a bill was drafted but never reached the floor and thus died in 1972. In Iowa, a bill was introduced but died in the same year. In Massachusetts, senate bill 114 was defeated in that body in 1972. In Minnesota; a bill passed the senate but died in the house in 1972. In Missouri; house bill 18 died in committee in 1971. In Texas; house bill 205 died in committee in 1972 and senate bill 558 died after committee amendment on the floor later that year. In Wisconsin, senate bill 585 (1971) passed and died in the house in 1972. The bill was sharply qualified by excluding from its protection the source of any allegedly defamatory information in any case where the defendant, in a civil action for defamation, asserts a defense based on the source of such information. The intent of the Wisconsin legislature was to deter those who disseminate libelous information from using the statute as a shield to prevent their detection.

Three states unsuccessfully sought to amend their existing privilege statutes.[3] In Alaska, senate bill 272 died in committee in 1972. The amendment would have created an absolute privilege in place of the qualified statute. In Kentucky, house bill 586 died in committee in 1972. The amended version would have broadened coverage for newsmen. In New Jersey, senate bill 1121 was passed but languished in the assembly. The amended version would extend the privilege beyond "newspaperman" to any person "connected with any news dissemination."

Many other state legislatures have successfully updated their journalist privilege statutes over the years. California's first shield statute was enacted in 1935, although there is some argument about its real origin being in an 1881 statute.[4] The 1935 statute[5] was revised in 1966[6] and again in 1974.[7] Kentucky's statute was revised in 1969,[8] Maryland's in 1971,[9] New Mexico's in 1967,[10] Ohio's in 1964,[11] and Pennsylvania's in 1970.[12]

The record is spotty on the subject of pressures that led to specific state statutes, but there are a few references to the causes of such enactments. For example, in 1896 the *Baltimore Sun's* confrontation with a grand jury subpoena led to a state campaign by the *Sun* for legislative protection. *Sun* reporter John Morris had been sentenced to jail for five days for refusing to divulge sources.[13] Two months after the *Morris* case, Maryland enacted the first reporters' privilege statute in the United States. The statute, still in effect, provides that a person "engaged in, connected with or employed by" a newspaper cannot be "compelled to disclose" in any legal proceeding "the source of news or information."[14]

This first action was followed thirty-seven years later by a statute in New Jersey and, after two vigorous drives by the newspaper profession in 1935 and again in 1948–50, by statutes in ten other states.[15]

The revisions of the 1960s and 1970s were responses to increased subpoena pressures resulting *inter alia* from reporting on the counterculture and the federal government's clash with the press.[16] The New York statute was passed in May 1970 subsequent to the issuance of a number of Justice Department subpoenas to newsmen requiring disclosure of information communicated in confidence.[17]

There are indications that in the absence of state shield laws judges have often denied the privilege, and in so doing, have referred to the absence of a state statute. Such was the case in New Jersey before that state had such a statute. In reference to newsman Julius Grunow, the judge noted that "he pleaded a privilege which finds no countenance in the law."[18]

In New York State before passage of a shield statute, a judge in sentencing Martin Mooney stated: "I know of no law, Mr. Mooney, and none has been presented to me so that the Court could consider its judgment in this State—at least either by the legislature or by recognized law—which gives the witness the privilege claimed by him."[19]

In the *Goodfader* case,[20] the Supreme Court of Hawaii noted that the state did not have a privilege statute. The same observation was made by the court in the *Buchanan* case in Oregon[21] and again in the *Pappas* case in Massachusetts, where the Supreme Court observed that the state did not have a journalist privilege statute.[22]

Thus in the past the press has generally been in favor of some kind of state journalist privilege statute because it acts as a buffer against judicial denial of a privilege or at least denies the judiciary the argument that there is no legislative enactment.

JOURNALIST PRIVILEGE MODEL LEGISLATION

In 1973 the National Conference of Commissioners on Uniform State Laws began the adoption of a model newsmen's privilege statute. The seven-man committee recommended that newsmen could never be compelled to testify before a grand jury or legislative committee but they could be so compelled during a trial if the party seeking their testimony showed that they had the relevant information and that the party had made a substantial effort to get the information elsewhere. The party would also have to show that the resolution of the issue would be impossible without the reporter's testimony.[23]

Any newsman claiming the immunity under the statute would be required to file an affidavit stating that his testimony would either violate an explicit promise of confidentiality or would do serious harm to a continuing relationship with a source.[24]

According to Vincent A. Blasi, a professor at the University of Michigan Law School who is advising the committee, these restrictions would so limit the number of subpoenas that sources and newsmen would rarely have anything to fear.[25]

The proposed measure drew criticism from the press. Representatives of the American Newspaper Publishers Association, the Reporters' Committee for Freedom of the Press, and the National Newspaper Association contended that any door left open for subpoenas to newsmen would make it impossible for reporters to assure fearful sources of information that their identities would be kept secret. For this reason, Jack Landau, a reporter for the Newhouse newspaper chain, said that he saw little merit in establishing different rules for investigative and adjudicative proceedings.[26]

LAW ENFORCEMENT OPINION ON STATE SHIELD LEGISLATION

Support for state journalist privilege statutes has come from both the media and law enforcement agencies: The general public has been polled on the subject of shield legislation as it pertains to both state and national jurisdictions.

Gallup researchers have found that the public, especially those who have attended college, generally support the right of the reporter to protect his source of information in court. In a survey conducted November 10 to 13 in 1973 in 300 localities across the country, researchers found that of 1,462 persons interviewed, 57 percent supported the right of newsmen to protect sources.[27] Of those who attended college, 68 percent felt that newsmen had a right to conceal sources. The question that was asked of the respondents was: "SUPPOSE A NEWSPAPER REPORTER OBTAINS INFORMATION FOR A NEWS ARTICLE HE IS WRITING FROM A PERSON WHO ASKS THAT HIS

NAME BE WITHHELD. DO YOU THINK THAT THE REPORTER
SHOULD OR SHOULD NOT BE REQUIRED TO REVEAL THE
NAME OF THIS MAN IF HE IS TAKEN TO COURT TO TESTIFY
ABOUT THE INFORMATION IN HIS NEWS ARTICLE?''[28]

Law enforcement opinion has been mixed. In March 1973 Arthur B.
Hansen of the American Newspaper Publishers Association (ANPA)
conducted a mail ballot poll among state attorneys general and received
replies from thirty-four states.[29] Those polled were asked to state their
views of the ANPA bill, which has been acknowledged by its authors to
be very broad in its guarantees for newsmen.[30]

Nineteen attorneys general stated that they were not aware of any
incidences concerning problems that may have arisen between the press
and the various state governmental investigative bodies of their jurisdictions.[31]

Attorneys general in seven states went into substantial detail on state
court cases in which the media and the government had confronted each
other.[32] The Alabama reply referred to the case of *Ex parte Sparrow*[33];
that of California to the *Farr* case[34]; that of Kentucky to the *Branzburg*
case[35]; that of Maryland to the *Lightman* case[36]; that of Oregon to the
State v. *Buchanan*.[37] The Tennessee letter referred to a news reporter
who had conducted a talk show and refused to disclose the identity of a
caller who turned out to be a grand juror who accused the grand jury of
conducting a whitewash in its investigation of a local judge.[38] The
answer from Texas referred to a gag order over a rape case and a
demand for negatives of photographs.[39]

Eight responses dealt squarely with the matter of whether or not the
respondents could support the bill proposed by ANPA.[40] Among them,
the Connecticut attorney general, Killian, stated that he was in favor of
the right of a newsman to protect his sources because he felt that the
news media is the "most effective shield ever devised for protection of
the people's right to know." The respondent from Maine, Attorney
General Lund, stated that the ANPA bill is almost identical to a bill
submitted to the Maine legislature, and he noted that he was considering
supporting it publicly. In New Mexico the ANPA bill went before the
legislature, and Attorney General David L. Norvell gave full public
support to the bill.[41] And in New Hampshire, Attorney General Warren
B. Rudman supported a house bill that was similar to the ANPA proposal.

The remaining four of the eight respondents giving their opinions of
the proposal were more qualified in their support. The attorney general

of Delaware, for example, believed that newsmen's privilege legislation should be approached with caution, but he indicated his concern that arbitrary subpoenaing of newsmen before grand juries is harmful.[42]

The attorney general of Rhode Island was not in favor of those provisions in the ANPA bill that he felt would allow a person claiming to be the potential author of a manuscript of a book that has not yet been written, to claim the privilege against testifying to a murder to which he was an eyewitness.[43]

Wyoming Attorney General Clarence A. Brimmer generally favored such legislation but was somewhat disturbed by the complete lack of qualification of such a privilege, since it had occurred to him that there could be instances in which information pertaining to the commission or the concealment of a crime ought to be disclosed to a grand jury.[44]

From what is revealed in the preceding survey, only eight out of fifty attorneys general indicated where they stood on the issue of the merits of shield legislation.

Several law enforcement spokesmen other than attorneys general have appeared before Congress to give their views. In testimony before the House committee studying the journalist privilege, Governor Meskill of Connecticut favored a qualified privilege bill; one that would not allow those committing libel to hid behind it. Such a bill, he felt, should not be so absolute in its coverage that it could protect criminals and eyewitnesses to crime. He would, however, require alternative source proof by the person seeking the testimony of a newsman.[45]

Former Governor Nelson Rockefeller signed the New York Freedom of Information bill, which contains the guarantees for a newsmen's privilege. He pointed out that the statute is one of the few that protects both sources and information. He praised the press for publishing stories on organized crime that reveal leads that make it easier for law enforcement agencies to follow through after press exposure. He referred to a case in which a particular prosecutor "once obtained 22 convictions in a drive against organized crime that grew initially out of newspaper revelations."[46]

Joseph Lordi, the prosecutor of Essex County in New York State, opposed an absolute privilege that would protect newsmen from disclosing any and all information involuntarily. He was especially concerned about crime and referred to a case in Essex County in which "the newsman tried to assert a privilege not to disclose information given to him concerning an attempt to bribe a public official. In doing this, he hindered the investigation of the grand jury concerning charges of official corruption.[47] He supported a privilege that would extend only to the source of the information and not the information itself.[48]

William Cahn, the district attorney for Nassau County in New York State, represents the National District Attorney's Association. He was of the belief that law enforcement has not suffered as a result of shield legislation in his jurisdiction. He noted that American newspapers have compiled outstanding records of investigative and interpretive reporting without the privilege statute, but he thought that they might do even better with the protection.[49] He stated:

In a society which features expanding governmental bureaucracies, enlarging governmental jurisdiction and progressive centralization of power, where powerful private interests such as organized crime challenge the primacy of government and corrupt its central processes, effective investigative reporting and opinion leadership based upon a solid underpinning of concrete factual information becomes an increasingly urgent public need.[50]

Cahn emphasized that in a particularly suppressive jurisdiction sources of information could be choked off "which would otherwise provide the factual basis for future news stories alerting investigatory agencies to sub rosa crime breeding conditions."[51]

Melvin Block, president of the New York Trial Lawyers Association stated: "We are in favor of an absolute and unqualified privilege for newsmen."[52] He noted that absoluteness is not a new concept in the area of privilege and that journalism should be trusted with "the keys that unlock the closets."[53]

In January 1973 the Massachusetts Bar Association endorsed a shield law that would protect a journalist's source of information. The proposal would provide for a balancing formula, however, and is therefore not absolute. A court could order disclosure when there is "substantial evidence" that the information is necessary to permit a criminal prosecution for a serious crime, or to prevent a threat to human life, and when such information is unavailable from other prospective witnesses.[54]

The Association of the Bar of the City of New York endorsed a qualified privilege. "An absolute protection for journalists from testimonial obligations seems to us not warranted."[55] The association was also concerned that "extending the statute to cover all free-lancers, scholars, lecturers, pamphleteers, etc., not only would complicate its administration"[56] but would be too difficult for legislators to draft because of the complications of First Amendment claims.

MEDIA OPINION ON STATE PRESS PRIVILEGE LEGISLATION

The Freedom of Information Committee of the Associated Press Managing Editors Association, in cooperation with the American Newspaper Publishers Association and the American Society of Newspaper Editors, conducted a state-by-state survey to determine the extent of the use of subpoena power in the fifty jurisdictions during the period between January 1, 1967, and December 31, 1972. They wanted to know how much pressure was being applied through subpoenas to force reporters to divulge confidential information.[57]

Editors and newspaper representatives in all fifty states were asked to respond. At the time when the study was made available to Subcommittee 3 of the House Judiciary Committee, forty-nine states were represented. A synopsis of the study follows:

ALABAMA: John W. Bloomer, managing editor of the *Birmingham News,* stated: "Alabama newspapermen are adequately protected from subpoenas by state courts by what, I think, is one of the finest subpoena laws in the nation."[58]

ALASKA: Robert B. Atwood, editor and publisher of the *Anchorage Daily Times,* noted that "no subpoena has ever been requested in Alaska that caused any concern."[59]

ARIZONA: Lowell Parker, managing editor of the *Phoenix Gazette,* referred to threats of subpoena by lawyers who wanted complete negative files of pictures taken at accident scenes and racial disturbances. Eventually, papers in Tucson and Phoenix adopted a policy of keeping only pictures that had been published. The *Phoenix Gazette* and the *Arizona Republic* finally adopted a policy of charging $1 per print, and word of this policy spread rapidly "through legal beagle circles and now we have very few requests for pictures and no threats of subpoena."[60]

ARKANSAS: A representative of the *Gazette* in Little Rock reported one subpoena. The state legislature was considering a casino gambling bill to legalize gambling at Hot Springs. Two reporters wrote that unnamed legislators had said that they had been offered bribes to vote for the bill. The reporters were summoned before a grand jury but refused to identify sources. They were found guilty of contempt and spent thirty hours in jail. Their sources then urged the reporters to identify them, and they did.[61]

CALIFORNIA: The *Caldwell, Farr, Bursey, Lawrence,* and *Baldwin* cases have been reported on elsewhere in this work. (For *Farr, Lawrence,* and *Baldwin* see chapter 1; for *Caldwell* see chapter 2; for

Bursey see chapter 5.) In addition to these there were many other references. We shall refer to only two of them. In August 1970 Orange County Superior Court Judge William S. Lee quashed a subpoena that would have required the *Los Angeles Times* to produce unpublished photos of campus disturbances at Cal State Fullerton. The judge said the prosecution had not shown the photographs would be material or admissible as evidence.[62]

Logan McKechnie of the *San Diego Union* had done a series of articles on land development and was subpoenaed in February 1971 by an attorney representing the developers in a libel suit against a homeowner. He was asked to give a deposition, but because the libel suit was dropped, the matter died.[63]

COLORADO: John Rogers, managing editor of the *Denver Post,* referred to a case in which one of his reporters was subpoenaed to testify about confidential sources.[64] The report did not indicate how the matter had been resolved.

CONNECTICUT: E. Bartlett Barnes, publisher of the *Bristol Press,* referred to only two subpoena incidents. In the one case the newsman refused to comply, without serious consequences. In the other case the newsman complied voluntarily.[65]

DELAWARE: The News-Journal of Wilmington was happy to report that the state supreme court had overturned a superior court order requiring a photographer to yield negatives. Counsel for the paper stated: "You will notice that they do it on state law grounds and not on constitutional law grounds."[66]

FLORIDA: George Beebe of the *Miami Herald* observed that Florida had no adverse cases to report, but he expected that the situation would change for the worse.[67]

GEORGIA: A spokesman for the *Atlanta Journal* and the *Atlanta Constitution* referred to three cases that occurred during the period referred to by the survey authors. One matter involved land development, another a murder, and the third a homicide. In none of the three cases were the reporters required to divulge confidences.[68]

HAWAII: The editor of the *Honolulu Star-Bulletin* was not aware of any subpoena problems in his state.[69]

IDAHO: The *Idaho State Journal* of Pocatello complied under protest with a subpoena issued by the deputy county defender for photos taken of a fatal 1972 traffic accident. The pictures were requested for use as evidence in a homicide case.[70]

ILLINOIS: The *Chicago Tribune* was served with what the paper referred to as "dragnet subpoenas," of unpublished notes, photos, and confidential sources, but successfully resisted all of them. The *Chicago Sun-Times* and *Chicago Daily News* reported thirty-nine subpoenas but noted that "to date we have been successful in protecting the unpublished notes, sources and photographs of our staff members in all instances."[71] Illinois has a shield statute.

INDIANA: Wendell Phillippi, managing editor of the *Indianapolis News,* mentioned two incidents that involved the *Warsaw Times-Union* in 1971 and the *Evansville Courier* in 1972. In the *Warsaw* case, a defense attorney for the man charged with peddling drugs subpoenaed all the files the newspaper had accumulated in an investigation of drug activity. The newspaper filed a motion to block the subpoena, and the judge ruled for the paper, citing Indiana's journalist privilege law and the First Amendment. In Evansville the judge directed a reporter to answer five of the twenty-eight questions a grand jury had asked. The reporter complied with the judicial order.[72]

IOWA: Edward Heins of the *Register and Tribune* of Des Moines stated that there have been "almost no requests for subpoenas of information from newspapers in Iowa."[73]

KANSAS: Confidentiality of a newsman's sources was upheld July 5, 1971, by Judge James V. Riddel, Jr., in Sedgwick County District Court. Three newsmen had been subpoenaed by the defense in a drug case to testify about whether they had been informed by sheriff's officers that a search warrant was to be served before it actually was served. Kansas does not have a shield law.[74]

KENTUCKY: In addition to the *Branzburg* matter there were many other subpoena confrontations. In summary, two reporters who resisted subpoenas were upheld by the judge; one matter was dropped after negotiations; and one newsman who resisted an out-of-state demand for information prevailed over the prosecutor seeking the information because of the legal complications involved.[75]

LOUISIANA: The editor of the *Times-Piscayune* in New Orleans stated that the only cases he could remember concerning subpoenas were the Black Panther and Clay Shaw trials. The city editor of the *State-Times* of Baton Rouge stated: "In Louisiana we have a shield law several years old which protects confidential sources only, as distinct from the information itself. When the law was proposed and passed there was not the threat to information that exists today."[76] Of the three editors who responded to the survey there was general agreement that the subpoena situation has not become very threatening yet.

MAINE: The editor for the *Portland Press Herald* and *Portland Evening Express* could only recall one incident involving a subpoena in which the reporters had complied.[77]

MARYLAND: In chapter 2 we have already referred to the one and only case that was cited in this state.

MASSACHUSETTS: The only case mentioned by the respondents from this state, the *Pappas* case, has been covered in this book in chapter 2.

MICHIGAN: Elmer E. White of the Michigan Press Association observed that there has been a little trouble in Michigan with subpoenas but not much. "A state law on the books for 20 years and previously considered applying only to grand jury investigations has been held applicable to any criminal case."[78]

MINNESOTA: The editor of the *St. Paul Dispatch* and *Pioneer Press* noted that there has been only one incident. One of his reporters for the *Pioneer Press* was subpoenaed for information in a murder case and refused to identify his sources. The judge in a county court sentenced him to ninety days for refusal. The state supreme court of Minnesota ruled that the questions asked of the reporter were too vague and were dangerously close to a "fishing expedition." The reporter did not have to testify.[79]

MISSISSIPPI: The executive editor of the *Clarion-Ledger* of Jackson stated that he was not aware of any subpoena cases in the state.[80]

MISSOURI: The assistant managing editor of the *St. Louis Globe-Democrat* stated that in civil matters "we receive an average of three or four subpoenas a year."[81] He noted that there are more cases involving criminal matters. The manging editor of the *Kansas City Star* stated that he had checked his files and found no subpoena cases that met the specifications of the survey question.

MONTANA: The editor of the *Billings Gazette* observed that there were no subpoenas of the type mentioned in Montana in the survey period.[82]

NEBRASKA: The executive editor of the *Lincoln Journal* said that "In 25 years I have been with the *Lincoln Journal,* we have never been subpoenaed, except in libel cases involving our own newspaper story."[83] He then noted that they were threatened with subpoenas on many occasions but that they had talked the parties out of pursuing the matter.

NEVADA: A reporter for the *Las Vegas Sun* noted that there was only one incident in which the court was asking for a disclosure of confidences, and the Nevada shield law protected those involved.[84]

NEW HAMPSHIRE: The executive editor of the *Manchester Union Leader* reported three instances in which staff members were subpoenaed to divulge confidences. Two of his reporters complied, and a third only in part. He took a position of partial noncompliance.[85]

NEW JERSEY: The Peter Bridge matter has already been discussed in this paper in chapter 1. The editor of the *Daily Journal* of Elizabeth, New Jersey, said that the paper had been served very few subpoenas during the survey period. The executive editor of the *Herald-News* of Passaic referred to an incident involving photos. The issue became moot because the paper had recently established the policy of destroying photos not published or those more than one year old. The general manager for the New Jersey Press Association was especially diligent in attempting to comply with the authors of the survey. He forwarded questionnaires to 150 weekly newspapers and received 32 responses, of which all but 3 reported that they had not been served subpoenas.[86]

NEW MEXICO: The editor of the *Albuquerque Tribune* responded to the survey by noting only one incident in which photos were sought. The reporters agreed to turn over the photos but could not find them. The prosecutor dropped the matter.[87]

NEW YORK: Burt Blazer of the *Star-Gazette* in Elmira referred to a case involving the suspension of a police chief. The chief was seeking information from the paper, and the reporters agreed to comment on anything published but would not go beyond that. In the meantime, the village and the chief reached an agreement and the issue became moot.[88]

NORTH CAROLINA: The editor of the *Charlotte Observer* reported that he knew of no subpoenas or even the threat of them.[89]

NORTH DAKOTA: The editor of the *Forum* in Fargo reported only one case in which the reporter cooperated because she had been assured that she would not be asked about confidences.[90]

OHIO: The editor of the *Cincinnati Enquirer* found no examples that he thought fit the requirements of the survey takers. The head of the Ohio Newspaper Association boasted about the Ohio shield law. The executive editor of the *Plain Dealer* in Cleveland observed, ''Ohio has had a shield law since the early 1940's and it is regarded as one of the best of any state. It has been tested many times, but in every case it has been upheld. There has never been an appeal to a higher court.''[91]

OKLAHOMA: The manging editor of the *Oklahoma City Times* said that only three incidents have been recorded. Reporters were summoned in all cases, and the editor told them to comply with the summons. He noted:

Our rule is that we will testify against an accused if we have knowledge. We do not consider this a misuse of the subpoena power. We would, of course, strenuously object to testifying about what a witness might tell us in confidence. But we haven't had any problems of the latter sort.[92]

OREGON: We have already referred to the *Buchanan* case in chapter 2. The only case since 1967 has been one in which student editors were subpoenaed from the *Daily Emerald,* the paper that Buchanan served, to disclose photos of an anti-ROTC demonstration. The student editors refused to turn over the photos, and eventually the matter was dropped. This was clearly a case of using the press as an ''investigative arm of government'' for the law enforcement agencies could take photos of the demonstration as well as a newspaper.[93]

PENNSYLVANIA: The general manager of the Pennsylvania Newspaper Publishers Association observed that the Pennsylvania journalist privilege law was tested in a case that involved the *Philadelphia Bulletin* and that the courts sustained the law and upheld the reporter's claim. He noted that there have been no cases since then.[94]

RHODE ISLAND: The managing editor of the *Evening Bulletin* of Providence reported two cases. The one subpoena challenge was quashed, and the other involved testimony under a protective order that barred inquiry into any confidential information the reporter possessed.[95]

SOUTH CAROLINA: The editor of the *Columbia Record* referred to two instances of subpoenas issued to obtain confidential sources of information from the media. One involved student reporters for the *Gamecock,* a student publication for the University of South Carolina that has published stories on narcotics. The students appeared before the grand jury but did not divulge confidences. The solicitor later admitted that he knew the identity of the informants all along from other sources. The South Carolina Press Association issued a statement declaring that particular investigation improper. The other case involved the *State,* Columbia's morning daily newspaper. Here a reporter wrote about bad conditions at the county jail from confidential tips in the form of signed statements of former inmates. The solicitor asked for the statements, and they were supplied sans names. Subpoenas for the names followed, but the reporters finally exhausted the prosecution and never supplied the names.[96]

SOUTH DAKOTA: The editor of the *Rapid City Journal* stated: "I know of no subpoenas used in South Dakota in recent memory."[97]

TENNESSEE: The *Weiler* case was the single reported case, and it has been discussed in chapter 1.

TEXAS: The managing editor of the *Dallas Morning News* knew of no subpoena power to force the media to disclose confidential sources. The *Corpus Christi Caller-Times* was involved in a minor incident that stopped short of a showdown.[98]

UTAH: The executive editor of the *Salt Lake Tribune* remarked that he was "unable to turn up one case where there was forced disclosure."[99]

VERMONT: The editor of the *Free Press* of Burlington knew of no subpoenas.[100]

VIRGINIA: The editor of the *Free Lance-Star* of Fredericksburg knew of only two subpoena cases in recent years. In both cases the reporters did not have to divulge confidences but did appear.[101]

WASHINGTON: Only one case was reported involving a reporter for the *Seattle Times.* This involved an out-of-state request from a federal grand jury investigation taking place in northern Iowa. Eventually, the United States attorney in that case had the subpoena withdrawn.[102]

WEST VIRGINIA: The executive editor of the *Charleston Gazette* reported only one case. The story involved narcotics. The reporter appeared before the grand jury and pleaded with the angry jurors that he had received his information in confidence. In the reporter's words:

When Simpson and the jurors asked over and over for the names of the students, I always looked at the jurors imploringly and said something like, "These young people trusted me. They believed in me, that I wouldn't betray them. Put yourself in my place. Would you violate their trust?" ...etc. etc.

At one point, Simpson told the jurors they could request a court order to force me to testify—meaning, I assume, that I would be jailed for contempt if I persisted in noncooperation. All the jurors were rather angry, but finally they just told me disgustedly, to get out. That was the end of it.[103]

WISCONSIN: The survey in Wisconsin was made by Lucas G. Staudacher of the Marquette University College of Journalism. He reported that the case involving illegal gambling and pornographic movies in 1969 led to subpoenas that dried up information for both the prosecution and the media.[104] This incident involved reporters for the *Capital Times* of Madison. A reporter for the *Milwaukee Sentinel* was protected by a court order in 1972. Seven other cases involved the *Milwaukee Journal*.

The first case, occurring in 1968, involved the bribing of legislators by lobbyists. A newsman with the proof based on confidential sources was deposed but eventually released from the subpoena because the information had been found elsewhere.

The second case, in the same year, turned on the suicide of a judge in which another judge sought testimony from a newsman to determine whether any judicial irregularities had contributed to the suicide. The reporter resisted, and the judge withdrew the questions.

A third case, also in 1968, continued with the judge's suicide issue. A state hearing was conducted into whether two attorneys who had been pressuring the judge were acting unprofessionally. *Journal* reporters were summoned to disclose information to the hearing referee. It is unclear from the reporter how the case was disposed of.

In the fourth case, in 1969, a reporter was called to testify about his knowledge concerning violation of a corrupt practices act by a city alderman. He complied and testified.

A fifth case, in 1970, involved the grand jury investigation into the bombing of the Army Mathematics Center on the University of Wisconsin, Madison campus. Donald Pfarrer, newly assigned to cover radical politics, was subpoenaed concerning his interview with Mark Knops. Pfarrer appeared and told what he knew, which seemed to include little information that was not already known.

The sixth case also concerned the bombing. Two *Journal* reporters were asked by the attorney general to supply the names of the bombers because the newsmen had hinted that they might know who was involved in the destruction. They pleaded for more time and expressed a need for further verification. In the end they could not come through with concrete information.

The seventh case, in 1972, involved antiwar protest and the uttering of "obscenities." A reporter was sought for any light he could shed on who had used abusive language. The effort came to naught.[105]

WYOMING: The editor of the *Star-Tribune* of Casper reported that "there have been no subpoena cases in Wyoming."[106]

The survey that appeared in congresional hearing publications did not draw any data out of the state-by-state elaboration for classificatory or comparative purposes. Because one of the concerns of this book has been the determination of the effect that press privilege legislation has had on the issuance of subpoenas and compliance with them, an effort at comparison has been undertaken employing two questions:

1. Based on the responses in the foregoing survey, are journalists safer from subpoena challenge in the shield law states as opposed to the states without such statutes? This question is concerned with the actual number of subpoenas issued.

The results are inconclusive. The shield states collected fifty-five subpoenas and the nonshield states fifty-seven subpoenas. But there were many survey respondents who spoke in generalities about subpoenas without referring to concrete instances. Thus it is difficult to obtain an accurate count.

2. Answers to the second question might be more useful. Of those concrete subpoena confrontations recorded, how many were successfully resisted in shield states as opposed to the states without such legislation?

The results indicate that forty-seven subpoenas were successfully resisted in the shield jurisdictions and sixteen subpoenas were successfully resisted in the states without such laws. The fact that many respondents to the survey did not supply figures on the subpoena situation in their states makes the classification incomplete. Nevertheless, there are the reported subpoenas and their disposition in definite cases indicating that reporters in states with journalist privilege statutes are more likely to block subpoenas than are reporters in states without such laws.

CLASSIFICATION OF STATE JOURNALIST PRIVILEGE STATUTES

This section is concerned with methods of classifying the various shield statutes as to how protective they are of the reporter's interest. Many efforts have been made to portray these statutes as "absolute" or "qualified": The former translates as broad protection for the press, the latter as less protection. Under this method one group of state laws is typically listed under one heading or the other. The problem with this approach has been that what is considered "qualified" by one student of the problem is considered "absolute" by another. For example, one commentator has stated that Michigan has granted "the most restrictive privilege,"[107] whereas another has classified the Michigan statute as absolute.[108] There is agreement among four students of the subject[109] that the states of Indiana, Montana, Nevada, and Pennsylvania have absolute statutes. There is also agreement among three writers that the states of Alaska, Arkansas, Louisiana, New Jersey, and New Mexico have qualified or more restrictive or limited statutes.[110]

The typology selected for classifying state statutes on reporter privilege for this book is an adaptation of those employed by Talbot D'Alemberte[111] as updated by a cognate classification approach used by the Radio-Television News Directors Association,[112] plus an analysis of state newsmen's privilege legislation conducted by Arthur B. Hansen of the American Newspaper Publishers Association.[113]

The various statutes in question will be examined under six general headings:

1. Persons Protected
2. Proceedings Covered
3. Nature of Materials Protected
4. Circumstances Under Which the Privilege May Be Denied
5. Whether an Informant May Invoke the Privilege
6. Rule of Construction of Newsman's Privilege Statute

Persons Protected

Disseminators of information are protected in four ways: (1) a statutory description of how the disseminator is related to formal news media; (2) a definition of news media; (3) degrees of protection as determined by relationship to the formal, established, professional press; and (4) determining the status of ex-reporters.[114]

DESCRIBING THE RELATIONSHIP BETWEEN THE PEOPLE PROTECTED AND THE NEWS MEDIA State shield laws employ three methods in this category: (1) They use a noun such as "reporter" or "cameraman." This definition can be used to exclude free-lance people. (2) They use the term "employed by." Any self-employed writer could presumably fall short of protection with this wording. (3) They list the functions performed by the reporter such as "gathering news."[115]

If courts narrowly construe these definitions, only certain kinds of reporters would be eligible for protection. Former reporters, free-lancers, and scholars might not be covered. Some states protect newspaper reporters but not radio reporters.[116] Others refer to "reporter, or other person connected with . . . newsmedia."[117]

This broad language could cover free-lancers. Similar broad language such as "gathering, procuring . . . news"[118] or "engaged in the work of a news media"[119] is also subject to a more liberal interpretation.

LISTING OF THE MEDIA This is a more restrictive area. Some states protect only newspapers.[120] Some have excluded magazines.[121]

PROTECTING ONLY THE PROFESSIONAL PRESS Some statutes specify when publication takes place, that is, on a weekly, monthly, etc., basis, or stipulate that there must be a certain number of subscribers.[122] Others even demand proof that income is derived from some employer.[123] There appears to be anxiety over protecting the "underground" or "unprofessional" disseminator.

THE INCLUSION OF EX-REPORTERS Where problems have developed in this area states have rectified the situation by including the ex-reporter.[124]

Proceedings Covered

Some states are very specific.[125] A typical specific statute reads:

(A person need not disclose) in any legal proceeding, trial or investigation before any court, grand jury, traverse or petit jury or any officer thereof, before the General Assembly or any committee thereof, before any commission, department or bureau of this Commonwealth, or before any county or municipal body, officer or committee thereof.[126]

The general statutes are less concerned with particular proceedings.[127] This allows judges to delineate the conditions.

Nature of the Material Protected

Arthur Hanson states:

The nature of the material protected can be defined by answering three questions;
   1) What the newsman must have been doing when he received the information
   2) Whether the information must have been given in confidence and what "in confidence" means.
   3) Whether information or its source only is protected and, if the source only is protected, what "the source" means.
By far the greatest number of cases which have arisen under the reporter's privilege legislation are concerned with answering the last two questions.[128]

WHAT THE NEWSMAN MUST HAVE BEEN DOING WHEN HE RECEIVED INFORMATION Some statutes specify "in the course of his employment"[129] or only when he works as a "newsman."[130] Some statutes are not concerned with this aspect.[131]

WAS THE INFORMATION GIVEN IN CONFIDENCE? Shield statutes have not distinguished between confidential and nonconfidential information generally, but judges have sometimes amended the legislation to include confidentiality requirements.[132]

IS THE SOURCE AND THE INFORMATION PROTECTED, AND IF ONLY THE SOURCE IS PROTECTED, HOW IS "SOURCE" DEFINED? Many privilege statutes protect only the source of the reporter's information.[133] A few states protect the information as well as the source.[134]

Circumstances Under Which the Privilege May Be Denied

A number of state shield statutes do not provide for a procedure challenging the privilege.[135] Other states have allowed greater opportunities for challenges to the shield.[136] In some cases the judge has considered the privilege waived because the reporter named one of his sources.[137] Reporter Bridge argued that he named the source who had not asked for anonymity, but he still intended to protect the other sources who sought protection. He told a house committee: "I refused to answer those questions because the answers comprised unpublished information, and might have exposed other sources for the story I wrote which was the reason I was called."[138]

Whether an Informant May Invoke the Privilege

Only one state allows an informant to invoke the privilege.[139] In other states the courts have repeatedly stated that newsmen's privilege is just that and does not cover nonreporters who are informants.[140]

The Rule of Construction of Newsmen's Privilege Statutes

Should privilege statutes be broadly or narrowly construed? Some courts have strictly interpreted the statutes and by so doing have restricted the media.[141] In Pennsylvania the Supreme Court ruled that the shield law must be construed in favor of the journalists:

The Act must therefore, we repeat, be liberally and broadly construed in order to carry out the clear objective and intent of the Legislature which has placed the gathering and the protection of the source of news as of greater importance to the public interest and of more value to the public welfare than the disclosure of the alleged crime or the alleged criminal.[142]

SUMMARY

State journalist privilege statutes have grown out of subpoena pressures. They have been very slowly and gradually sweeping the country, with just over half of the states employing shield laws.

The effort at uniform state legislation that could serve as a model for states to adopt has not been the source of one reporter privilege code to date. The press is generally not favorable to the balancing formula offered by the model statute.

Public opinion is, if anything, identified with the media's perception of the subpoena problem, that is, in support of the media spokesmen who want to broaden legislation to arrive at greater protection for newsmen who are trying to resist subpoenas. Law enforcement person-nel are divided on the issue of whether the privilege should be broadly or narrowly construed, but there is very little unqualified opposition to the newsmen's privilege by officers of the law enforcement institutions who testified before congressional committees and who were surveyed by the American Newspaper Publishers Association.

Press opinion expressed as apprehension or anxiety over subpoena pressures, varies according to whether the reporter is in a setting that is (1) urban as opposed to rural; (2) heavily penetrated with incidents involving the counterculture as opposed to little reportorial activity in this regard; (3) overshadowed by a relatively "hostile" legal environ-ment stressing compliance with subpoenas as opposed to a more "friendly" legal environment where the burden of proof is shifted to those seeking information from reporters.

It is a cumbersome task to classify state shield laws. Terms such as "absolute" or "qualified" cannot adequately label nor accurately clas-sify the various statutes with such dichotomous and oversimplified generalities. Far too many relevant distinctions are collapsed by that method. A statute that is broad and general in one area is often narrow and specific in another area.

Most state statutes appear to be replete with qualifiers. Courts have protected newsmen in states that do not have shield laws, but there seems to be a greater tendency by the judiciary to support newsmen where media privilege laws are present, especially if those laws are more general and broad.

Judges often narrow the application of statutes beyond what appears to have been the intent of the legislature. For this reason it is likely that efforts at broadening legal protection for newsmen will continue in the state legislature: Where there are no privilege statutes, bills will be introduced, and where they already exist, there will be an effort to "strengthen" them so far as the journalist's perspective is concerned.

Failing that, efforts will continue in the Congress to pass a newsmen's privilege statute or public information act that will be preemptive on the states and thus solve the problem in the states at the higher level of our federal system of government.

CHAPTER 2

Legislating a Privilege for News Disseminators: The Congressional Effort

After Senator Sam J. Ervin, Jr., had spent two months presiding over hearings on Senate bills to create a testimonial privilege for newsmen, he commented that he had never dealt with any more difficult issue in the years he had been in Congress.[1].

Legislative efforts in Congress to establish protection for journalists on the press privilege issue have been frequent but have yet to produce a statute. The complexities of the issue have spawned a long list of bills that contains many differing variations of protection. Furthermore, the press has been divided over the advisability of privilege legislation and what form it should take.

A BRIEF HISTORICAL SURVEY OF PRESS PRIVILEGE BILLS INTRODUCED IN CONGRESS

At the federal level, bills introduced in the House or the Senate have never been acted upon finally. Senator Arthur Capper (R–Kansas) introduced the first privilege legislation in Congress in 1929.[2] Similar measures have been introduced periodically ever since. The following representatives and senators have sponsored legislation to establish a privilege:

Congress

71st	1929–30	Sen. Arthur Capper (R–Kan.)
		Rep. Fiorello LaGuardia (R–N.Y.)
		Rep. Jacob Garber (R–Va.)
72d	1931–32	Rep. LaGuardia
74th	1935–36	Sen. Capper
		Rep. Edward Curley (D–N.Y.)
75th	1937–38	Sen. Capper
		Rep. Curely
76th	1939–40	Sen. Capper
		Rep. Curley
78th	1943–44	Sen. Capper
82nd	1951–52	Rep. Louis Heller (D–N.Y.)
83rd	1953–54	Rep. Frank Osmers (R–N.J.)
		Rep. Heller
84th	1955–56	Rep. Osmers
86th	1959–60	Rep. Francis Dorn (R–N.Y.)
		Rep. Donald Magnuson (D–Wash.)
		Rep. E. Ross Adair (R–Ind.)
		Sen. Kenneth Keating (R–N.Y.)
88th	1963–64	Sen. Keating
		Rep. Sherman Lloyd (R–Utah)
		Rep. Seymour Halpern (R–N.Y.)
91st	1969–70	Numerous sponsors
92nd	1971–72	Numerous sponsors
93rd	1972–74	Numerous sponsors[3]

Only one bill to create a testimonial privilege for newsmen was introduced when the Ninety-second Congress convened in January 1971. This was the bill by Senator James Pearson (R–Kansas).[4] The bill met with little response, and the press, although generally approving the intent of the bill, was cautious and preferred to wait for further congressional reaction and judicial developments before extending support. All of this pondering was still taking place prior to the *Branzburg* decision. Many press spokesmen who commented on the Pearson bill suggested that Congress proceed cautiously. They urged that a statutory privilege be enacted ''only if the Supreme Court refused to recognize a constitutional privilege.''[5] The situation could have been worse. The Ninth Circuit's stand in *Caldwell*[6] was on record, and the President had made favorable comments about the need for a testimonial privilege for newsmen.[7]

Senator Ervin's Subcommittee on Constitutional Rights held hearings on this legislation and other free-press issues in late 1971 and early 1972.[8] In the House, Congressman Robert Kastenmeier (D–Wisconsin), chairman of House Judiciary Subcommittee No. 3, conducted hearings in September and October 1972.[9]

When the Supreme Court's decision was handed down in the summer of 1972,[10] the press reaction was one of shock. There was immediate legislative reaction. Senator Alan Cranston (D–California) introduced an absolute-privilege bill the day after the decision. It would apply to all kinds of proceedings, ostensibly covering all kinds of information from just about anyone who communicates public information. It would be preemptive on the states.[11]

The press now believed that it had only the Congress for testimonial privilege protection. Press organizations such as the Joint Media Committee, consisting of representatives from the American Society of Newspaper Editors, the Associated Press Managing Editors Association, Sigma Chi Delta, and the National Press Photographers Association combined for the purpose of drafting legislation. Spokesmen for these groups appreciated the Cranston bill for its absoluteness but believed its chances for passage were remote.

The bill that they eventually agreed upon contained qualifications. It was introduced by Senator Walter Mondale (D–Minnesota) in August 1972.[12] The equivalent version of the Mondale bill on the house side was introduced by Congressman Charles Whalen (R–Ohio).[13] Senator Ervin of North Carolina also introduced a similarly qualified bill in August 1972.[14]

The public's attention was not really drawn to the press privilege issue until the Bridge,[15] Farr,[16] and Weiler[17] incidents dramatized the problem. Was the *Branzburg* decision acting as a green light for prosecutors? Press editorials framed the issue as one involving the public's right to know versus prosecutorial and judicial tyranny. The press posture on the issue seemed to have public support.[18]

In the early fall of 1972, a new press alliance the Ad Hoc Coordinating Committee, was formed.[19] It brought together elements from the print and electronic media but was initiated primarily by the American Newspaper Publishers Association. This group did not completely overlap with the earlier Joint Media Committee, which was still pressing for the qualified bill.

It now became apparent that journalists were losing interest in a qualified bill because some of the newsmen who were jailed came from states having qualified shield laws.

As press attitudes began to harden around support for an absolute privilege bill, the administration's attitude appeared to be shifting away from support for the testimonial privilege. President Nixon announced in November 1972 that he did not feel that federal legislation on that subject was warranted "at this time."[20] As Sam Ervin notes, "This was not an easy pill for the inflamed media to swallow."[21] Further stimulus was added to the legislative movement when John Lawrence of the *Los Angeles Times* was jailed in December. (See chapter 1.)

Thirty-two senators formally committed themselves to some kind of legislation by cosponsoring a bill.[22] In the House, fifty-six bills were introduced and about a third of the house members were in support of some kind of journalist privilege bill.[23]

DRAFTING DIFFICULTIES

Who Is a Newsman?

Press and legislative opinion span a broad spectrum of opinion over proposed legislation defining the newsman. Some would very carefully define the "professional and established press" as opposed to outsiders. Others would draw no distinction between a newsman and anyone else. Former Congressman Jerome Waldie (D–California) introduced one of the broadest bills on this aspect of the topic.[24] He established no qualifications. The language of his bill defines the newsman as "Any person engaged in the gathering of information."[25] Waldie's philosophy was expressed in Senate hearings:

I can't think of a worse area for Congress to get involved in than attempting to identify who is a news person. I just can't think of a worse area for Congress to suggest that and I have even heard it proposed—absurdly it seems to me—that that will require a definition of the person working 20 hours a week for a paycheck to become a news person. Those are artificial distinctions the first amendment never encompassed. The first amendment was seeking to protect a flow of information. . . . [26]

The Waldie approach seems to begin with the assumption that because courts have the power to narrow and constrict the scope of legislation, it might be better to start with breadth so as to hedge against restrictions. It would appear that such a bill has less chance of passage because most of the bills are qualified on this point. There are, however, three other bills that resemble Waldie's bill on the question of who is a newsman. They were introduced by Congressman Henry Helstoski[27] (D–New Jersey), Congressman Jack Brooks[28] (D–Texas), and Senator Richard Schweiker[29] (R–Pennsylvania). The rest of the bills contain definitions of the newsmen that parallel some of the state shield laws in that they emphasize "employed by," specify minimum time on the job with a carefully defined media, and so on.[30] The bills that exclude nonpress persons generally follow Benno Schmidt's suggestion that "a statutory privilege . . . be invokable only by professional journalists." For those hoping to include free-lancers Schmidt answers:

Free lance professional journalists should also be covered, provided their professional status is established by a showing of prior publication or broadcast of their materials in one of the covered media. We believe that Congress should go farther than a regular employment relation or prior experience and protect anyone clearly associated with an established medium or communication, in connection with the journalistic story for which he claims the privilege. This would include free-lancers who, though not having the professional experience referred to above, could demonstrate some tangible connection with a medium of news dissemination.[31]

Schmidt's definition of a free-lancer is closely tied to professionalism and established media. Free-lancers with irregular schedules would probably not be included.

Blasi would insist upon a "professional" definition:

"Professional disseminator of information to the public" means a person who, at the time he obtained the information that is sought, was earning his principal livelihood by, or for each of the preceding three weeks or for four of the preceding eight weeks had spent at least twenty hours per week engaged in the process of, obtaining or preparing information for dissemination to the general public with the aid of printing, reprographing, mimeographing, broadcasting, sound amplification, or sound reproduction facilities.[32]

Steven Fischer of the National Student Lobby disagreed with these requirements because they would exclude many student journalists who are among the most vulnerable reporters in a subpoena confrontation. According to Fischer:

I do not think it would be fair to get a time definition such as "A newsperson is one who spends 20 hours a week gathering news." Frankly, I don't know whether a college reporter can always devote that much time while he or she is in school, yet there are 2,500 American college newspapers with a circulation of 7½ million people, and we feel they deserve protection also.[33]

It appears that the pamphleteer could not be covered under Blasi's standards either. Much publication of that nature took place during the Revolutionary period and in the early years of the Republic. Much of it was anonymous and would still have to be to survive under Blasi's tests.

A scholar might qualify as a professional disseminator of information. Paul Nejelski would prefer to develop a media privilege or "Free Flow of Information Act" out of the research function that could include journalists, scholars, doctors, criminologists, psychologists, and so on.[34]

Should an author of a book be able to claim the privilege? Journalists have written books, and book writers have acted in the capacity of journalists. Joel M. Gora of the American Civil Liberties Union has stated:

We think that the definition of who is entitled to statutory protection should be broad enough to encompass authors of books as well as journalists for news media. An investigative reporter performs the same function whether the end product is a newspaper column, a magazine article, or a book. As Victor Navasky has suggested: "A nonfiction author, at least if he is dealing in contemporary affairs, is really just a slow journalist, perhaps more careful to document because of the hard covers, perhaps not, but in any event, no less connected to the public's right to know." And of course, some of our most important "muckraking" journalism has been in the form of a book.[35]

From Ida Tarbell's History of the *Standard Oil Company* to Seymour Hersh's *My Lai 4*, Rachel Carson's *Silent Spring*, Ralph Nader's *Unsafe at Any Speed*, and Alfred W. McCoy's *The Politics of Heroin in Southeast Asia*, much of the most valuable investigative reporting has been done in books on current social, political, and economic problems. Books have often blazed the trail for newspapers and television. Indeed, if one weighs the contributions of investigative reporting in books and on television, the scales might register a more valuable contribution by book authors.

Definitions of news gatherers that insist on established media linkages and minimum hours worked per week may exclude many investigative book authors from legislative protection. And why should reporters with the established media who have a publishing home base have a monopoly on privilege protection for books on the current scene?

The majority of the bills so far introduced do not sufficiently take care of this distinction between book authors and the press. Did the Founding Fathers wish to confine press to newspapers and exclude authors from the protection of the First Amendment? The only way out of the maze seems to point toward an analysis of the process of news flow rather than second-guessing the meaning of the nomenclature the writers of the Constitution had in mind.

Assuming the media can be defined, another problem area arises that involves the question of how far privilege protection should reach into the staff structure of a media organization. From staff reporters, one can slide to stringers, writers under contract, persons who write for the firm or publication when the mood moves them.

Some commentators have been concerned with subterfuge. They fear that too broad a definition of newsman would invite the use of press privilege as a cover for illegal operations. Joseph Lordi, prosecutor of Essex County in New York State, counseled careful definition of the newsman in any legislation, noting that "it would be absurd to permit the author of a leaflet for some revolutionary cause, or a member of organized crime who claims he is writing a book, to invoke a newsman's privilege when subpoenaed to testify concerning a criminal matter."[36]

Should ex-newsmen be covered by a testimonial privilege? That was a problem in some of the states that had shield laws when the ex-reporter was attempting to claim the privilege. (See *Farr,* chapter 1.) In contrast to the bills before the previous Congress, and probably as a reaction to the *Farr* and *Bridge* cases, some of the bills currently before Congress protect persons who were newsmen when they received certain information but who were not newsmen at the time they were requested to testify. Some bills define a news person very broadly, and others would specifically protect the ex-reporter.[37]

There is also some concern about whether a testimonial privilege for the news gatherer, the disseminator or communicator of information should include those who report for trade journals, "house organs," "public access channels," or whether even an insurance investigator could be included because he is gathering information.

It has been demonstrated in chapter 6 that courts have been reluctant to provide media privilege protection to reporters for trade journals.[38] The federal bills so far proposed do not address the problem.

There are publications that emanate from bureaucratic agencies and departments of government. Should publishers and reporters for those organs be able to invoke a media privilege? Does this not amount to a kind of executive privilege through another device? What would be the ramifications of such an extension of the privilege on the Freedom of Information Act?

Could "public access" channels create drafting problems? David Foster, president of the National Cable Television Association, thinks so:

Under the FCC's new rules for the cable television industry, new systems are required to provide what are called "public access channels," channels available to the public on a first-come, first-served basis, on which any public-spirited citizen could become a newsman. Anyone—an insurance man, a laborer—could find out a piece of information which he felt was newsworthy to his fellow citizens, could call his local cable television system and say, "I would like a half-hour on the access channel," and could go before the public and put on his own news show.[39]

What of the insurance investigator who is gathering information? Congressman Danielson of California put forth the question of whether such a person should be covered. Benno Schmidt answered as follows:

The aim of privilege legislation is protecting the ability of persons who disseminate the news to get the widest variety of news to the public. An insurance investigator by and large is not in that business. Therefore, there is no public interest in that case which outweighs his value as an investigative resource.[40]

There has been much concern over the on-duty/off-duty distinction. Is a reporter always a reporter? Or is he sometimes off duty as a private citizen? If he observes questionable activities when he is off duty, should he be more vulnerable to a subpoena as opposed to when he is on duty?[41]

Some commentators have tried to solve the problem of who qualifies for the privilege by assessing the intention to communicate publicly. John Kuhns suggests the following rule: "The person invoking the right must have intended to use material, gathered through a confidential informer relationship, in a process aimed at disseminating information to the public."[42]

Many congressional bills are concerned with protection for the established newsman. "Established" can be defined as specific media firms and periodic publications, but it can also be used to.separate the "establishment" from "underground" newspapers. It is conceivable that a judge could construe some of the bills as being intended for the "established" and not the "underground" press. Blasi has noted that:

In the Madison bombing case, the government originally contended that the underground press should not be entitled to assert the privilege, but reporters for the establishment media, including *The New York Times's* Lesley Oelsner, are quick to point out the unfairness of any such distinction.[43]

The question of who is a newsman was the first administrative difficulty raised by Justice White in his *Branzburg* opinion: ''The administration of a constitutional newsman's privilege would present practical and conceptual difficulties of a high order. Sooner or later, it would be necessary to define those categories of newsmen who qualified for the privilege . . . .'' [44]

The federal legislative effort thus far has struggled with the problem but has not resolved the question because terms such as ''professional'' and ''established media'' still leave considerable room for varying interpretations. This remains one of the more vexing drafting difficulties.

What Proceedings Should Be Covered?

Opinions vary as to whether all or only some of the proceedings should be excluded from the list of forums in which a journalist can invoke the testimonial privilege. Blasi has drawn a distinction between investigative and adjudicative proceedings:

Everybody I have seen has talked about this problem as though investigative subpoenas are the same as adjudicative subpoenas. A subpoena issued in the course of an investigative proceeding is generally not narrow in focus. There is not the procedural protection that comes from the rules of evidence and standards of relevance, and there is no credibility check in the sense you have a dispute that is already framed. Those kinds of subpoenas are vastly different, both in terms of their evidentiary gain and also in terms of the damage they do, the fears they generate, the climate they create which is the real problem. They are vastly different from adjudicative subpoenas, when you are talking about a trial, a focused issue, and using evidence in a legalistic sense, not the kind of exploratory, looking-for-leads kind of sense. So I think you should strongly differentiate adjudicative subpoenas from investigative subpoenas. I recommend an absolute privilege with regard to investigative subpoenas. [45]

The vast majority of bills introduced in the Ninety-third Congress carefully specified which proceedings were covered by journalist privilege. Forty-six bills were analyzed. [46] Several individual congressmen introduced additional bills from time to time. (Instead of counting all the revisions, I have used only the latest version.)

Twenty-eight [47] of the forty-six bills provided carefully detailed protection from forced testimony in proceedings initiated by grand juries, courts, legislative bodies, administrative agencies, departments, or commissions. Thus 61 percent of the bills in the sample tried to anticipate any and all proceedings in which a newsman might be forced to testify.

Thirteen of the bills, or 28 percent, did not provide for protection from grand jury investigations.[48] The bill by Congressman Kuykendall specifically protects newsmen in all other proceedings except grand jury investigations.[49] Bills by Congressmen Brooks[50] and Drinan[51] did not mention the matter of proceedings at all and could be interpreted to exclude grand jury investigations from legislative purview. The typical bill in this category would guarantee privilege protection in "executive, legislative and judicial proceedings."[52] The words "grand jury" were never actually employed in any of these bills. Judicial proceedings could be interpreted to apply to the courts but not the grand jury, and that has been one of Blasi's concerns.[53] Sixteen of the bills specifically excepted any proceedings involving defamation.[54] Three bills were sweeping in coverage in that they mentioned the broad range of possible forums but insisted on strict "threshold rules;" that is, newsmen and persons seeking the information would have to show an overriding need for journalist testimony. The reporter would have to demonstrate how news flow would be endangered. This proposed legislation specifically leaves the judge with the final determination.[55]

In sum, almost all of the proposed media privilege measures in Congress give detailed attention to the problem of forums and proceedings in which the privilege can be invoked.

What Types of Information Ought to Be Protected?

There are essentially three problems in this category. (1) Should the privilege extend to the naming of the source but not to the information given by the source? (2) Should the privilege apply only to published but not unpublished information? (3) Should the privilege apply only to information received in confidence?

Should the reporter possess the right to protect from compulsory disclosure both the identities of his informants *and* communications received from them? Opinions vary. John B. Kuhns has referred to the problem of disclosing private communications that may make it possible to trace the informer.[56] He believes that the protection of off-the-record communications is as important as the protection of names, in that informer-reporter relationships will be more secure if informers know that the reporter will shield name and story from, say, a grand jury. There the informant could only guess at how much damaging information may have been revealed. A prosecutor can deduce from information revealed by forced testimony and trace the facts to the informer. The informer may not have committed any crime but may fear exposure, for legitimate reasons. He may have exposed corruption and be anxious over consequences if the corrupt are his employers. According to Kuhns:

Empirical evidence and the recent *Caldwell* case indicate that off-the-record communications are a significant part of news gathering, for reporters often use background information in order to evaluate material for publication. A confidential informer-reporter relationship can only be honored, and deterrence minimized, if such confidential background communications are protected from compulsory disclosure.[57]

Another view of the source information problem is expressed by William F. Stewart.[58] He fears that the news media has dangerously expanded the traditional concept of "source of information." He notes that one ordinarily considers a source of information to be "a talebearer, a tipster, someone who exposes or divulges facts."[59] Such a person would bring information of illegal activities but would not be an actor or participant in crime himself. In recent years, Stewart observes "the news media have urged that performers or participants, that is the persons who actually participate in events observed by the reporter, form the core or background of a news story and are therefore sources of information."[60]

Stewart has developed a hypothetical case. If a newsman is writing a story on burglars, and accompanies one on his nightly rounds, does the observed burglar constitute a source of information so that the reporter cannot be compelled to testify to the burglar's identity?

The eyewitness to crime problem has been dealt with in court[61] and through legislative enactment[62] and does not exhaust the subject of source information protection. Expanding the definition of source from the conversational relationship to observation of participants in lawful demonstrations may present problems, but they are not necessarily confined to Stewart's criminal model.

A second problem is whether to protect the reporter and informant when the information passed has not been published. The argument for not protecting unpublished communications is that such material does not become part of the vital news flow that newsmen emphasize. On the other hand, it appears that it is hard to draw the line between the two areas. Background information not published today may be a buildup for a big exposé two months from now. Peter Bridge has presented the problem this way:

I think you will find that a newsman who spends a lot of time going to the same place every day gathers a great deal of information that is not necessarily news, but it is information. Much of it is gossip or rumor. Some of it is simply background information. It helps the reporter to add depth and meaning and explanation to his own reporting. When a reporter is called before a grand jury and is asked to divulge all of that background after years of developing sources, knowledge, whatever expertise he might have, he also is being asked to jeopardize his effectiveness as a reporter.[63]

What has worried Congressman Railsback of Illinois is that a broad privilege that protects the unpublished material, which is often in the form of "outtakes," could defeat necessary investigations. He referred to an incident in which he was representing a plaintiff who was severely injured. A television studio had filmed the accident, and part of the film had been shown publicly. The film showed the damage and where everything was located. Railsback noted that he had difficulty getting the tape but that the judge ruled in his favor. He feared that a statute that provided an absolute privilege on this aspect of the privilege issue would prevent discovery of the truth in situations in which it is absolutely essential to achieve justice.[64]

But some commentators fear that legislation without specific protection for unpublished information would not only have a chilling effect on sources but would encourage reporters to destroy notes and records. This would be an unfortunate loss for news flow because records are important for verification and the thorough development of a story. Judge Garippo expressed concern that perhaps too much was being expected of the press: "Must there be a burden on photographers to both catalog and preserve all the pictures that they take?... The press is not so geared, is not so designed. And I don't know if you really want it so geared and so designed."[65]

In May 1978 *The Stanford Daily,* a student newspaper at Stanford University in Palo Alto, California, was subjected to a surprise search of its files because its reporters had filmed demonstrators attacking police. The police did not find evidence beyond the photographs published in the paper and therefore obtained no further assistance in proceeding against demonstrators as a result of the search.[66]

James Reston has wondered how worthwhile it is getting entangled in such a discussion:

Have you ever seen a reporter's notes? Would any serious judge really accept most of them in evidence? They are a jumble of phrases, homemade shorthand, disconnected words, names, wisecracks by the press table companions, lunch dates, doodles, descriptions of somebody's necktie or expression, and large and apparently significant numbers, probably reminding the reporter of nothing more than his next deadlines.[67]

In summary, there are those who believe that a privilege covering both published and unpublished information could be abused by reporters, that outtakes are sometimes essential to resolve justiciably a criminal or civil case. The opposing view is centered on another concern, namely, that the published–unpublished distinction creates a vital uncertainty that might well nullify the proposed protective effect of the privilege.

A third problem in determining what information should be protected has to do with whether it was obtained in confidence. This was one of Henry Wigmore's[68] fundamental rules that had to be followed in granting any privilege.

What troubles those who are opposed to extending the media privilege to nonconfidential information? Perhaps they are inclined to believe that it is unnecessary because the purpose of a media privilege is to protect confidences in order that the chilling effect will not dampen news flow. If there are not confidences, how can news flow be affected one way or the other? But what if a statute is drafted that specifically rules out the nonconfidential information from protection? Will that not make it easier for a judge narrowly to define the confidential relationship? In a California case a judge made a distinction between confidential and nonconfidential information even though the legislature had not. The distinction served to deny the privilege to a manager of a radio station who thought that he was covered by the privilege statute.[69] In the KPFK matter in Los Angeles (see chapter 2) the Symbionese Liberation Army (SLA) obviously did not have a confidential relationship as that is generally understood.[70] It had not conversed with or asked for pledges of protection from Will Lewis of KPFK. The telephone call placed by the group was an anonymous one-way communication. However, now that the SLA knows that any of its tapes or communications can be seized by the government, because anonymous calls tipping off a reporter to whereabouts of messages are not considered confidential, it will probably be more reluctant to contact the media in any form and the public will be denied contact.

Another difficulty with legislatively drawing a distinction is that there is a certain artificiality about doing so. If there is a line between confidential and nonconfidential communications, it is either very fine or inchoate except as an intellectual abstraction. As an editor for a small-town newspaper observed: "They don't come up every time and say this is confidential. They know me and they know that with certain information that they are telling me they don't have to speak the words, 'This is confidential.' "[71]

It is true that the SLA did not know the staff at the Pacifica station the way that Einstoss knew his fellow townsmen. But they knew that KPFK was one of the more likely conduits for their message. KPFA and KPFK are Berkeley and Los Angeles stations respectively that have a reputation for covering the counterculture, and there is an unspoken rapport between underground spokesmen and that particular type of media.

In summary, the problem with distinguishing between confidential and nonconfidential information is one of reifying an intellectual and legal distinction. The real difficulties appear to lie with the concepts of *time* and *intent*. Thus an ordinary conversation can—after the fact—be transformed into a protected newsman-informant conversation. What was intended to be only a social conversation, upon later reflection is cognizable as a professional reporter-informant relationship.

If a distinction must be drawn, it might be better to distinguish between social and professional relations as opposed to confidential and nonconfidential relations. But this may also be only another legislative encouragement for judicial restriction.

The congressional response to the question of what information should be protected falls into five categories.

Fourteen bills specifically provided privilege protection for "published and unpublished" information.[72] Seventeen bills used the language "any information," which may not be as protective of sources and the press as specifying "published or unpublished." "Any" may be subject to a narrowing interpretation as with "any but."[73] Three bills required that material be "actually published or broadcast" before privilege protection can be extended.[74] Seven bills required that the information be confidential before the privilege applies.[75] Three bills were too laden with qualifiers to be classified within this category.[76]

The vast majority of bills indicated that their authors accepted the argument that legislative remedy should provide broader rather than narrower coverage in this area.

Should There Be Specific Exceptions to the Privilege?

Are there circumstances in which the public interest could be endangered by a journalist privilege that covers any and all information gathered or observed by a reporter? The most often contemplated exemption would apply in a situation in which the reporter is an eyewitness to the commission of crime. The question is whether a statute should specify that the privilege does not apply under circumstances where, say, a reporter observes murder.

During House hearings, Congressman Danielson expressed the view that the statute should spell out such an exemption that "we cannot leave this to the discretion or the option of the person who wishes to invoke it or not as he chooses."[77] A. M. Rosenthal, the managing editor of the *New York Times,* answered that it might be a mistake to "legislate primarily to take care of the eventualities that, so far as we know, have never come up, at the price of vitiating the flow of information."[78] Peter Bridge noted:

I think it ought not be written in the law that I would be compelled to testify as to what I saw in a murder. I think it almost goes without saying that if a reporter or newsman witnessed a murder, I don't know any reporter or newsman who would not testify, regardless of shielding laws. I cannot imagine any responsible newsman hiding behind a shield law when, in fact, he is the witness to that type of crime.[79]

Besides murder there are other violent crimes, such as skyjacking, espionage, arson, and kidnapping, which, in the opinion of some congressmen should be written into a statute so as to prevent any reporter from refusing to testify about them on the grounds of a privilege.[80] It could be argued that alternative sources should be sought first, but the imminence of the threat to public safety may override the free flow of news rationale in such circumstances.

It has also been suggested that where the "national interest" warrants it, the privilege could be set aside, but former Governor Meskill of Connecticut has stated that such a standard would be too general or vague. "It has been my experience that courts . . . have a difficult enough time finding compelling and overriding interests of any sort. . . . When the further requirement that the interest be national is added, I am afraid the courts would be unable ever to find such an interest."[81]

Only three House bills[82] had language that would set aside the privilege where newsmen are aware of or observe crimes such as skyjacking, espionage, kidnapping, murder, forcible rape, and aggravated assault. Only two Senate bills had similar language.[83]

Senator Ervin has expressed his view that excessive zeal in establishing exemptions from privilege protection when crimes are witnessed by reporters will have adverse effects on news flow: "In the *Branzburg* case, the reporter would never have seen a violation of law if those who violated it had not had confidence in him and permitted him to see. I think he almost had to see it to really be able to report on the matter he was reporting on."[84]

Anthony Amsterdam, who had represented Earl Caldwell, answered Ervin's comment by observing that:

. . . there is an inverse relationship between the need for reporters' testimony and the seriousness of crimes. Reporters very, very, very infrequently know anything about hardcore crime—street crimes, muggings, murders, rapes, those kinds of things. They are almost never used in those kinds of cases. They are primarily used in youth crimes, marijuana, open-ended investigations into subversive activity, and that sort of thing.[85]

If legislation contains too many exemptions or qualifications, these tend to swallow the privilege as well as mire the Congress in longer debate and irresolution.

Should the Legislation Apply to State as Well as Federal Proceedings?

Federal legislation that is not preemptive on the states will leave the overwhelming majority of reporters to face subpoenas without privilege protection in half the states where there are no shield laws. On the other hand, the preemptive approach will set aside state and local autonomy on the issue.

A statute that would apply in federal and state proceedings could be constitutionally authorized in one of two ways. The first method of authorizing such a statute is bottomed on the commerce clause.[86] This clause gives Congress the right to regulate, so as to promote the general welfare of the nation, whatever affects interstate commerce. The policy question of what regulation best promotes the general welfare is a decision for Congress alone to make.[87] The power granted to Congress under the commerce clause has been very broadly construed. The Supreme Court has decided that, under it, Congress has the power to regulate entities as diverse as those regulated by the National Labor Relations Act, the Sherman Anti-Trust Act, and the Civil Rights Act of 1964. The Supreme Court has also decided that, under it, Congress has the power to regulate newspapers, news-gathering agencies, and broadcasting companies.[88]

A federal-state shield law would be a regulation of the news media. By imposing certain restrictions on state and federal courts, Congress would be making use of an effective method of securing this regulation. A comprehensive federal-state privilege would, in effect, be a direction to newsmen not to reveal their undisclosed information or sources of information if they feared that disclosure might weaken the ability of themselves or others to guarantee the free flow of information to the public.

It is true that the commerce clause power granted to Congress may be limited by other constitutional provisions. The issue comes down to this: Is the need for the free flow of information great enough for the federal government to regulate the conditions under which newsmen can be forced to testify before state investigatory bodies? The drafters of the comprehensive federal-state bills clearly thought that it was great enough, and Congress in enacting and the Supreme Court in upholding such legislation on the basis of the interstate commerce clause would be in agreement with them.

Fifteen bills in the Ninety-third Congress would apply to both state and federal proceedings.[89] Twenty bills only applied to federal proceedings.[90]

Congressmen opposed to the preemptive approach have argued that it would be better for the federal government to offer a statute that states could copy if they wished. Congressman Coughlin stated:

Each state is unique with respect to its own particular laws and its own particular relationships between law-enforcement officials and the press. In 19 of the states, shield legislation already has been enacted [now 26], and several other states are contemplating similar protection. Certainly, it would be unwise for the Congress to preempt the States and interfere in their procedures. Let us instead enact legislation which would apply only on the Federal level, and let this law serve as a model upon which the states could build should they wish to further extend a newsman's immunity.[91]

But Congressman Meeds viewed news flow as a national matter and thought it a mistake to leave only spotty protection across the fifty states.[92]

Assistant Attorney General Roger C. Cramton argued that the commerce clause argument was not strong enough. He noted that although the Court has held the media to be an instrumentality of commerce, Congress should not therefore regulate state courts and legislatures with respect to the media.[93] He mentioned the need of the state courts to acquire information through subpoena without federal interference. It would appear that the counterargument is that state legislatures need a free flow of communications to inform their legislative discretion.

In addition to the commerce clause authorization for a preemptive federal media privilege statute, a rationale can be developed out of the First and Fourteenth Amendments. By relying on the enforcement clause[94] of the Fourteenth Amendment, Congress can regulate the testimony of newsmen before state courts, regardless of competing considerations. The Fourteenth Amendment in Section 5 gives Congress the specific authorization to enact whatever legislation is necessary to reach the goals of that amendment. The protection of "liberty" by the due process clause of the amendment has been interpreted as requiring the states to comply with the First Amendment guarantees of freedom of speech and press.[95]

For case authority to enact a preemptive newsman's privilege bill a court could look to *Katzenbach* v. *Morgan*,[96] in which the Court held by dint of the enforcement clause of the Fourteenth Amendment and the supremacy clause of Article Six, that the New York English literacy test voting requirement could not be enforced to the extent that it was inconsistent with certain provisions of the Voting Rights Act of 1965.

Justice White indicated in *Branzburg*[97] that Congress could draft a newsman's privilege statute and "fashion standards and rules as narrow or broad as deemed necessary to address the evil discerned . . . ."[98]

Would the Court uphold a federal shield law that is preemptive? Blasi believed that it would:

I read the court's opinions in the *Morgan* case and in the *Oregon* v. *Mitchell* voting rights case. If the Justices who wrote them adhere to their positions I have no doubt that five Justices would uphold such a statute. I think there is a good chance that seven Justices might even do that.[99]

Blasi is backed by people who agree with him on the need for a preemptive statute, namely, scholars Paul Freund,[100] Archibald Cox,[101] and Benno Schmidt,[102] and law enforcement officials Joseph P. Lordi[103] and Melvin Block.[104]

Even if a federal media privilege statute were to be passed that was not preemptive on the states, it is possible that the federal law would prevail over the state law, since reporter's privilege legislation has been declared procedural rather than substantive law.[105] However, this would only be true in federal court.

What Should Be the Procedure Through Which the Privilege Is Claimed or Divested?

Recognition of the right of a news gatherer to protect the confidentiality of his relations with informants raises the question whether this right may be waived. Since the major reason for recognizing this right is the deterrent effect of compulsory disclosure on informants, an informant should be able to waive the newsman's right of nondisclosure if confidentiality is no longer desired.

The courts' treatment of waiver of the newsman's privilege is anything but consistent. When the newsman has revealed some facts that indicate a source of information, the court has held, on at least one occasion, that a waiver had resulted,[106] and on another, to the contrary.[107] Generally speaking, the same cases that have held the privilege to be personal to the reporter have stated that he is free to waive it and divulge the confidential source's identity and the imparted information at his own will.[108]

Another method of waiver would be for the informant to appear at court or at a hearing brought about by the newsman's motion to quash the subpoena and testify that confidentiality of his communications with the reporter is no longer desired.

There were nineteen congressional bills that included divestiture provisions.[109] The most common wording read: "Any person seeking information or the course thereof protected under this Act may apply to the United States district court for an order divesting such protection."[110] This statement was often followed by the provision that the person seeking information must demonstrate need according to what has come to be called the three-pronged test.[111]

Many still unanswered questions have been raised with regard to the problems of claim and divestiture. If a newsman is solely in charge of waiver, will that give less assurance to sources? If a source waives his right, should newsmen be forced to divulge all? William Farr believed they must in that case.[112] Where should the burden of proof lie? The congressional bills that referred to divestiture placed the burden of proof on the parties seeking information, that is, the prosecutor and the defense.[113] There has been some objection to that trend among the bills.[114] Congressman Cohen believed that at present the burden of proof is generally on the newsmen.[115] He believed it should remain that way in the first instance, but once the reporter has made a case for refusing to divulge, the onus definitely should shift to the other side and there should be an application of a standard similar to the three-pronged test.

Some have suggested that the court should be empowered to order the proof presented in camera, out of the presence of the opposing side, under oath, and subject to cross-examination by the judge.[116] This method might avoid some of the costly confrontations that are so prevalent and well publicized.

Should an Informant Be Able to Invoke the Privilege?

The newsmen's argument for the press privilege is grounded on the need to protect confidential sources from the fear that their names will be disclosed. As we have already seen, the imminence and the impact of this fear on the flow of news have been said to have a chilling effect. If a secure source is the goal, why should the source not claim the privilege? Under the rules of attorney-client and doctor-patient privileges, clients and patients are protected rather than the professionals. But does the analogy from clients and patients to news sources fit? News sources convey information for the purpose of publication. Clients and patients are only trying to protect their privacy. There has been some discussion of the matter in congressional hearings but no concrete proposals.[117] Newsmen have not generally defended a right of reporters to refuse to divulge if sources should be allowed to waive the privilege.[118] This writer found no congressional bill that addressed the question of whether the source could or should claim the privilege. Certain interests among the news media spearheaded the drive for legislation, and the bills have emphasized newsmen's privilege rather than source privilege.

A FINAL LOOK AT DRAFTING PROBLEMS

There has been repeated reference in the literature on press privilege to "qualified" and "absolute" bills. An analysis of the preceding considerations for drafting such legislation should have demonstrated the following: Although a particular bill may be broadly protective of the press in one aspect, it often sharply qualifies the privilege in another respect.

The terms "absolute" and "qualified" are unfortunate in two ways. First, "absolute" implies irrational inflexibility, whereas "qualified" connotes moderation and fairness. Second, bills with minor qualifications are more like bills having no qualifications than measures replete with qualifications. Such distinctions are overlooked when "absolute" is contrasted with "qualified."

THE LEGISLATIVE EFFORT IN CONGRESS FALTERS

A great divergence among legislators in Congress only reflected the divergence in the press. The Ad Hoc Drafting Committee, which was seeking a universally acceptable approach, drafted not one, but six bills for the press to rally behind.[119] Members of the press had not only differing ideas on the best legislative draft but also differing estimates of what could get through Congress. Press support during the Ninety-third Congress drifted toward a qualified bill because more and more press spokesmen believed that a bill without exemptions would have little chance of passage. Another one of the many moderating factors was the concern of the American Civil Liberties Union for the rights of criminal defendants under the Sixth Amendment[120] as well as the issue of libel.

It appears that the diversity of press opinion on the issue is still one of the primary reasons why the legislative movement faltered. What were some of those differences? In the majority group are those reporters who have argued the classic case for journalist privilege with the use of arguments accompanying references to "chilling effects," "the public's right to know," "free flow of information," "protection for news gathering as well as news dissemination," "ferreting out corruption," "the press as watchdog," and so on.[121]

But there was a minority opinion out of press ranks that was much more skeptical about the motives of fellow journalists, sources, politicians, and bureaucrats. One former reporter, Lewis H. Lapham, has skillfully presented the bulk of antishield law arguments.[121] He has likened the press effort in Congress to "convicts building gallows from which they will hang."[123] Some journalists favorable to the privilege have also feared that what Congress gives in a statute, it can take away by the same means.

Lapham believed that a privilege statute would "encourage the press in its most cowardly instincts and so disembowel it."[124] He was concerned that protection of the source would not work to the advantage of the press or the free flow of information but would benefit the sources, most of whom are government officials. Sources would be encouraged to inhibit the circulation of news that "does not enhance the self-importance of the man circulating it."[125] The more secrecy that is created for government sources, the more power will shift to the bureaucracy. Sources will draw the reporters into a game. They will feed the press selective information in return for promises of confidentiality. Sometimes the selective information will constitute a "leak" to embarrass one of the source's enemies, another time to bolster his ego.

Lapham believed that the press is too frightened by its own editorials, exaggerated the Nixon threat, and was too worked up over the subpoena issue. He sneered at the "romantic view" of the press as "watchdog of the republic."[126] He suggested instead that the real press "seldom concerns itself with the routine injustices committed by the people who own the wealth of the country for the logical reason that the same people also own the press."[127]

The article observed that the press confers legitimacy on government, that "the government and the press entertain inflated opinions of one another."[128] Thus he did not see the critic's check on official excesses as Rosenthal, Hume, Anderson, Bernstein, and Woodward emphasized. Rather, correspondents exaggerate their influence on government and "are too often overtaken by the point of view" of the agency that they cover. He believed that a reporter privilege stature would only harden this phenomenon.

James J. Kilpatrick is more concerned with the subpoena threat than Lapham, but he does not believe that legislation is the answer. In his opinion, "We are experiencing no more than a muscular spasm in the body politic. It is painful, but it will subside. We will err, I believe, if we embark upon a cure that could be worse than the disease."[129]

Clark Mollenhoff of the *Des Moines Register* does not favor a privilege statute because:

There is a great deal of sympathy for public officials who are subjected to probably false attacks by other politicians or by the press. The public reactions against "smears" by the political critics or by the press is a proper reaction, and the last thing we need today is a law that could be a further invitation to irresponsibility.[130]

William Loeb of the *Manchester Union Leader* has expressed his view that "Newspapermen are not any better than anybody else. There is absolutely no reason why they should be granted any special privileges under a so-called 'shield' law."[131]

Vermont Royster, writing in the *Wall Street Journal,* has expressed chagrin over the subpoena threat but does not think that legislation could solve the problem because it would be too difficult to define a newsman.[132]

Some expressed the view that the press can take care of itself and does not need legislative protection.[133] Others noted that the best protection was in the First Amendment and that legislative tinkering might undermine that protection.[134]

The preceding minority views present a side of the press that is either opposed altogether to any kind of legislative solution or is skeptical of its usefulness. The remaining facets of press opinion are divided over draft versions. Interests vary considerably from publisher to reporter, from don't-rock-the-boat journalists to hard-hitting investigative sleuths, and from the "established" press to the "underground" press. Not everyone is as vulnerable to subpoena pressures. Those less threatened by subpoenas can more easily afford to talk about "no special treatment for the media."

At some undiscernible point the press began to see that although the commitment of 32 senators and over 100 congressmen was not insignificant, it was by no means overwhelming in light of the strong public interest in source disclosure that had been generated over more than a year (mid-1973 to mid-1974).

Faced with the warnings of Kastenmeier in the House and Ervin in the Senate that an absolute privilege was politically impossible to obtain, newsmen began speculating about whether any sort of qualified privilege was worth supporting. As Senator Ervin noted:

They feared that any qualification which would be susceptible of judicial interpretation must necessarily confuse newsmen as to their legal status and confuse sources as to the worth of the newsmen's assurances of confidentiality. These doubts, coupled with a fear that what Congress gives, Congress may one day take away, began to cause many newsmen to reconsider the legislative alternative.[135]

Despite Ervin's skepticism about passage, which is probably realistic for the long run, a year later NBC, CBS, the Authors League of America and the American Newspaper Publishers Association, which had formerly insisted on an absolute bill, endorsed a qualified bill by Congressman Kastenmeier.[136] Although the bill protected reporters from divulging in grand jury proceedings, it required their testimony at trial. It also required that there be a confidential relationship before a reporter can invoke the privilege. The three pronged test was also employed. It was not preemptive on the states.

In the Ninety-fourth Congress a journalist privilege bill was finally reported out of committee as H.R. 215.[137] Critics of the bill emerged from various sides of the issue. Those hoping for a qualified statute were disappointed that the bill had a preemptive feature. If adopted, the shield would be uniform for federal and state courts.

But most of the criticism was over the qualified aspects of the proposed shield. There seemed to be some potential difficulties because of the narrow interpretation of who is protected:

. . . any man or woman who is a reporter, photographer, editor, commentator, journalist, correspondent, announcer, or other individual (including partnership, corporation, association, or other legal entity existing under or authorized by the laws of the United States or any State) engaged in obtaining, writing, reviewing, editing, or otherwise preparing information in any form for any medium of communication to the public . . . [138]

"For any medium of communication to the public" could be interpreted so as to confine "medium" to only the established press, thus excluding underground publications. "Wire services might be denied the privilege since, arguably they communicate only to their customers and not the public in general."[139]

"In his capacity as newsman" could preclude a reporter from claiming the privilege if he was an eyewitness to a crime. This aspect has concerned some critics.

H.R. 215 provides an absolute privilege for grand jury proceedings, but for civil and criminal proceedings there are the qualifications stated by Justice Stewart in *Branzburg*,[140] namely, the relevance of the material and alternative sources. This approach would be more protective of the reporter than Justice White's standards but is not the absolute privilege some supporters have sought.

Journalists are becoming increasingly concerned over the libel aspects of the issue. The bill would not shield a reporter trying to protect confidences in a libel action. News people fear that this statutory feature could lead to many nuisance libel suits, as well-known public figures would sue in retaliation for embarrassing exposés.

Mark Neubauer believes that another serious failing of the House bill is the omission of protection "for newsmen against search warrants."[141] The newsroom search by the Palo Alto, California, police of the Stanford University student publication office underscores this concern. The United States Justice Department supports the elimination of the subpoena requirement for search by substituting the search warrant so that "valuable evidence will not be lost."[142]

Whether to support statutory protection for journalists protecting confidential sources presents a dilemma for reporters. Without statutory relief, judges can refer to the absence of such protection. But on the other hand qualified legislation can be narrowly construed against the press. Because there are more examples of narrow as opposed to broad construction, the media is increasingly reluctant to support statutory remedy.

In spite of that fact, each time a new confrontation occurs, there is usually a renewed round of speculation about new shield legislation. Such has been the case with the newsroom search issue[143] or the refusal by prison officials of media coverage of some aspects of prison life.[133]

8

CHAPTER

Conclusion

Legal protection of personal privacy is a cherished procedure in constitutional democracies. One of the manifestations of this protection has come through the protection of communications between parties who have preferred that their conversations remain confidential (for example, attorneys and clients, husbands and wives, priests and penitents).

Unlike the rationale for other privileges, the argument for a press privilege is not based on a need for confidentiality because the exposure would be personally embarrassing or would invade the privacy of the parties per se. Rather, it is that compulsory disclosure would lead to more serious consequences for both sources, who, for example, would pass information of government or other corruption, and reporters, who are subject to contempt charges if they protect the source.

The general argument against establishing any privilege is that the law has the right to everyman's evidence for the correct disposal of litigation. In addition to the general argument, it is argued that the government must operate to a degree in secrecy, and that the press privilege by undermining state privilege embarrasses public officials and threatens their authority. Without secrecy it is believed that there will be an interruption of the delicacy of crucial negotiations. Government officials argue that press exposure of secret talks causes the public to reflect unfavorably upon government's ability to properly control the communications process for the public good. Revealing secret talks may also embarrass private parties involved in some aspect of government.

It has also been argued that once in the possession of such a privilege the press would have license for irresponsible behavior. Instead of searching for facts, it would spin webs of fantasy. Public officials and private citizens would be maligned, with no means of redress, because the reporter could not be called as a witness either to corroborate his charges or to exonerate the defendant. This argument does have weight if there are no circumstances under which a reporter could ever be sought as a witness. But a privilege does not have to be unconditional. All privilege must yield to the logic of "the missing link in the chain of evidence" to prove guilt or innocence.

A press privilege should not be used to stall or interrupt the process of litigation in such a way as to bring about a miscarriage of justice, as when providing no injunctive relief to a defendant who has exhausted alternative sources and has solid evidence to prove that a reporter has the only testimony that can exonerate him in a libel action.

Prior to issuing a press subpoena in a criminal matter a prosecutor should have to demonstrate before a judge that there is probable cause to believe that a reporter has information relevant to a specific violation of law and that other sources have already been sought for establishing guilt or innocence. The reason for advocating the institution of this particular presubpoena showing is based on the following conclusions:

1. The press has been used as an investigative arm of government because it has gathered information that is relevant, complete, and often based on more reliable sources than the police are able to acquire.

2. The press has been subpoenaed because its members embarrass the government and community establishments with exposés of improper and illegal behavior.

3. The press has often been the fall guy for counterculture dissent. The reporting of such activities has been interpreted by some as approval of those activities. There is a measure of truth to that charge because tensions of confrontation often force polarization of beliefs. Reporters have become compatriots of radical dissenters. As a result of that phenomenon, police and reporters are often not in as close a working relationship as they have been in the past. This statement should be qualified with the observation that in small towns, rural areas, and in certain sections of the country very little has changed from the past as

far as police–press relations are concerned. However, in large cities with heavier concentrations of minority groups and on some university campuses the change is substantial.

Although the subpoena and newsroom search pressure is experienced by a minority of journalists, they are nevertheless the journalists at the pressure points who report the most significant developments about cultural cleavages, generation gaps, and ideological clashes. It is at this stage of reporting that privileged communication between informant and reporter is most delicate and can be kept from public perception by a fear of source disclosure. There are those who would cheer at this observation and echo the sentiments of former Vice-President Spiro Agnew's goad to the press, "If this leads to a chilling effect, so be it."

However, a good case can be made for conveying information about dissident activities to society at large. First, the press can serve as a catalyst for amalgamating subcultures into the mass culture through two-way communications that produce better understanding between counterculture and establishment culture, even if it does not change their separate life styles. Second, the media can act as a check on the excesses of dissenters who are interested in projecting more favorable images to the establishment. Third, by publishing accounts of excesses, journalists can act as a check on law enforcement interests that are image conscious. In such a situation a law officer's version of what happened can be compared with a dissident's account. Fourth, counter-culture reportage can serve as a check on those in government who create polarization of differences in our society. They can be made more aware of the views of those who are involved in the counterculture confrontations.

In support of the first goal the Kerner Commission made this observation in 1968: "Our nation is moving toward two socieites, one black, one white—separate and unequal."[1] Of particular importance here is the commission's concern over the failure of the news media to report adequately on race relations and ghetto problems. As the report states, the news media "have not communicated to the majority of their audience—which is white—a sense of the degradation, misery, and hopelessness of life in the ghetto."[2] The report reveals that ghetto blacks distrust and dislike the media, which they frequently refer to as the "white press."[3] Recognizing the obvious danger inherent in shutting off alienated groups from a communication forum through which they can effectively express their grievances, the commission recommended that the news media expand its coverage of the black community.[4] These goals can never be attained in an atmosphere of distrust of the newsman's promises of confidentiality.

In a survey by the commission of the attitudes of five thousand blacks and whites in fifteen major American cities, one question asked for ways in which a disturbance like the one in Detroit in 1967 could be avoided. The reply showing the highest correlation between the answers of blacks and whites cited the need for improving communications between the two groups.[5] *New York Times* reporter Earl Caldwell's confrontation with established views through reporting on Black Panthers led him into a thicket of subpoena challenges. The Ninth Circuit Court of Appeals, in overruling a lower court holding that Caldwell must appear before a grand jury to give testimony about the Panthers, gave fuel to the argument that the press needs to act as a communications link between dissenting groups and the public at large:

The need for an untrammelled press takes on special urgency in times of widespread protest and dissent. In such times the First Amendment protections exist to maintain communications with dissenting groups and to provide the public with a wide range of information about the nature of protest and heterodoxy.[6]

Earl Caldwell referred to the reporter as the funnel. "Pour the angry shouts of a black militant in one end, and at the other the white suburban father of four begins to receive the signal of maladjustment."[7] In support of this view Ben Bagdikian, national news editor of the *Washington Post,* commented:

Complaints and grievances are the only reliable signals of maladjustments, but there is no automatic way to hear them. And these complaints mean nothing unless they get into the media . . . . Tampering with the reporting of protest and dissent is tampering with the self-righting mechanism in society.[8]

Paul Branzburg, who reported on the drug scene in Kentucky for the *Louisville Courier-Journal,* feared that if he were required to disclose confidences to the grand jury, he would destroy his relations with sources in the drug culture.[9]

Social science researchers may discover that they encounter the same problems as newsmen as they attempt to study the counterculture. Informants—a very useful source of news—will become reluctant to reveal information if they believe that the reporter may be compelled to disclose his sources. Similarly, subjects of research would refuse to cooperate when the threat of government interference became obvious: Once a researcher honors a subpoena or cooperates with investigators, he is likely to lose credibility with the group being studied.[10] Samuel J.

Popkin, as a student of political movements and social forces in Vietnam, depended upon confidential sources for his research. When he was subpoenaed, he asked for a showing by the government that the information sought was relevant for the government's investigation into the publication of the Pentagon Papers.

This ubiquitous threat imposes a significant limitation on the topics studied: Researchers will be hesitant to study Vietnam-type controversies, deviant behavior, or unorthodox groups if their data may be expropriated by prosecutors.

In addition to serving a catalytic function, the media can serve as a moderating influence with those dissidents who are interested in projecting favorable images toward established society. As more dissidents became aware of journalistic concern for communicating their desires, they became more sophisticated in their strategy and tended to demand more explicit understandings concerning the details of confidentiality. Some police officers, and particularly police chiefs, also appeared to be very interested in their public image.

There was a time when the police had less to fear from reporters regarding their image. For years people have been going to jail on the basis of evidence originally acquired by newsmen. Police reporters have had a friendly rivalry with law enforcement officials to see who could solve a case first. As the dissent of the sixties moved toward a crescendo, reporters became more reluctant to cooperate with law officers. There were reasons for this change of attitude. First, many newsmen shared a general disillusionment with the process of government as a result of the Vietnam War and various government attempts to suppress dissent. Second, the journalistic fraternity felt a sense of indignity at the way it had been manipulated by three presidential administrations. As Sander Vanocur put it: "I have served as a conduit for lies."[11]

There is a fourth argument for getting journalists more involved in reporting dissent. As long as government sees only the day-to-day confrontations, with the emphasis on drama and violence, it will respond to the threats reported by establishment journalists who have traditionally emphasized the "story," that is, that which is stark, immediate, and seizes the attention. A newer brand of investigative reporting is moving away from the "story" toward in-depth coverage of an issue and therefore inquire into the causes of violence. But this kind of journalism requires considerable digging and cultivating of confidential relationships with sources. Unfortunately, the reporters most hindered by the subpoena are those who seek a composite picture and are more thorough in their investigations. The more informants who are contacted, the greater the vulnerability of the journalist to subpoenas. And because subpoenas have halted many investigations, it is essential that reporters as investigators have some insulation against the unrestrained use of subpoenas.

On what legal authority, then, can a media privilege be based? For many years attempts have been made to carve such a privilege out of the common law. The common law of evidence barely tolerates privileges of any kind. But it clearly extends the privilege to attorneys, priests, ministers, spouses, and police informers. It does not include those from other professions or occupations. The rationale under which it extends the privilege to some groups and not others rests primarily on arguments for privacy and arresting crime. It does not seem unreasonable that a common law rationale could be employed to create a journalist privilege based on a need to inform the public and the police of criminal activities. Judicial administration could be enhanced by protecting journalistic informants along with police informants.

The guideline approach, whether drawn up by private organizations (journalistic codes of ethics and the American Bar Association's suggestions for improvements in evidence law) or as found in governmental department guidelines (Justice Department memorandums), has not been very helpful because such guidelines are not established as law and they can be quickly changed by new administrations.

After failing to secure a common law media privilege, newsmen turned to the constitutional argument and sought to establish protection under the First Amendment. The Court did not accept their argument that the First Amendment restricts grand jury subpoena activity against competing considerations such as news flow.

The First Amendment has been interpreted to protect news dissemination, but it has yet to be applied to news gathering. It would not seem unreasonable to establish a First Amendment right to gather news that guarantees a journalist privilege within the restrictions of three conditions:

1. The information sought must bear a direct relationship to the subject of the litigation.

2. There must be probable cause to believe the witness has information that is clearly relevant to a specific issue of law.

3. It must be demonstrated that the information sought cannot be obtained by alternative means.

Subpoena by a grand jury was centrally involved in the press privilege issue before the *Branzburg* court. Investigations in this forum have had the effect of dampening investigation into and reporting of radical dissent both by design and inadvertence. Grand jury subpoenas discourage reporters from covering controversy that causes them to spend valuable time in court. They must often explain to their employer that the confrontation was unavoidable, knowing that a managing editor will not want to take on too many costly confrontations. Such a situation is even more threatening with small media enterprises. The reporter must try to reassure sources that he will not expose them in secret deliberations. If he cannot convince them, the public and the police may know a good deal less about crime, corruption, and dissent.

By the Court's flat rejection of a First Amendment right for journalists to refuse to divulge communications from confidential sources before a grand jury, the future of controversial reporting is clouded. There is a substantial record of case evidence that a chilling effect has set in. There are concrete illustrations of stories that were not published because assurances of confidentiality could not be extended to sources. Many more stories were not even begun because informants knew that journalists could not protect them because of a subpoena threat here or a newsroom search there. Even though the latter cannot be empirically known with exactitude regarding each real or potential news story, it can be deduced from the known variables. Human tendencies to fear coercive power produce conformity with governmental policy. The logical result is that rigorous investigative reporting is somewhat less likely to challenge the official press release.

Some will point out that the chilling effect was not sufficient to deter the press from exposing and pursuing with fury the Watergate scandals. But the same Court that overturned the reporter's claim on grounds that criminal investigations cannot be impeded by journalist privilege claims used the same reasoning to deny a claim of executive privilege.

The press was aware of that analogy and probably knew that its efforts to assist the Congress with leads would not be defeated by an executive privilege claim. In addition, the Court's *Branzburg* holding, with its four-way ideological split, was gradually being narrowed and restricted a year later, but this was also on the eve of the press's long ordeal in covering the Watergate investigations in Congress and the special prosecutor's efforts.

In spite of this rigorous coverage of an administration increasingly on the defensive, the press has not fared as well with local authorities on the subpoena offensive. The gag order and the press subpoena have both been employed to inhibit press coverage. Sometimes the press subpoena follows when a judge is of the opinion that his gag order has been disobeyed.

In its restlessness over judicial reluctance to protect journalists' sources under a First Amendment rationale, the press has turned to legislators for statutory definition of a reportorial privilege.

The better method of handling questions of evidence, privilege, and competing considerations on this issue would appear to occur in a judicial forum. It is unfortunate that the Court completely ruled out a First Amendment rationale for news gathering and press privilege and instead concluded that grand jury investigative interests are always greater than reportorial investigative interests.

At the state level, over half of the states have press privilege statutes. All of them are qualified in one way or another. These statutes have been the result of pressures by the journalists and their civil libertarian supporters. But state statutes have so many qualifications that they have not been able to protect reporters such as Paul Branzburg, Peter Bridge, and William Farr. Even in states where they appeared to have sufficient breadth, they have been narrowed by local courts.

The media has had even greater difficulty with the legislative process at the national level. Vast differences have developed within Congress and among journalists over the scope and emphasis of such legislation. There has been difficulty in defining the newsman. It does appear ill advised to extend a "press" privilege to every citizen in the land who communicates information. On the other hand, it seems unnecessary to restrict the definition of a journalist to one who works through the established media which must be, among other things, a frequent periodical publication with a minimum number of subscribers for a specified number of hours per week, for a certain percentage of salary each year.

What proceedings should be covered by such legislation? It should apply in all proceedings, but the burden of proof to support a subpoena request should be heavier for grand jury proceedings than for other forums. In libel litigation the onus should be on the defendant to prove the need for reportorial testimony.

What types of information ought to be protected? It would be better for lawmakers to stay out of this thicket because there is a fine line between the concepts of "source" and "source of information" as well as between "confidential" and "nonconfidential" information. It would appear that the more specific the legislation is at this stage of the problem, the more likely judges will narrowly construe privilege protection for reporters.

Should there be specific exceptions to the privilege? This is another thicket. If there must be legislation, it would be a mistake to try to anticipate conditions or circumstances under which a privilege would have to yield to a demand for evidence. It is not being suggested here that legislation be written so as to shield the press from testimonial obligation under any and all circumstances. Such legislation would be ill advised and would probably be ruled unconstitutional. But it would appear that any language on exceptions having to do with special circumstances would unnecessarily open a "can of worms." It is the task of judges to determine what constitutes an "emergency" or "imminent threat" when the need arises. In the age of "future shock," it is hard to foresee or imagine in a legislative committee setting what those contingencies will be.

Should a reporter be protected by a privilege when he is an eyewitness to crime? In general it appears more reasonable to say no, but as the seriousness of the crime diminishes, the burden of proof should be much heavier on the prosecution to apply the tests of relevancy, alternative means, and overriding factors. Was the cause of justice better served by holding Paul Branzburg in contempt for refusing to name his drug sources, or should he have been able to continue the stories in the hope that the community would come to understand itself better? Might it not have been better if he had laid out additional pieces of the narcotics mosaic in Franklin County so that law enforcement would have a larger composite of information from which to arrest not only the participants but begin to deal with some of the underlying causes, that is, alienation and the generation gap? In the Branzburg matter it might have been better to "write about crime rather than do something about it" too precipitously and therefore less effectively.

Should federal legislation apply to state as well as federal proceedings? If it applies only in federal proceedings, it will not shield the vast majority of investigative reporters who are most often vulnerable before county rather than federal grand juries. The enforcement clause of the Fourteenth Amendment is a good constitutional basis from which to initiate the preemptive effort.

The privilege should be divested only under the rules of relevancy and alternative means. An informant should be able to invoke the privilege on a showing that there has been a communications relationship with a particular media and particular reporters. Informants need protection through those means so as to assist and protect news flow.

Thus the issue boils down to information flow versus successful disposal of litigation. One does not of necessity have to sacrifice one completely at the expense of the other. The *Branzburg* holding on its face sacrifices the interest of news flow to the interest of litigation. But Justice Powell almost accepted the three conditions of relevancy, alternative means, and overriding factors, and his ideological position in the concurring opinion has come under close scrutiny for a better understanding of the meaning of the ruling. Judicially establishing the three-rule formula seems preferable to a statutory solution that is not only fraught with drafting difficulties, as has been demonstrated in the past few years, but now rests in congressional limbo. Even if the legislative drive for a shield statute succeeds on Capitol Hill, there is the danger that First Amendment guarantees could be undermined by proceeding in that fashion. What Congress gives, it could later take away, and what it denies at first, it could compound with more restrictive denial later.

Although there is some evidence of increasing judicial recognition of the three-rule formula, the limited impact of that development has not changed the fact that substantial numbers of reporters continue to be subpoenaed as a result of their reporting of corruption in high places.

Could it be that despite increasing civic awareness of this pressing issue the institutions of our government will be unable to seize the moment and provide a freer and more orderly flow of information or, despite recent evidence, could not a more concerted effort by Congress or well-balanced and bold judicial pronouncements be forthcoming in the near future? And would it not indeed be a fitting tribute to a republic still recovering from the disillusionment of Watergate but determined to find a more harmonious resolve in the after glow of the Bicentennial?

Afterword

This work begins and ends with the question of how the public interests in press information and adjudication of legal disputes can be reconciled. Since completing the manuscript, it has become increasingly apparent that the classic difficulties over press restrictions—controlling what journalists both cannot reveal and must reveal—continue to haunt the processes of gathering and disseminating the news.

The contours of the reporter-source issue continue to change in shape and complexity and increasingly overlap with cognate constitutional issues. This is especially true of privacy and the Fourth Amendment—the *Stanford Daily* ruling raises questions about constitutional search that need to be answered in a context larger than reportorial privilege. Likewise, recently the rights of defendants to a fair trial have been repeatedly juxtaposed against the interest of public knowledge concerning court proceedings and pretrial hearings. Should the press have access to public facilities such as prisons, where coverage could embarrass authorities? Does the press not represent the public more than the average citizen? Comments from the Court during the past year have left that principle in grave doubt. Recent press cases lead one to speculate more than ever that judges, attorneys, and political authorities feel threatened by the press and that journalists in turn seem to feel intimidated by these officials. According to leading pollsters, today's public is less sympathetic toward the press, attorneys, judges, and politicians than it used to be. In the absence of a clear public mandate, is there anything that can be done to harmonize these interests? Has post-Watergate coverage, with its penetration of private as well as public affairs, created distrust from which there is no immediate relief?

What solutions have been offered recently? The courts have become more vigilant in defending zones of privacy against reporters. Two kinds of orders have been invoked: the gag rule and the closure rule.

The gag order bars the press from publishing what it knows. The closure order bars the press from knowing what to publish. Both orders have the effect of prior censorship. There is not much difference between telling a newspaper what it cannot print and prohibiting it from covering something. It is true, of course, that gags have been reduced by the *Nebraska* case. In general, members of the Court have been unpredictable in recent months. Stewart disappointed the media on the access issue, and Stevens pleased them on the newsroom search issue. In the *Farber* case, the courts sided with the doctor defendant by sending the reporter to jail and fining his paper, the *New York Times*, $5,000 per day while he was confined. Court remedies were clearly not in the direction of balancing factors such as relevance of material and alternative sources.

Press complaints that recent decisions *(Stanford, KQED*, and *Farber)* have chilling effects on future candid news coverage have been met in part by proposed solutions designed to help news flow. The Justice Department has revived the guideline concept, and shield legislation is being discussed once again. But attorney-general guidelines on newsroom search would apply only at the federal level and could be easily withdrawn because they are not law. Discussion of shield legislation still continues to divide journalists. What legislators give, they can take away and thus undercut the First Amendment. Judges tend to narrow shield legislation despite qualifications built into the statutes. Public opinion seems less committed now than previously to using shield-law remedy. Instead of a crisis-to-crisis approach, it would be better to obtain comprehensive legislation; one time the problem can be source relationships; another time, unpublished notes or a fishing expedition. Instead of specific remedies for newsroom search emanating from legislators as ideologically different from one another as Drinan and Dole, a comprehensive bill covering many news gathering problems should be addressed. With that methodology, press and nonpress privileges might survive the sweeping invasions that undermine First and Fourth amendment rights. Could such comprehensive legislation also provide greater protection for the FBI and its secret sources of information?

Many vexing questions remain, of course, and two of them in particular were raised more vividly in 1978 than previously. Will notes and outtakes become more "sanitized," stored elsewhere, or destroyed? Will reporters be forced to shy away from authoring manuscripts because a judge may believe that it is ignoble for a journalist to write a book?

The story about chilling effects and embarrassing exposés is unfinished. Each year will most likely bring forth not only customary cases but also some so unique that few can have anticipated their novelty.

Notes

CHAPTER 1

1. Bernard M. Ortwein, "Evidence—Privileged Communication—*In re Pappas*," 6 *Suffolk University Law Review* 186 (1971). James E. Beaver, "The Newsman's Code: The Claim of Privilege and Everyman's Right to Evidence," 47 *Oregon Law Review* 245 (1968).

2. *Branzburg* v. *Hayes*, 408 U.S. 665 (1972).

3. *Caldwell* v. *United States*, 434 F. 2d 1081 (9th Cir. 1970).

4. *Supra,* note 2.

5. H.R. 215, 94th Cong., 1st Sess. (1975).

6. *Zurcher* v. *The Stanford Daily*, 46 LW 4546 (1978).

7. Ira R. Allen, "Senators Eye Bills to Protect Media in 'News Search' Rule," *The Fresno Bee,* June 25, 1978, p. A10.

8. John Tebbel, *The Media in America* (New York: Thomas Y. Crowell Company, 1974), p. 26.

9. Charles W. Whalen, Jr., *Your Right to Know* (New York: Random House, 1973), p. 12.

10. Leonard W. Larrabee et al. eds., *The Autobiography of Benjamin Franklin* (New Haven, Conn.: Yale University Press, 1964), p. 69.

11. "Piracies of the Washington Lobby—the Land Robbers," *New York Times,* January 6, 1857, p. 4.

12. *Supra,* note 9, at 22.

13. *Senate Doc.* 278, 325. Cited in Whalen, *Your Right to Know,* p. 192.

14. *Senate Doc.* 278, 856. Cited in Whalen, *Your Right to Know,* p. 192.

15. *Ex Parte Lawrence,* 116 Cal. 398, 300, 48 P. 124 (1897).

16. *Supra,* note 9, at 26.

17. Walter A. Steigleman, "Newspaper Confidence Laws," 20 *Journalism Quarterly* 236 (1943).

18. *Supra,* note 9, at 27.

19. "Senators Stop Quiz into Reporter's Sources," 85 *Editor and Publisher* 8 (May 10, 1952).

20. *New York Times,* April 10, 1963, p. 22.

21. "Reporter Refuses to Tell Senate Who Gave Him Data on TFX," *New York Times,* May 25, 1963, p. 6.

22. "Television—the Art of 'Cut and Paste,' " 97 *Time* 56 (April 12, 1971).

23. U.S. House of Representatives. *Hearings on Subpoenaed Material Re Certain TV*

News Documentary Programs Before the Special Subcommittee on Investigations of the Committee on Interstate and Foreign Commerce, 92d Cong., 1st. sess., 1971, p. 98.

24. American Enterprise Institute for Public Policy Research: *Legislative Analysis No. 11,* p. 3 (August 17, 1971).

25. *Id.* at 6.

26. *Hearings Before Subcommittee No. 3, House Judiciary Committee, House of Representatives,* 92d Cong., 2d sess., 1972, Statement of Rep. Dan Kuykendall, 195.

27. "U.S. Investigation Charges of 'Leak' on Soybean Crop." *New York Times,* May 27, 1966, p. 30.

28. "FTC Subpoena of Writer Voided," *New York Times,* September 28, 1971, p. 17.

29. *Supra,* note 2, at 688.

30. *People* v. *Durrant,* 116 Cal. 179, 220, 48 p. 75 (1897).

31. *Plunkett* v. *Hamilton,* 136 Ga. 72, 81, 70 S.E. 781 (1911).

32. *In re Grunow,* 84 N.J.L. 235, 85 A. 1011 (1913).

33. James E. Beaver, "The Newsman's Code: The Claim of Privilege and Everyman's Right to Evidence," 47 *Oregon Law Review* 254 (1968). *Burdick* v. *United States,* 236 U.S. 79 (1915).

34. "Three Reporters Are Sent to Jail in Contempt Case," *Washington Star,* October 30, 1929, 2.

35. "Virginia Editor Jailed for Contempt," 65 *Editor and Publisher* 7 (January 9, 1932); "Chicago Court Defers Contempt Ruling," 67 *Editor and Publisher* 3 (August 4, 1934); "Court Drops Sloan Contempt Charge," 67 *Editor and Publisher* 10 (August 11, 1934); *People ex. rel. Mooney* v. *Sheriff of New York County,* 269 N.Y. 291, 199 N.E. 415, 416 (1936); "Guilty of Concealing News Source," *New York Times,* September 13, 1939.

36. "Jailed Newsmen Plead for Confidence Law," 81 *Editor and Publisher* 7 March 6, 1948).

37. *Id.*

38. *Rosenberg* v. *Carroll, In re Lyons,* 99 F. Supp. 629 (1951).

39. *Murphy* v. *Colorado* (Colo. Sup. Ct., unreported opinion), *cert. denied.* 365 U.S. 843 (1961).

40. *In re Goodfader's Appeal,* 45 Hawaii 317, 367 P. 2d 472 (1961).

41. *Id.*

42. *Id.*

43. Margaret Sherwood, "The Newsman's Privilege: Government Investigations, Criminal Prosecutions and Private Litigation," 58 *California Law Review* 1218 (1970).

44. *Id.* at 1219.

45. *Thompson* v. *State,* 284 Minn. 274, 275, 170 N.W. 2d 101 (1969).

46. *Lipps* v. *State,* Ind. App., 258 N.E. 2d 622 (1970).

47. *Supra,* note 9, at 97.

48. *Id.*

49. "Foard Attacks News Articles," *Columbia State,* August 15, 1972, Bl. Cited in Whalen, *Your Right to Know,* p. 194.

50. *"Los Angeles Times,* Released from Pledge of Confidentiality by A. C. Baldwin III, Key Government Witness in Watergate Case," *New York Times,* December 22, 1972, p. 1.

51. *Supra,* note 9, at 43.

52. "Court Upholds Journalist's Right to Refuse to Disclose Confidential News Sources," *New York Times,* December 8, 1972, p. 37.

53. *Baker* v. *F & F Investment,* 670 F. 2d 778 (2d Cir. 1972).

54. *Pledger* v. *State,* 77 Ga. 242, 245, 2 S.E. 320 (1886).

55. *Brogan* v. *Passaic Daily News,* 22 N.J. 139, 152, 123A 2nd 473, 480 (1956).

56. *Garland* v. *Torre,* 259 F. 2d 545 (2d Cir.), *cert. denied,* 358 U.S. 910 (1958).

57. James A. Guest and Alan L. Stanzler, "The Constitutional Argument for Newsmen Concealing Their Sources," 64 *Northwestern University Law Review* 23 (1969).

58. "Newsmen's Privilege Against Compulsory Disclosure of Sources in Civil Suits—Toward an Absolute Privilege?" 45 *University of Colorado Law Review* 174 (1973).

59. *Application of Cepeda,* 233 F. Supp. 465 (1964).

60. Stephen F. Peifer, "State Newsman's Privilege Statutes: A Critical Analysis," 49 *Notre Dame Lawyer* 160 (1973). William F. Stewart, "The Newsman's Source Privilege—a Balancing of Interests," 2 *University of San Fernando Valley Law Review* 104 (1973).

61. *Alioto* v. *Cowles Communications, Inc.* No. 52150 (N.D. Cal., December 4, 1969).

62. David A. Marcello, "Freedom of the Press: The Journalist's Right to Maintain the Secrecy of His Confidential Sources," 45 *Tulane Law Review* 614 (1971).

63. "Alioto Given $350,000 in Suit Against *Look:* Judge Rules Mafia Story Malicious," *Los Angeles Times,* May 4, 1977, p. 1.

64. *Id.* at 26.

65. *New York Times* v. *Sullivan,* 376 U.S. 254 (1964).

66. *Cervantes* v. *Time, Inc.,* 330 F. Supp. 936, 940 (1970).

67. *Cervantes* v. *Time, Inc.,* 464 F. 2d 986, 993 (1972).

68. Cal. Evid. Code Ann. ss 1070 (West Supp. 1971); "(a) A publisher, editor, reporter, or other person connected with or employed upon a newspaper, *magazine, or other periodical publication . . . ."*

69. "Seattle Reporter Is Ordered Jailed," *New York Times,* May 20, 1939, p. 10. *Supra,* note 5, at 55–56.

70. *Sheppard* v. *Maxwell,* 384 U.S. 333 (1966).

71. Petition for a Writ of Certiorari, *Farr* v. *Superior Court of Los Angeles County,* U.S. Supreme Court, October Term 1971, No. 71-1642, 168, 169.

72. *Joe Rosato, William K. Patterson, George F. Gruner and Jim Bort* v. *Superior Court of Fresno County* 5 Civil 2623.

73. *Supra,* note 9, at 56.

74. Petition for Writ of Certiorari, *Farr* v. *Superior Court of Los Angeles County,* U.S. Supreme Court, October Term 1971, No. 71-1642, 168, 169.

75. "Newsman on Coast Sent to Jail Until He Reveals Source of Data," *New York Times,* November 17, 1972, p. 24.

76. *In re Farr,* 36 Cal. App. 3d 577, 584, Ill Cal. Rptr. 649, 653 (1974).

77. "Who's Hobbling the Press?" 167 *New Republic* 6 (December 16, 1972).

78. "Imprisoned Press," *New York Times,* November 17, 1972, p. 44.

79. "The Jailing of the First Amendment," *Los Angeles Times,* November 29, 1972, p. 6, Part II.

80. *Supra*, note 78.

81. Kenneth W. Devaney, "Attorney Defends Judges' Right to Jail Newsmen," *Fresno Bee*, May 9, 1975, p. A15.

82. "*Bee* Plans Appeal This Week to Overturn Jail Sentences," *Fresno Guide*, May 12, 1975, p. 3.

83. Joe Rosato and W. K. Patterson, "McKelvey Told Grand Jury of Anger at 'Bribe Offer,'" *Fresno Bee*, January 12, 1975, p. A1. Joe Rosato and W. K. Patterson, "Stefano Denied Aluisi Refund Was Factor In Firing Reiss," January 13, 1975, *Fresno Bee*, p. 1A. Joe Rosato and W. K. Patterson, "Stefano: Firm Paid Councilman," *Fresno Bee*, January 14, 1975, p. A1.

84. *Joe Rosato, William K. Patterson, George F. Gruner and Jim Bort* v. *The Superior Court of Fresno County*, Brief for Respondent, Fifty District Court of Appeals, Calif. 5 Civil 2623., p. 3.

85. Cal. Evid. Code Ann. ss 1070 (West Supp. 1971).

86. Petition for Writ of Certiorari and Request for Stay, *Rosato, et al.* v. *Superior Court of Fresno County* 5 Civil No. 2623, Brief for Petitioners.

87. Ellen Hume and Linda Mathews, "Douglas Halts Probe into *Fresno Bee* News Sources," *Los Angeles Times*, March 22, 1975, Part II, p. 1.

88. Cal. Code Civ. Pro. ss 128, subds. (3)–(5) (West Supp. 1976).

89. Application of Cepeda, 233 F. Supp. 465.

90. *Wood* v. *Georgia*, 370 U.S. 375, 383 (1972).

91. *Supra*, note 85.

92. "Assembly Okays News Shield Vote," *Fresno Bee*, June 25, 1977, p. B7.

93. "Wrong Way to Go," *Fresno Bee*, June 1, 1977, p. A10.

94. "Burger Sees Press-Courts Rift," *Fresno Bee*, August 14, 1975, p. D23.

95. *In re Wayne*, 4 Hawaii Dist. Ct. 475, 476 (1914).

96. *Supra*, note 4, at 45. *Id.* at 46. "Two Newsmen Freed in Contempt Case," *New York Times*, March 31, 1967, p. 24. *Supra*, note 24, p. 67. Robert Rawitch, "KPFK Chief Turns Hearst Tape Over to Federal Jury," *Los Angeles Times*, February 21, 1975, Part II, p. 4.

CHAPTER 2

1. Paul J. Buser, "The Newsman's Privilege: Protection of Confidential Sources of Information Against Government Subpoenas," 15 *Saint Louis University Law Journal* 183 (1970).

2. *Id.*

3. Address by Ben Bagdikian, national news editor of the *Washington Post*, Annual Meeting of the Association for Education in Journalism, as reported in 103 *Editor and Publisher* 11 (August 22, 1970).

4. U.S. House of Representatives. *Hearings on Newsmen's Privilege Before Subcommittee Number Three of the Committee on the Judiciary*, 93rd Cong., 1st. sess., 1973, pp. 334–336

5. "Bee Three Seek Writ—Court Is Asked to Halt Testimony Probe," *Fresno Bee*, February 15, 1975, p. 1.

6. E. Barrett Prettyman, Jr., "Press Freedom: Legal Threats," *New York Times*, January 22, 1975, p. 39.

7. "Constitutional Law—Freedom of the Press—Reporter Has No Constitutional Right to Preserve Anonymity of an Informer If Court Orders Disclosure," 82 *Harvard Law Review* 1384 (1969).

8. Richard O. Sharpe, "The Newsman's Qualified Privilege Under the First Amendment," 16 *South Dakota Law Review* 336 (1971).

9. James E. Beaver, "The Newsman's Code: The Claim of Privilege and Everyman's Right to Evidence," 47 *Oregon Law Review* 244 (1968).

10. Talbot D'Alemberte, "Journalists Under the Axe: Protection of Confidential Sources of Information," 6 *Harvard Journal on Legislation* 319 (1969).

11. 250 Ore. 244, 436 P. 2d 729 (1968).

12. Petition for Certiorari, *Branzburg* v. *Hayes,* U.S. Supreme Court, October term 1970, No. 70-85, 67.

13. Kentucky Revised Statutes, 421.100.

14. U.S. Supreme Court Records 1971 Term 408 U.S. 665.

15. *Supra,* note 12, at 33.

16. *Id.* at 36, 37.

17. *Lightman* v. *State,* 15 Md. App. 713, at 714–15 (1972).

18. Md. Code, Art. 25, paragraph 2.

19. *Supra,* note 17, p. 725.

20. *Id.* at 726.

21. U.S House of Representatives, *Hearings on Newsmen's Privilege Before Subcommittee Number Three of the Committee on the Judiciary,* 93rd Cong., 1st sess. 1973, p. 444.

22. *Id.* at 67.

23. Petition for Certiorari, *United States* v. *Caldwell,* U.S. Supreme Court, October Term 1970, No. 70-57, Appendix 17.

24. "Ask Me." I Know. I Was the Test Case," 55 *Saturday Review* 4, 5 (August 5, 1972).

25. *Id.*

26. *Supra,* note 23.

27. *Id.* at 9.

28. *Caldwell* v. *United States,* 434 F. 2d 1081, 1086 (1970).

29. Brief for Petitioner, *In re Pappas,* U.S. Supreme Court, October Term, 1971, No. 70-94, 9.

30. *Id.* at 10.

31. *In re Pappas,* 266 N.E. 2d 297 (Mass., 1971).

32. Petition for a Writ of Certiorari, *In re Pappas,* U.S. Supreme Court, October Term, 1970, No. 70-94, 12a.

33. *Supra,* note 29.

34. *Id.* at 43.

35. "Newsmen Subpoena Refused by Judge," *Washington Post,* April 8, 1970.

36. *People* v. *Dohrn,* No. 69-3808 (Cir. Ct. of Cook County, Ill, May 20, 1970), at 8.

37. David A. Marcello, "Freedom of the Press: The Journalist's Right to Maintain the Secrecy of His Confidential Sources," 45 *Tulane Law Review* 615 (1971).

38. James A. Baxter, "Constitutional Law: Testimonial Privilege of Newsmen," 55 *Marquette Law Review* 186 (1972).

39. *State* v. *Knops,* 49 Wis. 2d 647, 183 N.W. 2d 93, 98 (1971).

40. "Reporter's Privilege Under the First Amendment," 36 *Albany Law Review* 411 (1972).

41. *Supra,* note 8, at 348.

42. 49 Wis. 2d at 657-58, 183 N.W. 2d at 98.

43. Harold L. Nelson, "The Newsmen's Privilege Against Disclosure of Confidential Sources and Information," 24 *Vanderbilt Law Review* 676 (1971).

44. *Id.* at 677.

45. *Supra,* note 43, at 677.

46. *Supra,* note 38, at 188.

47. *Id.* at 190.

48. *Id.*

49. Paul Nejelski and Lindsey Miller Lerman, "A Researcher-Subject Testimonial Privilege: What to Do Before the Subpoena Arrives," 1971 *Wisconsin Law Review* 1121 (1971).

50. *Supra,* note 43, at 678.

51. Vince Blasi, "The Newsman's Privilege: An Empirical Study," 70 *Michigan Law Review* 231 (1971).

52. *Supra,* note 38, at 191.

53. *Supra,* note 21, at 413.

54. Robert L. Nisely, "Evidence: New York Shield Law Applies Only When Confidential Relationship Exists Between a Newsman and His Source," 23 *Buffalo Law Review* 529 (1971).

55. *Id.*

56. Brief for Respondent-Appellants, *New York* v. *Dan and Barnes,* N.Y. Supreme Court, Appellate Division, Fourth Dept., 5–6.

57. *Id.* at 7.

58. Robert D. McFadden, "Two Newsmen Told to Recall Attica: Court Says Exemption Law Does Not Apply to Them," *New York Times,* February 24, 1973, p. 18.

59. "Buffalo TV Newsman Agrees to Tell Grand Jury Everything He Knows," *New York Times,* June 29, 1973, p. 37.

60. Vince Blasi, "Privilege in a Time of Violence," 211 *The Nation* 654 (December 21, 1970).

61. R. de Leon, "Rebellion in the Tombs," *The Village Voice,* November 5, 1970, p. 9.

62. *Supra,* note, 54, at 539.

63. *Id.*

64. *Id.*

65. David K. Shipler, "Rockefeller Backs News Source Law," *New York Times,* February 23, 1973, p. 5.

66. Governor's Memorandum, N.Y. Sess. Laws 1970, at 3112.

67. Paul J. Buser, "The Newsman's Privilege: Protection of Confidential Sources of Information Against Government Subpoenas," 15 *Saint-Louis University Law Journal* 196 (1970).

68. "Another Press Setback," *The Fresno Bee,* June 29, 1978, p. A10.

69. Robert Rawitch, "KPFK Manager Jailed After Failing to Give Up SLA Tape," *Los Angeles Times,* June 20, 1974, Part I, p. 3.

70. John Kendall, "KPFK Manager Released from Federal Prison," *Los Angeles Times,* July 6, 1974, Part II, p. 1.

71. *Supra,* note 69.

72. *Id.*

73. Jack Jones, "Justice Douglas Orders KPFK Manager Freed," *Los Angeles Times,* July 5, 1974, Part I, p. 3.

74. Gene Blake, "U.S. Court Upholds Jailing of KPFK Official Over Tape," *Los Angeles Times,* July 23, 1974, Part II p. 1.

75. Daryl Lembke, "Pacifica Backs Station Manager's Tape Stand," *Los Angeles Times,* June 22, 1974, Part I, p. 21.

76. Editorial: "Press Freedom—and Responsibility," *Los Angeles Times,* June 20, 1974, Part II, p. 6.

77. Gene Blake, "He Will Surrender Tape If Fund Drive Fails, KPFK Official Says," *Los Angeles Times,* July 24, 1974, Part II, p. 1.

78. Gene Blake, "Douglas Stays Jailing of FM Station Manager," *Los Angeles Times,* August 3, 1974, Part I, p. 14.

79. Linda Mathews, "U.S. Supreme Court Upholds Conviction of KPFK Official in Hearst Tape Case," *Los Angeles Times,* February 15, 1975, Part I, p. 23.

80. Robert Rawitch, "KPFK Chief Turns Hearst Tape Over to Federal Jury," *Los Angeles Times,* February 21, 1975, Part II, p. 4.

81. *Id.*

82. John Kendall, "Pacifica Radio: Different Tune on the FM Dial," *Los Angeles Times,* July 5, 1974, Part I, p. 1.

83. *Supra,* note 80.

84. Charles W. Whalen, Jr., *Your Right to Know* (New York: Random House, 1973), p. 105.

85. Appellant-Petitioner's Brief in the Supreme Court of the State of Delaware, No. 209, Dec. 22, 1972, 5. (Petition of Charles McGowan.)

86. *Supra,* note 21, at 67.

87. "U.S. Asks Court O.K. Newspaper Raids," *Fresno Bee,* January 17, 1978, p. 1.

88. Editorial: "Newsroom Searches," *Fresno Bee,* December 26, 1977.

89. *Zurcher* v. *The Stanford Daily,* 46 LW 4546 (1978).

90. Jim Mann, "Court Upholds Police Searches of News Offices," *Los Angeles Times,* June 1, 1978, Part I, p. 6.

91. *Supra,* note 1, at 4548.

92. *Id.* at 4551.

93. *Id.* at 4552.

94. *Branzburg* v. *Hayes,* 408 U.S. 665 (1972).

95. *Supra,* note 1, at 4555.

96. *Supra,* note 6, at 726.

97. *Supra,* note 1, at 4553-54.

98. James J. Kilpatrick, "High Court and the Press," *Fresno Bee,* June 12, 1978, p. A15.

99. "A Different Land," *Los Angeles Times,* June 12, 1978, Part II, p. 8.

100. Anthony Lewis, "The Court and the Press," *Fresno Bee,* June 9.

101. *Houchins* v. *KQED,* 76-1310 (1978).

102. James D. Carroll, "Confidentiality of Social Science Research Sources and Data: The Popkin Case," 1973 PS 268 (1973).

103. *Supra,* note 49, at 1085.

104. *Supra,* note 102, at 2700.

105. *Id.* at 271.

106. *Id.*

107. In the Supreme Court of the United States, October Term, 1972, No. 72-974, *Samuel L. Popkin* v. *United States,* Motion for Leave to File Brief as Amicus Curiae and Brief of American Anthropological Association, American Political Science Association, and American Sociological Association, pp. 6–7.

108. United States District Court for the District of Massachusetts, *United States* v. *John Doe,* Memorandum of Law of Samual Lewis Popkin in Support of His Motion for Protective Order, October 27, 1971, p. 13.

109. *Id.*

110. *New York Times,* December 3, 1972, IV, p. 5.

111. *New York Times,* December 5, 1972, p. 46.

CHAPTER 3

1. 5 Eliz., c. 9 and 12 (1562).

2. *Countess of Shrewsbury's Case,* 12 Coke 94 (1613).

3. Talbot D'Alemberte, "Journalists Under the Axe: Protection of Confidential Sources of Information," 6 *Harvard Journal on Legislation* 311 (1969).

4. *Lawson and Harrison* v. *Odhams Press, Ltd.* (1949).

5. *Supra,* note 3, at 312.

6. *Id.*

7. Harry Trimborn, "TV Wins British Press Freedom Ruling," *Los Angeles Times,* April 9, 1975, Part 1 A, p. 4.

8. *Id.* at 5.

9. McCormick, *Evidence* 165 (954).

10. 7 J. Wigmore, *Evidence* ss 2192 (3rd ed. 1940).

11. 8 J. Wigmore, *Evidence* (McNaughton, rev. 1961), 2285.

12. David G. Jennings, "The Newsman's Privilege and the Constitution," 23 *South Carolina Law Review* 446 (1971).

13. James A. Guest and Alan L. Stanzler, "The Constitutional Argument for Newsmen Concealing Their Sources," 64 *Northwestern University Law Review* 18 (1969).

14. "Fifty-seven Percent Don't Want Newsmen to Name Their Sources," 105 *Editor and Publisher* 13 (December 9, 1972).

15. "Judicial Relief for the Newsman's Plight: A Time for Secrecy?", 45 *St. John's Law Review* 486 (1971). "The Newsman's Privilege after Branzburg v. Hayes: Whither Now?" 64 *Journal of Criminal Law and Criminology* 226 (1973). Paul Nejelski and Lindsey Miller Lerman, "A Researcher-Subject Testimonial Privilege: What to Do Before the Subpoena Arrives," 1971 *Wisconsin Law Review* 1134 (1971). Harold L. Nelson, "The Newsmen's Privilege Against Disclosure of Confidential Sources and Information," 24 *Vanderbilt Law Review* 668 (1971). Bernard M. Ortwein, "Evidence—Privileged Communication—In re Pappas," 6 *Suffolk University Law Review* 186 (1971). Judith A. Smith, "The Reporter's Right to Shield His 'Reliable' Source," 11 *Publishing, Entertainment, Advertising, and Allied Fields Law Quarterly* 500 (1973). Richard O. Sharpe, "The Newsman's Qualified Privilege Under the First Amendment," 16 *South Dakota Law Review* 330 (1971). James D. Hendersen, "The Protection of Confidences: A Qualified Privilege for Newsmen," 1971 *Law and the Social Order* 394 (1971). Wayne

C. Dabb, Jr., and Peter A. Kelley, "The Newsman's Privilege: Protection of Confidential Associations and Private Communications," 4 *Journal of Law Reform* 89 (1970). Margaret Sherwood, "The Newsman's Privilege: Governmental Investigations, Criminal Prosecutions and Private Litigation," 58 *California Law Review* 1212 (1970). Richard E. Anderson, "Branzburg v. Hayes: A Need for Statutory Protection of News Sources," 61 *Kentucky Law Journal* 551 (1973). "Privileged Communications: A Case by Case Approach," 23 *Maine Law Review* 443 (1971). James E. Beaver, "The Newsman's Code, the Claim of Privilege and Everyman's Right to Evidence," 47 *Oregon Law Review* 246 (1968). Nathan Norton, Jr., "Privileges," 27 *Arkansas Law Review* 200 (1973).

16. 8 J. Wigmore, *Evidence* ss 2290, at 547 (3rd ed., 1940).

17. *Id.*

18. "Privileged Communications: A Case by Case Approach," 23 *Maine Law Review* 444, (1971).

19. Roger M. Grace, "Attorney-Client Privilege Now Under Attack," *Los Angeles Daily Journal,* April 2, 1975, p. 1.

20. Nathan Norton, Jr., "Privileges," 27 *Arkansas Law Review* 207 (1973).

21. 20 How. St. Tr. at 573.

22. G. Keeton and G. Schwarzenberger, *Jeremy Bentham and the Law* (Toronto: Carswell Company, Ltd., 1948), p. 95.

23. *Id.* at 210.

24. *Id.*

25. "Privileged Communications: A Case by Case Approach," 23 *Maine Law Review* 444 (1971).

26. United States Senate, *Hearings on Newsman's Privilege Before the Subcommittee on Constitutional Rights of the Committee on the Judiciary,* 93rd Cong., 1st. sess., 1973, p. 745.

27. *Cal. Evid. Code* ss 1014, Comment (West 1966).

28. Alabama, Connecticut, Delaware, Florida, Georgia, Maryland, Massachusetts, Rhode Island, South Carolina, Tennessee, Texas, and Vermont.

29. Connecticut, Florida, Georgia, Illinois, and Maryland.

30. California and Maryland.

31. Maryland.

32. The jurisdictions that do not have the privilege are: the District of Columbia, Hawaii, Iowa, Louisiana, Minnesota, Missouri, North Dakota, Ohio, Pennsylvania, Rhode Island, South Carolina, South Dakota, Texas, Vermont, West Virginia, Indiana.

33. *Supra,* note 11.

34. Alabama, Arizona, Arkansas, Delaware, Georgia, Idaho, Kansas, Kentucky, Nebraska, Nevada, New Hampshire, New Jersey, New York, Oklahoma, Tennessee, and Washington.

35. Arizona, Arkansas, Georgia, Idaho, Kansas, Kentucky, Nebraska, Nevada, New Hampshire, New Jersey, Oklahoma, and Washington.

36. Kentucky and New Hampshire.

37. California, Illinois, Kentucky, Maryland, and New Hampshire.

38. *N.Y. Civ. Pract. Law* ss 4508 (McKinney Supp. 1970).

39. *Colo. Rev. Stat* ss 46-5-6 (1963); *Mich. Comp. Laws Ann.* ss 338.1043 (1967); *N.J. Rev. Stat* ss 45:8B-29 (Supp. 1970).

40. *Supra,* note 11.

41. *Id.*

194   Notes

42. *Id.*

43. *Roviaro* v. *United States* 353 U.S. 53 (1957).

44. *United States* v. *Caldwell* 408 U.S. 665 (1972).

45. Roger D. Graham "Constitutional Law—Disclosure of Journalist's Confidential News Sources," 73 *West Virginia Law Review* 323 (1971).

46. *Hearings Before Subcommittee No. 3 House Judiciary Committee,* House of Representatives, 93rd Cong., 1st sess., 1973, p. 523.

47. *Supra,* note 26, at 99.

48. *Id.* at 141.

49. *Supra,* note 15, Dabb and Kelley, at 93.

50. *Supra,* note 43, at 59.

51. *United States* v. *Tucker* 380 F. 2d 206 (2d Cir 1967).

52. *Supra,* note 26, at 149.

53. *Supra,* note 15, Ortwein, at 186.

54. *Supra,* note 25, at 454.

55. *Supra,* note 15, Nejelski, at 1140.

56. *Supra,* note 46, at 140.

57. *Id.* at 34.

58. *United States Department of Justice Memorandum No. 692,* Department of Justice, Washington, D.C.

59. William F. Stewart, "The Newsman's Source Privilege—Balancing of Interests," 2 *University of San Fernando Law Review* 109 (1973).

60. *Supra,* note 15, 64 *Journal of Criminal Law and Criminology* 232.

61. *Id.* at 215.

62. *Id.* at 217.

63. David Gordon, *Newsman's Privilege and the Law* (Published by the Freedom of Information Foundation, Columbia, Mo.), August 1974, p. 45.

64. *Supra,* note 15, Sharpe, at 344.

65. *In re Mack,* 386 Pa. 251, 265, 126, A.2d. 679, 685 (1956).

66. *Supra,* note 46, at 270.

67. *Supra,* note 14, at 13.

68. *United States* v. *Nixon* 94 S. Ct. 3090, 3108 (1974).

69. Mason Ladd, "Privileges," 1979 *Law and the Social Order* 555, 556 (1969).

70. "Constitutional Law—Newsman's Privilege: A Challenge to Branzburg," 53 *Boston University Law Review* 511 (1973).

71. *Id.*

72. *New York Times,* March 7, 1973, p. 18, col. 5.

73. Rules of Evidence for United States Courts and Magistrates, 56 F.R.D. 183 (1972).

74. *Id.*

75. *Id.* at 26.

76. *Supra,* note 70, p. 512.

77. *In re Wayne* 4 Hawaii Dist. Ct. 475 (1914).

78. *Plunkett* v. *Hamilton* 136 Ga. 72, 81, 70 S.E. 781, 785 (1911).

79. 2 *Hun* 226 (N.Y. 1874).

80. *In re Goodfader,* 45 Hawaii 317, 367 P. 2d 472 (1961).

81. *Garland* v. *Torre* 259 F. 2d 545 (2d Cir.) *cert. denied* 358 U.S. 910 (1958).

82. *Supra,* note 58.

83. *In re Caldwell,* No. 26, 025 (9th Cir. November 16, 1970).

84. *Id.*

85. Richard D. Younger, *The People's Panel* (Providence, R.I.: Brown University Press, 1963), pp. 1–4.

86. *Id.* at 2–3.

87. Charles Goodell, "Where Did the Grand Jury Go?" 246 *Harper's* 16 (May 1973).

88. *Id.* at 224–26.

89. *Id.* at 182–224.

90. *Hurtado* v. *California,* 110 U.S. 516 (1884).

91. *Wood* v. *Georgia,* 370 U.S. 375, 390 (1962).

92. Melvin P. Antell, "The Modern Grand Jury: Benighted Supergovernment," 51 *American Bar Association* Journal 154 (1965). "The Rights of a Witness Before a Grand Jury," 1967 *Duke Law Journal* 97 (1967).

93. Sanford Jay Rosen and William Birtles, "What's Wrong with Grand Juries?" 283–99 *Civil Liberties* 1 (1972).

94. *Branzburg* v. *Hayes,* 408 U.S. 665 (1972).

95. *Id.*

96. *Dennis* v. *United States,* 384 U.S. 855 (1966).

97. Frank J. Donner and Eugene Cerruti, "The Grand Jury Network: How the Nixon Administration Has Secretly Perverted a Traditional Safeguard of Individual Rights," 214 *The Nation* 5 (January 3, 1972).

98. *Supra,* note 87, at 14.

99. *Supra,* note 87, at 22.

100. *Supra,* note 87, at 20.

101. *Supra,* note 97, at 8.

102. "A 'Bill of Rights' for Grand Juries," 9 *Trial* 55 (September/October 1973).

103. *Supra,* note 92, at 16.

104. *Supra,* note 87, at 16.

105. *Supra,* note 26, at 103.

106. *In re Cohen,* 295 Mich. 748 (1940).

107. *Reina* v. *United States,* 364 U.S. 507 (1960); and *Murphy* v. *Waterfront Commission,* 378 U.S. 52 (1964).

108. *Supra,* note 26, at 142.

109. *Id.*

110. *Supra,* note 46, at 99–100.

CHAPTER 4

1. *Burdick* v. *United States,* 236 U.S. 70 (1915); *Curtin* v. *United States,* 236 U.S. 96 (1915).

2. Charles Wright, "LA Times Counsel Labels Court Orders 'Judicial Dictatorship,'" *Fresno Bee,* April 25, 1975, D1.

3. *State* v. *Buchanan, Ore.,* 436 P.2d 729, at 731 (1968).

4. See Comment, "Developments in the Law—Equal Protection," 82 *Harvard Law Review* 1065 (1969).

5. *United States Constitution, Amendment V:* "No person . . . shall be compelled in any criminal case to be a witness against himself. . . . "

6. *United States Constitution, Amendment IV:* "The right of the people to be secure in their persons, houses, papers, and effects, against unreasonable searches and seizures, shall not be violated. . . . "

7. *United States Constitution, Amendment VI:* " . . . to have compulsory process for obtaining witnesses in his favor. . . . "

8. *In re Groban,* 352 U.S. 330, 333 (1957).

9. *United States Constitution, Amendment I:* "Congress shall make no law respecting an establishment of religion, or prohibiting the free exercise thereof; or abridging the freedom of speech, or of the press. . . . "

10. *Gitlow* v. *New York,* 268 U.S. 652 (1925).

11. *Garland* v. *Torre,* 259 F. 2d 545 (2d Cir.), *cert. denied,* 358 U.S. 910 (1958).

12. *Id.* at 548.

13. *Id.* at 549.

14. 45 *Hawaii* 317, 367 P. 2d 472 (1961).

15. Id. at 329.

16. *Supra,* note 3.

17. *Id.* at 248–49.

18. Margaret Sherwood, "The Newsman's Privilege: Government Investigations, Criminal Prosecutions and Private Litigation," 58 *California Law Review* 1218 (1970).

19. *Id.* at 1219.

20. *Supra,* note 14, at 324.

21. Alexander Meiklejohn, "The First Amendment Is an Absolute," 1961 The Supreme Court Review 245, 255, in Phillip B. Kurland (ed.), *The Supreme Court Review* 245, 255 (1961).

22. Saul K. Padover, ed., *The Complete Madison* (New York: Harper & Row Publishers, Inc., c.1953).

23. Julian P. Boyd, ed., *The Papers of Thomas Jefferson* (Princeton: Princeton University Press, 1955), italics mine.

24. *Grosjean* v. *American Press Co.,* 297 U.S. 233 (1936).

25. *Id.* at 243.

26. *Thornhill* v. *Alabama,* 310 U.S. 88 (1940).

27. *Id.* at 102.

28. *Associated Press* v. *United States,* 326 U.S. 1, 20 (1945).

29. *Estes* v. *Texas,* 381 U.S. 532, 539 (1965).

30. *Red Lion Broadcasting Co.* v. *FCC,* 395 U.S. 367, 392 (1969).

31. *New York Times Co.* v. *United States,* 403 U.S. 826-7 (1971).

32. Thomas I. Emerson, *Toward a General Theory of the First Amendment* (New York: Random House, 1963), p. 3.

33. *Id.* at 12.

34. *Supra,* note 21, at 254.

35. James A. Guest and Alan L. Stanzler, "The Constitutional Argument for Newsmen Concealing Their Sources," 64 *Northwestern University Law Review* 31 (1969).

36. *Brief of the American Civil Liberties Union, The American Civil Liberties Union of Northern California, and the American Civil Liberties Union of Southern California,* AMICI CURIAE (In the Supreme Court of the United States, October Term, 1971, No. 70-57) *United States* v. *Caldwell* at 9 and 10.

37. *Stanley* v. *Georgia,* 394 U.S. 557, 564 (1969).

38. *Supra,* note 29, at 539.

39. *Talley* v. *California,* 362 U.S. 60 (1960).

40. Jeffrey D. Sherman, "Constitutional Protection for the Newsman's Work Product," 6 *Harvard Civil Rights—Civil Liberties Law Review* 128 (1970).

41. *Lamont* v. *Postmaster General,* 381 U.S. 301 (1965).

42. *Id.*

43. *Supra,* note 39, at 64–65.

44. Meg Greenfield, "Telling It (Sort of) Like It Is," 83 *Newsweek* 50 (July 22, 1974).

45. Lewis H. Lapham, "The Temptation of a Sacred Cow," 24 *Harper's Magazine* 44 (August 1973).

46. John B. Kuhns, "Reporters and Their Sources: The Constitutional Right to a Confidential Relationship," 80 *The Yale Law Journal* 330 (1970).

47. *Supra,* note 18, at 1204.

48. Vince Blasi, "The Newsman's Privilege: An Empirical Study," 70 *Michigan Law Review* 271 (1971).

49. *United States* v. *Caldwell,* 311 F. Supp. at 361–62.

50. *Brief of the New York Times Company, Inc., National Broadcasting Company, Inc., Columbia Broadcasting System, Inc., American Broadcasting Companies, Inc., Chicago Sun-Times, Chicago Daily News, Associated Press Managing Editors Association, Associated Press Broadcasters' Association and Association of American Publishers Inc.* as AMICI CURIAE (in the Supreme Court of the United States, October Term, 1971, No. 70-57) *United States* v. *Caldwell* at 18.

51. Floyd Sherman Chalmer, *A Gentleman of the Press: The Biography of Colonel John Bayne MacClean* (Garden City, N.Y.: Doubleday Co., Inc., 1969), pp. 74–75. Herman Klurfeld, *Behind the Lines: The World of Drew Pearson* (Englewood Cliffs, N.J.: Prentice-Hall, Inc., 1968), pp. 50, 52–55. Arthur Krock, Memoirs: *Sixty Years on the Firing Line* (New York: Funk and Wagnalls, 1968), pp. 181, 184–85. Egon Larsen, *First with the Truth* (New York: Roy Publishers, Inc., 1968), pp. 22–23, 94–95. Roi Vincent Ottley, *The Lonely Warrior—the Life and Times of Robert S. Abbott* (Chicago: H. Regnery Co., 1955) pp. 143–45. George Seldes, *Never Tire of Protesting* (Boston: Stuart Publications, 1968), pp. 83–84. Richard Brandon Morris and Louis Leo Snyder, eds., *A Treasury of Great Reporting* (New York: Simon and Schuster, 1949), p. 180. Cyrus Leo Sulzberger, *A Long Row of Candles, Memoirs and Diaries, 1934–54* (New York: Macmillan, 1969), pp. 24, 241, 249.

52. Curtis Daniel MacDougall, *Newsroom Problems and Policies* (New York: Dover Publications Inc., 1964), p. 301.

53. Hugh C. Sherwood, *The Journalistic Interview* (New York: Harper & Row Publishers, Inc., 1969), p. 89.

54. *Wieman* v. *Updegraff,* 344 U.S. 183 (1952).

55. *Id.* at 195.

56. Peter Weisman and Andrew D. Postal, "The Grand Jury: The First Amendment as a Restraint on the Grand Jury Process: *The American Criminal Law Review* 674 (Summer 1972).

57. *Keyishian* v. *Board of Regents,* 385 U.S. 589 (1967), and *Baggett* v. *Bullit,* 377 U.S. 360 (1964). Robert M. Tyler and Doris Kaufman, "The Public Scholar and the First Amendment: A Compelling Need for Compelling Testimony?" 40 *George Washington Law Review* 22 (1971–72).

58. Order Quashing Subpoenas, *People* v. *Dohrn,* No. 69-3808 (Cir. Ct. of Cook County—Crim. Div. June 12, 1970).

59. *Supra,* note 48, at 265.

60. *Id.* at 265.

61. U.S. House of Representatives. *Hearings on Newsmen's Privilege Before Subcommittee Number Three of the Committee on the Judiciary,* 93rd Con., 1st. sess., 1973, p. 241.

62. Charles Long, ''Are News Sources Drying Up?'' 61 *The Quill* 12 (March 1973).

63. *Id.*

64. *Supra,* note 61, at 488.

65. *Id.*

66. *Supra,* note 61, at 220.

67. *Id.*

68. *Supra,* note 61, at 520.

69. *Supra,* note 46, at 331.

70. *Id.*

71. Affidavits of Anthony Ripley, John Kifner, Thomas A. Johnson, Earl Caldwell, and Gerald Fraser, accompanying Petitioner's Brief, Application of Caldwell, 311 *F. Supp.* 358 (N.D. Cal. 1970).

72. James D. Hendersen, ''The Protection of Confidences: A Qualified Privilege for Newsmen,'' 1971 *Law and the Social Order* 389 (1971).

73. *Id.* at 390.

74. *Supra,* note 61, p. 115.

75. *Supra,* note 57, Tyler and Kaufman, at 18.

76. *Id.* at 21.

77. *Supra,* note 50, at 34.

78. *United States* v. *Rumely,* 345 U.S. 41 (1953).

79. *Watkins* v. *United States,* 354 U.S. 178 (1957).

80. *Sweezy* v. *New Hampshire,* 354 U.S. 234 (1957).

81. *Supra,* note 50, at 35; see also ''The First Amendment Overbreadth Doctrine,'' 83 *Harvard Law Review* 845 (1970).

82. *NAACP* v. *Button,* 371 U.S. 415, 438 (1963).

83. *Thomas* v. *Collins,* 323 U.S. 516, 530 (1945).

84. *Sherbert* v. *Verner,* 374 U.S. 398, 408 (1963).

85. *Gibson* v. *Florida Legislative Investigation Committee,* 372 U.S. 539 (1963).

86. *DeGregory* v. *New Hampshire Attorney General,* 383 U.S. 825 (1966).

87. *Bates* v. *Little Rock,* 361 U.S. 516 (1960).

88. *NAACP* v. *Alabama,* 357 U.S. 449 (1958).

89. *Shelton* v. *Tucker,* 364 U.S. 479 (1960).

90. *Supra,* note 85, at 557.

91. *Supra,* note 86, at 829.

92. *Supra,* note 87, at 527.

93. *Supra,* note 96, at 461.

94. *Id.*

95. *Id.* at 466.

96. *Supra,* note 50, at 39.

CHAPTER 5

1. *Branzburg* v. *Hayes,* 408 U.S. 665 (1972).

2. *Id.* at 690, 691.

3. Raymond F. Sebastian, "Obscenity and the Supreme Court: Nine Years of Confusion," 19 *Stanford Law Review* 167 (1966).

4. "Newsmen's Privilege Against Compulsory Disclosure of Sources in Civil Suits—Toward an Absolute Privilege?" 45 *University of Colorado Law Review* 188 (1973).

5. Susan Steiner Sher, "Constitutional Law—Requiring Newsmen to Appear and Testify Before Federal and State Grand Juries Does Not Abridge Freedom of Speech or Freedom or Press Guaranteed by First Amendment," 4 *Loyola University Law Journal* 243 (1973).

6. *Supra,* note 1, at 709.

7. *Supra,* note 5, at 245.

8. "The Newsman's Privilege After Branzburg v. Hayes: Whither Now?" 64 *Journal of Criminal Law and Criminology* 219 (1973).

9. *Supra,* note 1.

10. 402 U.S. 942 (1971).

11. 408 U.S. 671.

12. *Supra,* note 10.

13. *Id.*

14. 434 F. 2d 1081 (9th Cir. 1970).

15. "Confidentiality of News Sources: Emerging Constitutional Protection," 60 *Georgia Law Journal* 867 (1972). Also see Richard O. Sharpe, "The Newsman's Qualified Privilege Under the First Amendment," 16 *South Dakota Law Review* 328 (1971).

16. *Supra,* note 1, at 691.

17. *In re Pappas,* 266 N.E. 2d 297 (Mass., 1971).

18. *Supra,* note 1, at 748, n. 38.

19. *Supra,* note 1, at 748, n. 39.

20. Margaret Sherwood, "The Newsman's Privilege: Government Investigations, Criminal Prosecutions and Private Litigation," 58 *California Law Review* 1209 (1970).

21. *Supra,* note 1, at 691.

22. *Id.*

23. *Supra,* note 1, at 688.

24. *Id.* at 682.

25. Frank J. Donner and Eugene Cerutti, "The Grand Jury Network: How the Nixon Administration Has Secretly Perverted a Traditional Safeguard of Individual Rights," 214 *The Nation* 5 (January 3, 1972). Charles E. Goodell, "Where Did the Grand Jury Go? From a Legal to a Political Engine," 246 *Harper's* 14 (May 1973). Jay Sanford Rosen, "What's Wrong with Grand Juries?" *Civil Liberties* 1 (May 1972). Melvin P. Antell, "The Modern Grand Jury: Benighted Supergovernment," 51 *American Bar Association Journal* 154 (1965).

26. *Supra,* note 1, at 687, 688.

27. *Supra,* note 1, at 707, 708.

28. *Id.* at 692.

29. *Supra,* note 1, at 695.

30. *Supra,* note 1, at 684.

31. *Id.* at 693.

32. *Id.* at 699.

33. *Id.* at 698.

34. *Id.* at 704.

35. *Id.* at 702.

36. *Id.* at 695, 696.

37. *Id.* at 706.

38. *Id.*

39. *Id.* at 737.

40. *Id.* at 712.

41. *Id.* at 713.

42. *Id.*

43. *Supra,* note 5, at 244.

44. *Id.* at 249. Also see David G. Jennings, "The Newsman's Privilege and the Constitution," 23 *South Carolina Law Review* 453 (1971).

45. *Supra,* note 1, at 715.

46. *Id.* at 742.

47. *Id.* at 709.

48. *Id.*

49. *Supra,* note 1, at 710.

50. Lawrence R. Velvel, "The Supreme Court Stops the Presses," 22 *Catholic University Law Review* 341 (1973).

51. *Id.* at 342.

42. *Supra,* note 1, at 731.

53. *Id.* at 741.

54. *Watkins* v. *United States,* 354 U.S. 178.

55. *NAACP* v. *Alabama,* 357 U.S. 449 (1958).

56. *Supra,* note 1, at 719.

57. *Id.* at 722.

58. *Supra,* note 25, at 6.

59. *Supra,* note 1, at 742.

60. *Id.* at 744.

61. *Id.* at 692.

62. U.S. House of Representatives, *Hearings on Newsmen's Privilege Before Subcommittee Number Three of the Committee on the Judiciary,* 93rd Cong., 1st. sess., 1973, p. 490.

63. *Supra,* note 1, at 721.

64. *Sweezy* v. *New Hampshire,* 354 U.S. 245 (1957).

65. *Supra,* note 1, at 690.

66. *Id.* at 684.

67. *Supra,* note 5, at 247.

68. David A. Marcello, "Freedom of the Press: The Journalist's Right to Maintain the Secrecy of His Confidential Sources," 45 *Tulane Law Review* 625, (1971).

69. *Supra,* note 1, at 698.

70. *Id.* at 697.

71. *Supra,* note 5, at 248.

72. *Id.*

73. *Supra,* note 1, at 733.

74. Vince Blasi, "The Newsman's Privilege: An Empirical Study," 70 *Michigan Law Review* 229 (1971).

75. *Supra,* note 1, at 694.

76. *Supra,* note 74, p. 252.

77. *Id.* at 268.

78. *Id.* at 271.

79. *Id.*

80. *Supra,* note 74, p. 283.

81. *Id.* at 284.

82. United States Senate, *Hearings on Newsmen's Privilege Before the Subcommittee on Constitutional Rights of the Committee on the Judiciary,* 93rd Cong., 1st sess., 1973, p. 142.

83. *Id.*

84. James A. Guest and Alan L. Stanzler, "The Constitutional Argument for Newsmen Concealing Their Sources," 64 *Northwestern University Law Review* 18 (1969).

85. *Supra,* note 1, at 694.

86. *Supra,* note 84.

87. *Id.* at 45, 46.

88. *Supra,* note 1, at 699.

89. *Supra,* note 84, at 47.

90. *Supra,* note 1, at 746.

91. *Id.* at 722.

92. *Id.*

93. *Supra,* note 1, at 724.

94. *Id.* at 736.

95. The reasons included: judicial arguments that no confidential relationships existed (Dan and Barnes) (Lewis) (Lightman), the source had already been disclosed (Bridge), scholars are not protected (Popkin), and the privilege does not extend to photographs (McGowan).

96. *Supra,* note 62, Testimony of Peter J. Bridge, at 69.

97. *Brown* v. *Commonwealth,* 214 Va. 755, 204 S.E. 2d 429 (1974).

98. *State* v. *St. Peter,* Vermont, 315 A. 2d 254 (1974).

99. *Supra,* note 97.

100. *Baker* v. *F. & F. Investment,* 339 F. Supp. 942, 943 (S.D.N.Y. 1972).

101. *Id.* at 943.

102. 470 F. 2d at 784.

103. *Democratic National Committee* v. *McCord,* 356 F. Supp. 1394 (D.D.C. 1973).

104. *Garland* v. *Torre,* 259 F. 2d 545, 548 (2d Cir. 1958).

105. *Supra,* note 103.

106. *Supra,* note 103, at 1397.

107. "Newsmen's Privilege Against Compulsory Disclosure of Sources in Civil Suits—Toward an Absolute Privilege?" 45 *University of Colorado Law Review* 184 (1973). Also see "Constitutional Law—Newsmen's Privilege: A Challenge to Branzburg *Baker* v. *F & F Investment,*" 53 *Boston University Law Review* 474 (1973).

108. Editorial: "A New Setback," *Fresno Bee,* November 4, 1977. p. A14.

109. "Judge Postpones Editor's Jail Term: Mulls Tougher Penalty," *Fresno Bee,* November 12, 1977, p. A3.

110. Benno C. Schmidt, Jr., "Beyond the Caldwell Decision: II The Decision Is Tentative," 11 *Columbia Journalism Review* 25 (1972). Also see "Newsmen's Privilege—Where to from Here?" 11 *Publishing, Entertaining, Advertising and Allied Fields Law Quarterly* 479 (1973), and William F. Stewart "The Newsman's Source Privilege—a Balancing of Interests," 2 *University of San Fernando Law Review* 95 (1973).

111. *Supra,* note 50, at 324. Also see Norman E. Isaacs, "Beyond the Caldwell

Decision—There May Be Worse to Come from This Court?'' 11 *Columbia Journalism Review* 18 (1972), or William S. Hurst, "Has Branzburg Buried the Underground Press?'' 8 *Harvard Civil Rights—Civil Liberties Law Review* 181 (1973), and "Public and Press Rights of Access to Prisoners After *Branzburg* and *Mandel,''* 82 *Yale Law Journal* 1337 (1973), and "The Newsman's Privilege After *Branzburg* v. *Hayes:* Whither Now?'' 64 *Journal of Criminal Law and Criminology* 218 (1973).

112. Petition for a Writ of Certiorari, *Farr* v. *Superior Court of Los Angeles County,* U.S. Supreme Court, October Term 1971, No. 71-1642, 168, 169 and *Joe Rosato, William K. Patterson, George F. Gruner and Jim Bort* v. *Superior Court of Fresno County* Petition for Writ of Certiorari and Request of Stay Before Court of Appeal of the State of California (Fifth App. Dist) 5 Civil No. 2623.

113. *Bursey* v. *United States* 466 F. 2d 1059 (9th Cir. 1972).

114. 18 U.S.C. ss 871 (1970).

115. "Constitutional Law—First and Fifth Amendments—Grand Jury Witnesses May Assert First Amendment Rights of Press and Association as a Basis for Refusing to Answer Questions—Immunity Extends Only to Subjects Specifically Mentioned in a Grant of Immunity—*Bursey* v. *United States,''* 48 *New York University Law Review* 171 (1973).

CHAPTER 6

1. In chronological order of passage they are: Maryland (1896), New Jersey (1933), Alabama (1935), California (1935), Kentucky (1936), Arkansas (1936), Arizona (1937), Pennsylvania (1937), Indiana (1941), Ohio (1941), Montana (1943), Michigan (1949), New Mexico (1953), Alaska (1967), Nevada (1969), Louisiana (1970), New York (1970), Illinois (1971), Nebraska (1973), Oregon (1973), North Dakota (1973), Tennessee (1973), Rhode Island (1973), Minnesota (1973), Delaware (1974), Tennessee (1975).

2. U.S. House of Representatives. *Hearings on Newsmen's Privilege Before Subcommittee Number Three of the Committee on the Judiciary,* 93rd Cong., 1st. sess., 1973, pp. 290, 291.

3. *Id.*

4. Cal. Code Civ. Proc. Ann. ss 1881 (6) (Deering 1946).

5. *Id.*

6. Cal. Evidence Code ss 1070 (West 1966).

7. Ct. of App., 5th App. Dist. 5 Civil No. 2623 "Exhibit A."

8. Ky. Rev. Stat. ss 421.100 (1969).

9. Md. Ann. Code Art. 35, ss 2. (1971).

10. N. M. Stat. Ann. ss 20-1-12.1 (1953, 1967 rev.).

11. Ohio Rev. Code Ann. ss 2739.12 (1953) (Supp. 1966).

12. Pa. Stat. Ann. Tit. 28, 330 (1969, 1970 Cum. Supp.).

13. Charles W. Whalen, Jr., *Your Right to Know* (New York: Random House, 1973), pp. 54, 55.

14. *Supra,* note 9.

15. "Summary of State 'Shield' Laws Presently in Effect," *Congressional Digest* 132 (May 1973).

16. Frank J. Donner and Eugene Cerruti, "The Grand Jury Network: How the Nixon Administration Has Secretly Perverted a Traditional Safeguard of Individual Rights," 214

The Nation 5 (January 3, 1972). Paul J. Buser "The Newsman's Privilege: Protection of Confidential Sources of Information Against Government Subpoenas," 15 *Saint Louis University Law Journal* 183 (1970).

17. John B. Kuhns "Reporters and Their Sources: The Constitutional Right to a Confidential Relationship," 80 *The Yale Law Journal* 321 (1970).

18. *In re Grunow,* 84 N.J.L. 235, 236, 85A. 1011 (1913).

19. *State of New York Law Revision Commission,* Leg. Doc. No. 65(A), 1949, 22.

20. *In re Goodfader's Appeal,* 45 Hawaii 317, 319, 167 P.2d 472 (1961).

21. *State* v. *Buchanan,* 250 Ore. 244, 436 P.2d 729, *cert. denied,* 392 U.S. 905 (1968).

22. Petition for a Writ of Certiorari, *In re Pappas,* U.S. Supreme Court, October Term, 1970, No. 70-94, 12a.

23. David K. Shipler "Model Newsmen's Privilege Law Being Drafted," *New York Times* March 26, 1973, p. 1.

24. *Id.*

25. *Id.*

26. *Id.*

27. *Supra,* note 2, at 294.

28. *Id.*

29. United States Senate. *Hearings on Newsmen's Privilege Before the Subcommittee on Constitutional Rights of the Committee on the Judiciary,* 93rd Cong., 1st. sess., 1973, p. 721.

30. *Supra,* note 2, p. 63.

31. Arkansas, Colorado, Georgia, Hawaii, Idaho, Illinois, Kansas, Louisiana, Michigan, Minnesota, Missouri, Montana, New York, North Carolina, North Dakota, Vermont, Virginia, Washington, and West Virginia. *Supra,* note 27, at 721.

32. Alabama, California, Kentucky, Maryland, Oregon, Tennessee, and Texas. *Supra,* note 27, pp. 721, 722.

33. *Ex parte Sparrow,* 14 F.R.D. 351 N.D. Ala. (1953).

34. *Supra,* note 27, at 721.

35. Petition for Certiorari, *Branzburg* v. *Hayes,* U.S. Supreme Court, October Term 1970, No. 70-85, 67.

36. *Lightman* v. *State,* 15 Md. App. 713, at 714–715 (1972).

37. *Supra,* note 21.

38. *Supra,* note 27, at 722.

39. *Supra,* note 29, at 722.

40. Connecticut, Maine, New Mexico, New Hampshire, Delaware, Rhode Island, Wyoming, and Ohio. *Supra,* note 27, p. 722, 723.

41. *Id.* at 722.

42. *Id.*

43. *Id.* at 723.

44. *Id.*

45. *Supra,* note 2, at 195–206.

46. *Supra,* note 29, at 154.

47. *Supra,* note 2, at 475.

48. *Id.* at 476.

49. *Id.* at 455.

50. *Id.* at 454.

51. *Id.*
52. *Id.* at 328.
53. *Supra,* note 2, at 329.
54. *Supra,* note 2, p. 9.
55. *Supra,* note 29, at 713.
56. *Id.* at 718.
57. *Supra,* note 2, p. 297.
58. *Id.* at 299.
59. *Id.*
60. *Id.*
61. *Id.* at 314.
62. *Id.* at 300.
63. *Id.*
64. *Id.*
65. *Id.*
66. *Id.*
67. *Id.* at 301.
68. *Id.*
69. *Id.* at 315.
70. *Id.* at 301.
71. *Id.*
72. *Id.* at 302.
73. *Id.*
74. *Id.*
75. *Id.*
76. *Id.* at 304.
77. *Id.*
78. *Supra,* note 2, p. 305.
79. *Id.*
80. *Id.* at 306.
81. *Id.*
82. *Id.* at 307.
83. *Id.*
84. *Id.*
85. *Id.* at 308.
86. *Id.*
87. *Id.* at 309.
88. *Id.*
89. *Id.*
90. *Id.*
91. *Id.* at 309, 310.
92. *Id.* at 310.
93. *Id.* at 311.
94. *Id.*
95. *Id.*
96. *Id.* at 312.
97. *Id.*
98. *Id.* at 313.

99. *Id.*

100. *Id.* at 315.

101. *Id.* at 313.

102. *Id.* at 314.

103. *Id.*

104. *Id.* at 315.

105. *Id.* at 317.

106. *Id.* at 314.

107. Judith A. Smith "The Reporter's Right to Shield His 'Reliable' Source," 11 *Publishing, Entertainment, Advertising, and Allied Fields Law Quarterly* 502 (1973).

108. Wayne C. Dabb, Jr., and Peter A. Kelley "The Newsman's Privilege: Protection of Confidential Associations and Private Communications," 4 *Journal of Law Reform* 97 (1970).

109. Edward L. Graf "Newsmen's Privilege—Where to from Here?" 11 *Publishing, Entertainment, Advertising, and Allied Fields Law Quarterly* 482 (1973). Also see Paul J. Buser "The Newsman's Privilege: Protection of Confidential Sources of Information Against Government Subpoenas," 15 *Saint Louis University Law Journal* 197 (1970), and *supra,* note 102, pp. 96, 97.

110. *Id.,* Graf and Buser, at 198. Also see Peter J. Goldsworthy, "The Claim to Secrecy of News Source: A Journalistic Privilege?" 9 *Osgoode Hall Law Journal* 166, 167 (1971).

111. Talbot D'Alemberte "Journalists Under the Axe: Protection of Confidential Sources of Information," 6 *Harvard Journal on Legislation* 327—30 (1969).

112. "Confidential News Source Legislation by State," 24 *RTNDA Bulletin,* 6, 7 (May 1970).

113. Arthur B. Hanson, *An Analysis of State Newsmen's Privilege Legislation and Cases Arising Thereunder* (Washington, D.C. 1972).

114. *Id.* at 1.

115. *Id.* at 2.

116. Ark. Stat. Ann. ss 43-917 (1964).

117. Pa. Stat. Ann. Tit. 28, 330 (1969, 1970 Cum Supp.)

118. *Id.*

119. Ohio Rev. Code Ann. ss 2739.12 (1953).

120. Michigan Stat. Ann. ss 28.945 (1) and N.J. Stat. Ann. Tit. 2A, ch. 84A, ss 21, 29 (Supp. 1969).

121. Cal. Evid. Code Ann. ss 1070 (West Supp. 1971).

122. *Supra,* note 113, at 10.

123. Ind. Ann. Stat. ss 2-1733 (1968).

124. *Supra,* note 121.

125. Ala. Code Recompiled, Tit. 7, ss 370 (1960).

126. *Supra,* note 117.

127. *Id.*

128. *Supra,* note 113, at 21.

129. *Supra,* note 119.

130. Alaska Stat. ss 09.25.150-220 (1967, 1970 Cum Supp.)

131. N.Y. Civ. Rights Law ss 79-h (McKinney 1970).

132. *In re WBAI-FM,* 68 Misc. 2d 355, 326 N.Y.S. 2d 434 (1971).

133. Arkansas, Alabama, Alaska, Arizona, Illinois, Indiana, Kentucky, Louisiana,

Maryland, Montana, Nevada, New Jersey, New Mexico, Ohio, and Pennsylvania.

134. New York, Michigan, and California.

135. *Supra,* note 113, at 34.

136. Alaska, New Mexico, and Louisiana.

137. Petition for a Writ of Certiorari, *Bridge* v. *New Jersey,* U.S. Supreme Court, October Term, 1972, No. 72-923, 55a–57a.

158. *Supra,* note 2, at 70.

139. Alaska, *Supra,* note 113, at 50.

140. *Lipps* v. *State,* Ind., 21 Ind. Dec. 342, 258 N.E. 2nd 40 (1970).

141. *People* v. *Wolfe,* 69 Misc 2d 256, 329 N.Y.S. 2nd 291 (S. Ct. 1972).

142. *Supra,* note 117.

CHAPTER 7

1. *Hearings on Newsmen's Privilege Before the Subcommittee on Constitutional Rights of the Senate Committee on the Judiciary,* 93rd Cong., 1st sess., 1973, p. 387.

2. Charles W. Whalen, Jr., *Your Right to Know* (New York: Random House, 1973), p. 175.

3. *Id.* at 176.

4. *Hearings Before the Subcommittee on Constitutional Rights of the Committee on the Judiciary, U.S. Senate,* 92nd Cong., 1st. and 2d sess., 1971 and 1972, pp. 23–24, 336–37.

5. Sam J. Ervin, Jr., "In Pursuit of a Press Privilege," 11 *Harvard Journal on Legislation* 255 (1974).

6. *Caldwell* v. *United States,* 434 F. 3d 1081, 1086 (1970).

7. President's News Conference of May 1, 1971, in 7 *Weekly Comp. Press. Doc.* 703, 705 (1971).

8. *Supra,* note 4.

9. *Hearings on Newsmen's Privilege Before Subcommittee No. 3 of the House Committee on the Judiciary,* 92nd Cong., 2nd sess., 1972.

10. *Branzburg* v. *Hayes,* 408 U.S. 665 (1972).

11. *Supra,* note 1, at 412.

12. *Id.* at 435.

13. *Hearings on Newsmen's Privilege Before Subcommittee No. 3 of the House Committee on the Judiciary,* 93rd Cong., 1st. sess., p. 618 (1973).

14. *Supra,* note 1, at 452.

15. Petition for Writ of Certiorari, *Bridge* v. *New Jersey,* U.S. Supreme Court, October Term, 1972, No. 72-923, 55a57a.

16. Petition for Writ of Certiorari, *Farr* v. *Superior Court of Los Angeles County,* U.S. Supreme Court, October Term 1971, No. 71-1642, 168, 169.

17. *Supra,* note 9, at 195.

18. *Supra,* note 13, at 294.

19. *Supra,* note 5, at 258.

20. *Id.* at 259.

21. *Id.*

22. *Id.* at 261.

23. *Id.*

24. *Supra,* note 13, at 589.

25. *Supra,* note 13, at 449, 613.

26. *Supra,* note 1, at 256.

27. *Supra,* note 13, at 591.

28. *Id.* at 661.

29. *Supra,* note 1, at 409.

30. *Supra,* note 13, at 598, 618.

31. *Id.* at 29.

32. *Id.* at 131.

33. *Id.* at 441.

34. Paul Nejelski and Lindsey Miller Lerman, "A Researcher-Subject Testimonial Privilege: What to do Before the Subpoena Arrives," 1971 *Wisconsin Law Review* 1085 (1971).

35. *Supra,* note 1, at 126.

36. *Supra,* note 13, at 476; also see p. 516. *Supra,* note 1, at 683.

37. *Supra,* note 13, at 604, 653.

38. *Deltec, Inc.* v. *Dun and Bradstreet, Inc.* 187 F. Supp. 788 (N.D. Ohio 1960).

39. *Supra,* note 13, at 438.

40. *Id.* at 33.

41. *Id.* at 82, 83.

42. John B. Kuhns, "Reporters and Their Sources: The Constitutional Right to a Confidential Relationship," 80 *The Yale Law Journal* 365 (1970).

43. Vince Blasi, "Privilege in a Time of Violence," 221 *The Nation* 655 (December 21, 1970).

44. *Branzburg* v. *Hayes,* 408 U.S. 703, 704 (1972).

45. *Supra,* note 13, at 129.

46. Senatorial bills by Schweiker, Cranston, Weicker, Hatfield, Mondale, Byrd, Eagleton, and Ervin. *Supra,* note 1, pp. 409–63. House bills by Kuykendall, Waldie, Abzug, Helstoski, Maraziti, Mills, Bell, Danielson, Hillis, Pepper, Wilson, Whalen, Stanton, Bevill, Dellums, Boland, Johnson, Coughlin, Meeds, Reid, Brooks, Fascell, Findley, Giaimo, Mathis, Mitchell, Patten, Hudnut, Bingham, Crane, Matsunaga, Roybal, Anderson (Calif.), Grasso, Broomfield, Anderson, (Ill.), Cohen, and Drinan. *Supra,* note 13, at 588–754.

47. Schweiker, Cranston, Hatfield, Mondale, Byrd, Eagleton, Ervin, Waldie, Abzug, Helstoski, Mills, Bell, Danielson, Pepper, Bevill, Dellums, Boland, Meeds, Reid, Findley, Mathis, Mitchell, Hudnut, Crane, Matsunaga, Grasso, Broomfield, and Anderson of Illinois.

48. Kuykendall, Maraziti, Hillis, Wilson, Stanton, Johnson, Fascell, Patten, Bingham, Roybal, Anderson of California, Brooks, and Drinan.

49. *Supra,* note 13, at 588.

50. *Id.* at 661.

51. *Id.* at 742.

52. *Id.* at 614.

53. *Supra,* note 45.

54. Weicker, Hatfield, Byrd, Helstoski, Pepper, Broomfield, Whalen, Bevill, Boland, Coughlin, Meeds, Findley, Giaimo, Mathis, Mitchell, and Crane.

55. Coughlin, *supra,* note 13, at 640., Giaimo, p. 670., Cohen, p. 734.

56. *Supra,* note 42, at 345.

57. *Id.*

58. William F. Stewart, "The Newsman's Source Privilege—a Balancing of In-

terests," 2 *University of San Fernando Valley Law Review* 105 (1973).

59. *Id.*

60. *Id.*

61. *Branzburg* v. *Pound,* 461 S.W. 2d 348 (Ky. 1971).

62. In 1973 Nebraska enacted a privilege statute that expressly excepted from its application witnesses to crimes (1973). Laws of Neb. 957.

63. *Supra,* note 13, p. 82. On "outtakes" also see David A. Marcello, "Freedom of the Press: The Journalist's Right to Maintain the Secrecy of His Confidential Sources," 45 *Tulane Law Review* 622 (1971).

64. *Id.* at 80.

65. James D. Hendersen, "The Protection of Confidences: A Qualified Privilege for Newsmen," 1971 *Law and the Social Order* 392 (1971).

66. *Zurcher* v. *The Stanford Daily,* 46 LW 4547 (1978).

67. Charles Long, "Are News Sources Drying Up?" 61 *The Quill* 12 (March 1973).

68. J. H. Wigmore, 8 Evidence ss 2286 at 537 (3rd ed. 1940).

69. Cal. Evid. Code Ann. ss 1070 (West Supp. 1971).

70. Robert Rawitch, "KPFK Manager Jailed After Failing to Give Up SLA Tape," *Los Angeles Times,* June 20, 1974, Part I, p. 3.

71. *Supra,* note 13, at 225.

72. Maraziti, Waldie, Wilson, Johnson, Reid, Rascell, Patten, Bingham, Anderson of California, Grasso, Cranston, Weicker, Mondale, Ervin.

73. Helstoski, Mills, Danielson, Hillis, Stanton, Dellums, Boland, Coughlin, Meeds, Brooks, Findley, Mitchell, Hudnut, Crane, Roybal, Broomfield, and Schweiker.

74. Bevill, Mathis, and Hatfield.

75. Bell, Pepper, Matsunaga, Anderson of Illinois, Cohen, Drinan, and Eagleton.

76. Whalen, Giaimo, and Byrd.

77. *Supra,* note 13, at 246.

78. *Id.*

79. *Id.* at 74.

80. *Id.* at 14, 15, 79.

81. *Id.* at 196.

82. *Id.,* Coughlin, at 640, Giaimo, p. 670, and Grasso, p. 710.

83. *Supra,* note 1, Weicker, at 419; Mondale, at 435.

84. *Id.* at 178.

85. *Id.* at 179.

86. Article I, Section 8, Clause 3: "To regulate commerce with Foreign Nations, and *among the several States,* and with the Indian tribes . . . " (emphasis added).

87. *Heart of Atlanta Motel, Inc.* v. *U.S.,* 397 U.S. 241 (1964). *Stewart Die Casting Corporation* v. *N.L.R.B.,* 132 F. 2d 801 (7th Cir. 1942).

88. 15 C.J.S. Commerce ss 98.

89. Hartke, Kuykendall, Waldie, Findley, Mathis, Mitchell, Cranston, Mondale, Maraziti, Wilson, Johnson, Fascell, Patten, Danielson, and Waldie II, *supra,* note 1, p. 682.

90. Abzug, Hillis, Stanton, Dellums, Whalen, Bevill, Boland, Meeds, Helstoski, Bell, Pepper, Weicker, Coughlin, Giaimo, Schweiker, Hatfield, Mills, Reid, Brooks, and Stanton II.

91. *Supra,* note 13 at 382

92. *Id.* at 408.

93. *Supra,* note 13, at 91.

94. Fourteenth Amendment, Section 5: "The Congress shall have the power to enforce, by appropriate legislation, the provisions of this article."

95. *Gitlow* v. *New York,* 268 U.S. 652 (1925). *Murdock* v. *Commonwealth of Pennsylvania,* 319 U.S. 105 (1943). *Grossjean* v. *American Press Co.,* 297 U.S. 233 (1936).

96. *Katzenbach* v. *Morgan,* 384 U.S. 614 (1966).

97. *Branzburg* v. *Hayes,* 408 U.S. 665.

98. *Id.* at 706.

99. *Supra,* note 13, at 135.

100. *Id.* at p. 53.

101. *Id.*

102. *Supra,* note 13, at 10.

103. *Id.* at 478.

104. *Id.* at 331.

105. *Id.* at 271.

106. *In re Bridge* (N.J. 1972), 295 A 2d 3.

107. *In re Howard,* 136 C.A. 2d 816, 289 P 2d 537 (1955).

108. Stephen F. Peifer, "State Newsman's Privilege Statutes: A Critical Analysis," 49 *Notre Dame Lawyer* 154 (1973).

109. Helstoski, Pepper, Whalen, Bevill, Boland, Coughlin, Findley, Giaimo, Mathis, Mitchell, Crane, Grasso, Broomfield, Drinan, Schweiker, Cranston, Weicker, Mondale, Eagleton, and Ervin.

110. *Supra,* note 13, at 633.

111. The application shall be granted only if the court after hearing the parties determines that the person seeking the information has shown by clear and convincing evidence that (1) there is probable cause to believe that the person from whom the information is sought has information that is clearly relevant to a specific probable violation of law; (2) the informaiton sought cannot be obtained by alternative means; and (3) there is a compelling and overriding national interest in the information.

112. *Supra,* note 13, at 342.

113. *Supra,* note 109.

114. *Supra,* note 13, at 461.

115. *Id.* at 473.

116. *Id.* at 460.

117. *Id.* at 126.

118. *Supra,* note 112.

119. *Supra,* note 5, at 261.

120. *Id.* at 265.

121. "The Case for a Shield Law," *The Boston Globe,* January 27, 1973; Brit Hume, "A Chilling Effect on the Press," *New York Times Magazine,* December 17, 1972; A. M. Rosenthal, "The Press Needs a Slogan: 'Save the First Amendment!' " *New York Times Magazine,* February 11, 1973; "A Shield for Your Right," *Newsday,* February 1, 1973; "Who's Hobbling the Press?" 167 *The New Republic* 6 (December 16, 1972).

122. Lewis H. Lapham, "The Temptation of a Sacred Cow," 24 *Harper's* 43 (August 1973).

123. *Id.*

124. *Id.*

125. Id. at 44.

126. *Id.* at 46.

127. Id.

128. *Id.* at 48.

129. *Supra,* note 1, at 80.

130. Clark Mollenhoff, "Let's Take a Closer Look at 'Shield' Laws," *Human Events,* February 24, 1973.

131. William Loeb, "A Shield for Liars," *The Manchester Union Leader,* January 20, 1973.

132. Vermont Royster, "Dubious Shield," *supra,* note 1, p. 642.

133. Kenneth Crawford, "The Press Can Defend Its Own Freedom," *Washington Post,* March 18, 1973.

134. John S. Knight, "Shield Laws Can Be Risky: First Amendment Protects Best," *Charlotte Observer,* March 18, 1973.

135. *Supra,* note 5, at 271.

136. "Media Groups Back News Shield Bill: But Not 'Ideal Solution,' " *Fresno Bee,* April 25, 1975, p. A10.

137. H.R. 215, 94th Cong., 1st. sess. (1975).

138. *Id.*

139. Mark Neubauer, "The Newsman's Privilege," 24 *UCLA Law Review* 189 (1976).

140. *Branzburg* v. *Hayes,* 408 U.S. 665 (1972).

141. *Supra,* note 139 at 191.

142. "U.S. Asks Court O.K. Newspaper Raids," *Fresno Bee,* January 17, 1978, p. 1.

143. Ira R. Allen, "Senators Eye Bills to Protect Media in 'News Search' Rule," *Fresno Bee,* June 25, 1978, p. A10.

144. Jim Mann, "Supreme Court Rules Prisons May Bar Press and Public," *Los Angeles Times,* June 27, 1978, Part I, p. 6.

CHAPTER 8

1. *Report of the National Advisory Committee on Civil Disorders* (1968).

2. *Id.* at 10.

3. *Id.* at 206.

4. *Id.* at 10.

5. *Supplemental Studies for the National Advisory Committee on Civil Disorders,* Table V-d, p. 48 (1968).

6. *Caldwell* v. *United States,* 434 F. 2d 1081, 1088 9th Cir. (1970).

7. Kenneth C. Bryant, "Newsmen's Immunity Needs a Shot in the Arm," 11 *Santa Clara Lawyer* 62 (1970).

8. Address by Ben Bagdikian, national news editor of the *Washington Post,* Annual Meeting of the Association for Education in Journalism, 103 *Editor and Publisher* 11 (August 22, 1970).

9. 92 Kentucky S. Ct. 2646, 2650, n. 5.

10. Paul Nejelski and Lindsey Miller Lerman, "A Researcher-Subject Testimonial Privilege: What to Do Before the Subpoena Arrives," 1971 *Wisconsin Law Review* 1120 (1971).

11. Vince Blasi, ''The Newsman's Privilege: An Empirical Study,'' 70 *Michigan Law Review* 254 (1971).

Bibliography

Official Documents

Governor's Memorandum, N.Y. Sess. Laws 1970, at 3112.

President's News Conference of May 1, 1971, in 7 *Weekly Comp. Press. Doc.* 703, 705 (1971).

Report of the National Advisory Committee on Civil Disorders (1968).

Supplemental Studies for the National Advisory Committee on Civil Disorders, Table V-d at 48 (1968).

U.S. Department of Justice Memorandum No. 692, Department of Justice, Washington, D.C.

U.S. House of Representatives. *Hearings on Newsmen's Privilege Before Subcommittee Number Three of the Committee on the Judiciary,* 92nd Cong., 2d. sess., 1972.

U.S. House of Representatives. *Hearings on Newsmen's Privilege Before Subcommittee Number Three of the Committee on the Judiciary,* 93rd Cong., 1st. sess., 1973.

U.S. House of Representatives. *Hearings on Subpoenaed Material Re Certain TV News Documentary Programs Before the Special Subcommittee on Investigations of the Committee on Interstate and Foreign Commerce,* 92nd Cong., 1st. sess., 1971.

U.S. Senate. *Hearings on Newsmen's Privilege Before the Subcommittee on Constitutional Rights of the Committee on the Judiciary,* 93rd Cong., 1st. sess., 1973.

United States Department of Justice Memorandum No. 692, Department of Justice, Washington, D.C.

CASES

Alioto v. *Cowles Communications, Inc.* No. 52150 (N.D. Cal., December 4, 1969).

Application on Cepeda, 233 F. Supp. 465 (1964).

Application of Howard, 36 C.A. 2d 816, 289 P. 2d 537 (D.C. of Appeal, 3rd Dist., Cal. 1955).

Associated Press v. *United States,* 326 U.S. 1 (1945).

Baker v. *F. and F. Investment,* 470 F. 2d 778 (2d Cir. 1972).

Baker v. *F. and F. Investment,* 339 F. Supp. 942 (S.D.N.Y. 1972).

Bates v. *Little Rock,* 361 U. 516 (1960).

Beecroft v. *Point Pleasant Print and Publishing Co.,* 82 N.J. Super. 269, 197 A. 2d 416 (1964).

Branzburg v. *Hayes*, 408 U.S. 665 (1972).

Branzburg v. *Pound*, 461 S.W. 2d 348 (Ky. 1971).

Brogan v. *Passaic Daily News*, 22 N.J. 139, 123A 2nd 473 (1956).

Brown v. *Commonwealth*, 214 Va. 755, 204 S.E. 2d 429 (1974).

Burdick v. *United States*, 236 U. 79 (1915).

Bursey v. *United States*, 466 F. 2d 1059 (9th Cir. 1972).

Caldwell v. *United States*, 434 F. 2d 1081 (9th Cir. 1970).

Caldwell v. *U.S.*, 311 F. Supp. 358 (N.D. Cal. 1970), 434 F. 2d 1081 (9th Cir. 1970).

Cervantes v. *Time, Inc.*, 330 F. Supp., 936, 940 (1970).

Cervantes v. *Time, Inc.*, 464 F. 2d 986, 993 (1972).

Countess of Shrewsbury's Case, 12 Coke 94 (1913).

Curtin v. *United States*, 236 U.S. 96 (1915).

DeGregory v. *New Hampshire Attorney General*, 383 U.S. 825 (1966).

Deltec, Inc. v. *Dun and Bradstreet, Inc.*, 187 F. Supp. 465 (S.D.N.Y. 1964).

Deltec, Inc. v. *Dun and Bradstreet, Inc.*, 187 F. Supp. 788 (N.D. Ohio 1960).

Democratic National Committee v. *McCord*, 356 F. Supp. 1394 (D.D.C. 1973).

Dennis v. *United States*, 384 U.S. 855 (1966).

5 *Eliz.*, c. 9 and 12 (1562).

Estes v. *Texas*, 381 U.S. 532, 539 (1965).

Ex Parte Lawrence, 116 Cal. 298, 300, 48 P. 124 (1897).

Ex Parte Sparrow, 14 F.R.D. 351 N.D. Ala. (1953).

Garland v. *Torre*, 259 F. 2d 545, 548 (2d Cir. 1958).

Garland v. *Torre*, 259 F. 2d 545 (2d Cir.), *cert. denied*, 358 U.S. 910 (1958).

Gibson v. *Florida Legislative Investigation Committee*, 372 U.S. 539 (1963).

Gitlow v. *New York*, 268 U.S. 652 (1925).

Grosjean v. *American Press Co.*, 297 U.S. 233 (1936).

Heart of Atlanta Motel, Inc. v. *U.S.*, 397 U.S. 241 (1964).

Hestland v. *State, Ind.*, 27 Ind. Dec. 85, 273 N.E. 2d 282 (1971).

Hill's Trial, 20 How. St. Tr. 1318 (1977).

20 How St. Tr. at 573.

20 How. St. Tr. 586 (1776), *Notable British Trials Series* 256 (Melville ed. 1927).

2 *Hun* 226 (N.Y. 1874).

Hurtado v. *California*, 110 U.S. 516 (1884).

In re Bridge (N.J. 1972), 295 A 2d 3.

In re Caldwell, No. 26, 025 (9th Cir. November 16, 1970).

In re Cohen, 295 Mich. 748 (1940).

In re Dan, N.Y. Sup. Ct. 294 A. 2d at 156.

In re Farr, 36Cal. App. 3d 577, 584, 111 Cal. Rptr. 649, 653 (1974).

In re Goodfader, 45 Hawaii 317, 367 P. 2d. 472 (1961).

In re Groban, 352 U.S. 330, 333 (1957).

In re Grunow, 84 N.J. L. 235, 236, 85 A. 1011 (1913).

In re Howard, 136 C.A. 2d 816, 289 P 2d 537 (1955).

In re Mack, 386 Pa. 251, 265, 126 A. 2d. 679, 685 (1956).

In re Pappas, 266 N.E. 2d 297 (Mass., 1971).

In re WBAI-FM, 68 Misc. 2d 355, 326 N.Y.S. 2d 434 (1971).

In re Wayne 4 Hawaii Dist. Ct. 475 (1914).

Joe Rosato, William K. Patterson, George F. Gruner and Jim Bort v. *Superior Court of Fresno County* 5 Civil 2623.

Katzenbach v. *Morgan,* 384 U.S. 614 (1966).

Lamont v. *Postmaster General,* 381 U.S. 301 (1965).

Lawson and Harrison v. *Odhams Press, Ltd., (1949) 1 K.B. 129, 134*–36 (C.A.).

Lightman v. *State,* 15 Md. App. 713, at 714–15 (1972).

Lipps v. *State, Ind. App.* 258 N.E. 2d 622 (1970).

Lipps v. *State, Ind.,* 21 Ind. Dec. 342, 258 N.W. 2nd 40 (1970).

Miami Herald Publishing Company v. *Tornillo,* 94 S. Ct. 2831 (1974).

Murdock v. *Commonwealth of Pennsylvania,* 319 U.S. 105 (1943).

Murphy v. *Colorado* (Colo. Sup. Ct., unreported opinion), *cert. denied,* 365 U.S. 843 (1961).

NAACP v. *Alabama,* 357 U.S. 449 (1958).

NAACP v. *Button,* 371 U. 415, 438 (1963).

New York Times Co. v. *United States,* 403 U.S. 713 (1971).

Order Quashing Subpoenas, People v. *Dohrn,* No. 69-3808 (Cir. Ct. of Cook County— Crim. Div. June 12, 1970).

People v. *Dohrn,* No. 69-3808 (Cir. Ct. of Cook County, Ill., May 20, 1970), at 8.

People v. *Durrant,* 116 Cal. 179, 220, 48 F. 75 (1897).

People v. *Wolfe,* 69 Misc. 2d 256, 329 N.Y.S. 2nd 291 (S. Ct. 1972).

Petition for Certiorari, *Branzburg* v. *Hayes,* U.S. Supreme Court, October term 1970, No. 70-85, 67.

Petition for Certiorari, *United States* v. *Caldwell,* U. Supreme Court, October Term 1970, No. 70-57, Appendix 17.

Petition for a Writ of Certiorari, *Bridge* v. *New Jersey,* U.S. Supreme Court, October Term, 1972, No. 72-923, 55a-57a.

Petition for a Writ of Certiorari, *Farr* v. *Superior Court of Los Angeles County,* U.S. Supreme Court, October Term 1971, No. 71-1642, 168, 169.

Petition for a writ of Certiorari, *Farr* v. *Superior Court of Los Angeles County,* U.S. Supreme Court, October Term 1971, No. 71-1642, 168, 169, and *Joe Rosato, William K. Patterson, George F. Gruner and Jim Bort* v. *Superior Court of Fresno County* Petition for Writ of Certiorari and Request of Stay before Court of Appeal of the State of California (Fifth App. Dist.) 5 Civil No. 2623.

Petition for a Writ of Certiorari, *In re Pappas,* U.S. Supreme Court, October Term, 1970, No. 70-94, 12a.

Pledger v. *State,* 77 Ga. 242, 245, 2 S.E. 320, (1886).

Plunkett v. *Hamilton,* 136 Ga. 72, 81, 70 S.E. 781 (1911).

Red Lion Broadcasting Co., Inc. v. *Federal Communications Commission,* 395 U.S. 367 (1969).

Reina v. *United States,* 364 U.S. 507 (1960); and *Murphy* v. *Waterfront Commission,* 378 U. 52 (1964).

Rosenberg v. *Carroll, In re Lyons,* 99 F. Supp. 629 (1951).

Roviaro v. *United States* 353 U.S. 53 (1957).

Shelton v. *Tucker,* 364 U.S. 479 (1960).

Sheppard v. *Maxwell,* 384 U.S. 333 (1966).

Sherbert v. *Verner,* 374 U. 398, 408 (1963).

Stanley v. *Georgia,* 394 U.S. 557, 564 (1969).

State v. *Buchanan,* Ore., 436 P. 2d 729, at 731 (1968).

State v. *Buchanan,* 250 Ore. 244, 436 P. 2d 729, *cert. denied,* 392 U.S. 905 (1968).

State v. *Knops,* 49 Wis. 2d 647; 183 N.W. 2d 93, 98 (1971).

State v. *Lightman*, 294 A. 2d 149 (Md. Spec. App. 1972).

State v. *St. Peter*, Vermont, 315 A. 2d 254 (1974).

Stewart Die Casting Corporation v. *N.L.R.B.*, 132 F. 2d 801 (7th Cir. 1942).

Sweezy v. *New Hampshire*, 354 U.S. 234 (1957).

Talley v. *California*, 362 U.S. 60 (1960).

Thomas v. *Collins*, 323 U.S. 516, 530 (1945).

Thompson v. *State*, 284 Minn. 274, 275, 170 N.W. 2d 101 (1969).

Thornhill v. *Alabama*, 310 U.S. 88 (1940).

United States District Court for the District of Massachusetts, *United States* v. *John Doe*, Memorandum of Law of Samuel Lewis Popkin in Support of His Motion for Protective Order, October 27, 1971, p. 13.

United States v. *Caldwell*, 311 F. Supp. at 361–62.

United States v. *Nixon* 94 S. Ct. 3090, 3108 (1974).

United States v. *Rumely*, 345 U.S. 41 (1953).

United States v. *Tucker* 380 F. 2d 206 (2d Cir. 1967).

Watkins v. *United States*, 354 U.S. 178 (1957).

Wieman v. *Updegraff*, 344 U.S. 183 (1952).

Wood v. *Georgia*, 370 U.S. 375, 390 (1962).

BRIEFS

Affidavits of Anthony Ripley, John Kifner, Thomas A. Johnson, Earl Caldwell, and Gerald Fraser, accompanying *Petitioner's Brief, Application of Caldwell*, 311 F. Supp. 358 (N.D. Cal. 1970).

Appellant-Petitioner's Brief in the Supreme Court of the State of Delaware, No. 209, December 22, 1972, 5. (Petition of Charles McGowan.)

Brief for Petitioner, In re Pappas, U.S. Supreme Court, October Term, 1971, No. 70-94, 9.

Brief for Respondent-Appellants, New York v. *Dan and Barnes*, N.Y. Supreme Court, Appellate Division, Fourth Dept., 5, 6.

Brief for Respondent, United States v. *Caldwell*, U.S. Supreme Court, October Term 1971, No. 70-57, 7.

Brief of the American Civil Liberties Union, The American Civil Liberties Union of Northern California, and the American Civil Liberties Union of Southern California, Amici Curiae (In the Supreme Court of the United States, October Term, 1971, No. 70-57) *United States* v. *Caldwell.* at 9 and 10.

In the Supreme Court of the United States, October Term, 1972, No. 72-974, *Samuel L. Popkin* v. *United States*, Motion for Leave to File Brief as *Amicus Curiae* and *Brief of American Anthropological Association, American Political Science Association, and American Sociological Association*, pp. 6–7.

Joe Rosato, William K. Patterson, George F. Gruner and Jim Bort v. *The Superior Court of Fresno County, Brief for Respondent*, Fifth District Court of Appeals, Calif. 5 Civil 2623.

Petition for Writ of Certiorari and Request for Stay, *Rosato, et al.* v. *Superior Court of Fresno County* 5 Civil No. 2623, *Brief for Petitioners*.

U.S. Supreme Court Records. *Amicus Brief of The American Society of Newspaper Editors, Sigma Delta Chi, and Dow Jones and Company, Inc. in Support of Earl Caldwell*, October Term, 1971.

U.S. Supreme Court Records. *Amicus Brief of The Authors League of America, Inc.,* October term, 1971.
U.S. Supreme Court Records. *Brief of the American Civil Liberties Union, The American Civil Liberties Union of Northern California, and The American Civil Liberties Union of Southern California, Amici Curiae,* October Term, 1971.
U.S. Supreme Court Records. *Brief of the New York Times Company, Inc., National Broadcasting Company, Inc., Columbia Broadcasting System, Inc., American Broadcasting Companies, Inc., Chicago Sun-Times, Chicago Daily News, Associated Press Managing Editors Association, Associated Press Broadcasters' Association and Association of American Publishers Inc. as Amici Curiae,* October term, 1971.
U.S. Supreme Court Records. *United States of America v. Earl Caldwell, on Writ of Certiorari to the United States Court of Appeals for the Ninth Circuit, Brief for Respondent,* October term, 1971.
U.S. Supreme Court Records. *United States of America v. Earl Caldwell on Writ of Certiorari to the United States Court of Appeals for the Ninth Circuit. Brief for the Government,* October term, 1971.

STATUTES

Ala. Code tit. 7, ss 370 (1960).
Alaska Stat. ss 09.25.150 (1973).
Ariz. Rev. Stat. Ann ss 12-2237 (Supp. 1974–1975).
Ark. Stat. Ann. ss 43-917 (1964).
Cal. Evid. Code ss 1070 (Deering Supp. 1974).
Del. Code Ann. tit. 10 ss 4320-26 (Supp. 1974).
Ill. Ann Stat. ch. 51, ss 111-19 (Smith-Hurd Supp. 1974).
Ind. Ann Stat. ss 2-1733 (Burns Supp. 1972). Ind. Code 34-3-5-1 (1971).
Ky. Rev. Stat. Ann. ss 421.100 (1969).
La. R.S. 45:1451-54 (Supp. 1974).
Md. Ann. Code art. 35 ss 2 (1971).
Mich. Stat. Ann. ss 28.945 (1) (1972).
Minn. Stat. Ann. ss 595.021-595.025 (Supp. 1973).
Mont. Rev. Codes Ann. ss 93-601-2 (1964).
Laws of Neb. 957.
Nev. Rev. Stat. ss 49.275 (1971).
N.J. Stat. Ann. ss 2A:84A-21, 2A:84A-29 (Supp. 1974–1975).
N.M. Stat. Ann. ss 20-1-12.1 (Supp. 1973).
N.Y. Civ. Rights Law ss 79-h (McKinney Supp. 1973–1974).
N.D. Cent. Code ss 31-01-06.2 (Supp. 1973).
Ohio Rev. Code Ann. ss 2739.12 (Baldwin 1971).
Ore. Laws 62.
Pa. Stat. Ann. tit. 28, ss 330 (Supp. 1974–1975).
R.I. Gen Laws Ann. ss 9-19.1-1 to 9-19.1-3 (Supp. 1973).
Tenn. Code Ann. ss 24-113 (Supp. 1974).

BOOKS

Barron, Jerome A. *Freedom of the Press: For Whom? The Right of Access to Mass Media*. Bloomington: Indiana University Press, 1973.

Bernstein, Carl, and Bob Woodward. *All the President's Men*. New York: Simon and Schuster, 1974.

Boyd, Julian P., ed. *The Papers of Thomas Jefferson*. Princeton, N.J.: Princeton University Press, 1955.

Chalmers, Floyd Sherman. *A Gentleman of the Press: The Biography of Colonel John Bayne MacClean*. Garden City, N.Y.: Doubleday, 1969.

Emerson, Thomas I. *Toward a General Theory of the First Amendment*. New York: Random House, 1963.

Emery, Michael C., and Ted Curtis Smythe, eds. *Readings in Mass Communications Concepts and Issues in the Mass Media*. Dubuque: William C. Brown Co., 1974.

Glessing, Robert J. *The Underground Press in America*. Bloomington: Indiana University Press, 1970.

Hanson, Arthur B. *An Analysis of State Newsmen's Privilege and Cases Arising Thereunder*, Washington, D.C. (November 10, 1972).

Keeton, George Williams, and Georg Schwarzenberger. *Jeremy Bentham and the Law*. Toronto: Carswell Company, Ltd.

Klurfeld, Herman. *Behind the Lines: The World of Drew Pearson*. Englewood Cliffs, N.J.: Prentice-Hall, Inc., 1968.

Krock, Arthur. Memoirs: *Sixty Years on the Firing Line*. New York: Funk and Wagnalls, 1968.

Larrabee, Leonard W., et al., eds. *The Autobiography of Benjamin Franklin*. New Haven, Conn.: Yale University Press, 1964.

Larsen, Egon. *First with the Truth*. New York: Roy Publishers, Inc., 1968.

MacDougall, Curtis Daniel. *Newsroom Problems and Policies*. Lenoir: Smith Printing Co., 1964.

Morris, Richard Brandon, and Louis Leo Snyder, eds., *A Treasury of Great Reporting*. New York: Simon and Schuster, 1949.

Ottley, Roi Vincent. *The Lonely Warrior–the Life and Times of Robert S. Abbott*. Chicago: H. Regnery Co., 1955.

Padover, Saul K., ed. *The Complete Madison*. New York: Harper & Row, 1953.

Pember, Don R. *Privacy and the Press: The Law, the Mass Media, and the First Amendment*. Seattle: University of Washington Press, 1972.

Pritchett, C. Herman. *The American Constitution*. New York: McGraw-Hill, 1968.

Rogers, Henry Wade. *The Law of Expert Testimony*. Albany, N.Y.: Matthew Bender and Company, 1941.

Roszak, Theodore. *The Making of a Counter Culture*. Garden City, N.Y.: Doubleday, 1969.

Seldes, George. *Never Tire of Protesting*. Boston: Stuart Publications, 1968.

Sherwood, Hugh C. *The Journalistic Interview*. New York: Harper & Row, 1969.

Small, William J. *Political Power and the Press*. New York: W. W. Norton, 1972.

Sulzberger, Cyrus Leo. *A Long Row of Candles, Memoirs and Diaries, 1934–1954*. New York: Macmillan, 1969.

Whalen, Charles W., Jr. *Your Right to Know*. New York: Random House, 1973.

Wigmore, John Henry. *Wigmore on Evidence*. Boston: Little Brown and Company, 1961.

Wolff, Robert Paul. *A Critique of Pure Tolerance*. Boston: Beacon Press, Inc., 1965.
Younger, Richard D. *The People's Panel*. Providence, R.I.: Brown University Press, 1963.

ARTICLES

Anderson, Richard E. *"Branzburg* v. *Hayes:* A Need for Statutory Protection of News Sources'' 61 *Kentucky Law Journal* 551 (1973).

Antell, Melvin P. "The Modern Grand Jury: Benighted Supergovernment," 51 *American Bar Association Journal* 154 (1965).

Bagdikian, Ben. "Address to Association for Education in Journalism Annual Meeting,' 103 *Editor and Publisher* 11 (August 22, 1970).

———. "Access—the Only Choice for Mass Media," 48 *Texas Law Review* 766 (1970).

Barron, Jerome A. "Access to the Press—a New First Amendment Right," 80 *Harvard Law Review* 57 (1967).

Baxter, James A. "Constitutional Law: Testimonial Privilege of Newsmen," 55 *Marquette Law Review* 184 (1972).

Beasley, Joseph W. "Newsman's Privilege: The First Amendment Grants None," 25 *University of Florida Law Review* 381 (1973).

Beaver, James E. "Privileged Communications—News Media—a 'Shield Statute' for Oregon," 46 *Oregon Law Review* 99 (1966).

———. "The Newsman's Code, The Claim of Privilege and Everyman's Right to Evidence," 47 *Oregon Law Review* 243 (1968).

Bennett, Richard V. "Constitutional Law: *Branzburg* v. *Hayes,* Must Newsmen Reveal Their Confidential Sources to a Grand Jury?" 8 *Wake Forest Law Review* 567 (1972).

Blasi, Vince. "Privilege in a Time of Violence," 211 *The Nation* 653 (December 21, 1970).

———. "The Newsman's Privilege: An Empirical Study," 70 *Michigan Law Review* 229 (1971).

Block, Stephen M. "Journalist-Informant Privilege: The Government Must Demonstrate Compelling Need for a Journalist's Presence at Secret Grand Jury Proceedings Before His Attendance Can Be Required," 49 *Texas Law Review* 807 (1971).

Boyer, John H. "Supreme Court and the Right to Know," *Freedom of Information Center Report #272 (1971)*.

Bryant, Kenneth C. "Newsman's Immunity Needs a Shot in the Arm," 11 *Santa Clara Lawyer* 56 (1970).

Buser, Paul J. "The Newsman's Privilege: Protection of Confidential Sources of Information Against Government Subpoenas," 15 *Saint Louis University Law Journal* 181 (1970).

Caginalp, Aydin S. "Constitutional Law—First Amendment—Newsman's Privilege," 47 *Tulane Law Review* 1183 (1973).

Caldwell, Earl. "Ask Me. I Know. I Was the Test Case," 55 *Saturday Review* 4 (August 5, 1972).

Carroll, James D. "Confidentiality of Social Science Research Sources and Data: The Popkin Case," 1973 *PS* 268 (1973).

Carter, P. B. "The Journalist, His Informant, and Testimonial Privilege," 35 *New York University Law Review* 1111 (1960).

Cohen, William. "A New Niche for the Fault Principle: A Forthcoming Newsworthiness Privilege in Libel Cases?" 18 *U.C.L.A. Law Review* 371 (1970).

Cohen, Marla. "Shield Legislation in the United States," *Freedom of Information Center Report No. 212* (November 1968).

Coopersmith, Douglas Paul. "Newsmen's Privilege—Requiring Newsmen to Testify Before State or Federal Grand Juries Held Not Violative of the First Amendment," 18 *Villanova Law Review* 288 (1972).

Costello, Mary. "Newsmen's Rights," 2 *Editorial Research Reports* 949 (December 20, 1972).

Cranston, Alan. "First Means First," 9 *Trial* 31 (May/June 1973).

Cronkite, Walter. "Legal Issues Confronting Media Today," 60 *Georgetown Law Journal* 1001 (1972).

Dabb, Wayne C., Jr., and Peter A. Kelley. "The Newsman's Privilege; Protection of Confidential Associations and Private Communications," 4 *University of Michigan Journal of Law Reform* 85 (1970).

D'Alemberte, Talbot. "Journalists Under the Axe: Protection of Confidential Sources of Information," 6 *Harvard Journal on Legislation* 307 (1969).

Defouloy, Elizabeth Allen. "Constitutional Law—Freedom of the Press—Obligation of Reporters, as Citizens, to Respond to a Grand Jury Subpoena and Answer Questions Relevant to a Criminal Investigation" 50 *Journal of Urban Law* 306 (1969).

De Zutter, Henry. "Why SDS Banned Press at Coliseum," 2 *Chicago Journalism Review* 11 (July 1969).

Dixon, Robert G. "The Constitution Is Shield Enough for Newsmen," 60 *American Bar Association Journal* 707 (1974).

Donner, Frank J., and Eugene Cerruti. "The Grand Jury Network: How the Nixon Administration Has Secretly Perverted a Traditional Safeguard of Individual Rights," 214 *The Nation* 5 (Jan. 3, 1972).

Ervin, Sam J., Jr. "In Pursuit of a Press Privilege," 11 *Harvard Journal on Legislation* 233 (1974).

Friendly, Fred W. "Beyond the Caldwell Decision III—Justice White and Reporter Caldwell: Finding a Common Ground," 11 *Columbia Journalism Review* 31 (1972).

Golden, Patrick G. "Absolute Privilege in California: The Scope of the California Civil Code, Section 47(2)," 7 *University of San Francisco Law Review* 176 (1972).

Goldstein, Abraham. "Newsmen and Their Confidential Sources," 162 *The New Republic* 13 (March 21, 1970).

Goldsworthy, Peter J. "The Claim to Secrecy of News Sources: A Journalistic Privilege," 9 *Osgoode Hall Law Journal* 157 (1971).

Goodale, James C. "Branzburg v. Hayes and the Developing Qualified Privilege for Newsmen," 26 *Hastings Law Journal* 709 (1975).

Goodell, Charles E. "Where Did the Grand Jury Go?" 246 *Harper* 14 (May 1973).

Gordan, David. "The Confidences Newsmen Must Keep," 10 *Columbia Journalism Review* 15 (1971).

———. "Newsman's Privilege and the Law," *Freedom of Information Foundation* (August 1974).

Graf, Edward L. "Newsmen's Privilege—Where to from Here?" 11 *Publishing, Entertainment, Advertising and Allied Fields Law Quarterly* 479 (1973).

Graham, Fred P., and Jack C. Landau. "The Federal Shield Law We Need," 11 *Columbia Journalism Review* 26 (1973).

Graham, Roger D. "Constitutional Law—Disclosure of Journalist's Confidential News Sources," 73 *West Virginia Law Review* 318 (1971).

Green, Leon. "The Right to Communicate," 35 *New York University Law Review* 903 (1960).

Greenfield, Meg. "Telling it (Sort of) Like It Is," 83 *Newsweek* 50 (July 22, 1974).

Guest, James A., and Alan L. Stanzler. "The Constitutional Argument for Newsmen Concealing Their Sources," 64 *Northwestern University Law Review* 18 (1969).

Gunther, Gerald. "Newsmen's Privilege to Withhold Information From Grand Jury," 86 *Harvard Law Review* 137 (1972).

Hall, James A., and Stephan C. Jones. "Pappas and Caldwell—the Newsmen's Privilege—Two Judicial Views," 1971 *Massachusetts Law Quarterly* 155 (1971).

Hamilton, William. "Constitutional Law—the First Amendment Does Not Relieve a Newspaper Reporter of the Obligation That All Citizens Have to Respond to a Grand Jury Subpoena and Answer Questions Relevant to a Criminal Investigation," 2 *Texas Southern Law Review* 369 (1973).

Harris, Marjory, and Mary L. Brutocao. "Governmental Privileges: Roadblock to Effective Discovery," 7 *University of San Francisco Law Review* 282 (1973).

Henderson, James D. "The Protection of Confidences: A Qualified Privilege for Newsmen," 1971 *Law and the Social Order* 385 (1971).

Henkin, Louis. "The Right to Know and the Duty to Withhold: The Case of the Pentagon Papers," 120 *University of Pennsylvania Law Review* 271 (1971).

Hurst, William S. "Has Branzburg Buried the Underground Press?" 8 *Harvard Civil Rights–Civil Liberties Law Review* 181 (1973).

Huston, Luther A. "Supreme Court Will Hear Reporter Shield Cases," 104 *Editor and Publisher* 9 (May 8, 1971).

———. "Conflicting Views Presented at House News Shield Hearings," 106 *Editor and Publisher* 9 (February 17, 1973).

———. "Split Views on Immunity Bill Dim Hope for a Full Shield," 106 *Editor and Publisher* 7 (February 24, 1973).

———. "Editors Split Over Need for Absolute Shield Law," 106 *Editor and Publisher* 9 (May 12, 1973).

Isaacs, Norman E. "Beyond the Caldwell Decision—There May Be Worse to Come from This Court," 11 *Columbia Journalism Review* 18 (1972).

J.W.P. III. "The Emerging Constitutional Privilege to Conceal Confidential News Sources," 6 *University of Richmond Law Review* 129 (1971).

Jennings, David G. "The Newsman's Privilege and the Constitution," 23 *South Carolina Law Review* 436 (1971).

Johnson, Lee. "Oregon's Witness Immunity Law," 51 *Oregon Law Review* 573 (1972).

Kuhns, John B. "Reporters and Their Sources," The Constitutional Right to a Confidential Relationship," 80 *Yale Law Journal* 371 (1970).

Ladd, Mason. "Privileges," 1969 *Law and the Social Order* 555 (1969).

Lapham, Lewis H. "The Temptation of a Sacred Cow," 24 *Harper's* 43 (August 1973).

Lewis, Fred R. "Newsman's Privilege—the First Amendment," 25 *University of Miami Law Review* 521 (1971).

Lewis, Scott M. "The Reporter's Privilege: Perspectives on the Constitutional Argument," 32 *Ohio State Law Journal* 340 (1971).

Long, Charles. "Are News Sources Drying Up?" 61 *The Quill* 10 (March 1973).

Lumpp, James A. "Branzburg, Caldwell and Pappas Cases," *Freedom of Information*

Center Report No. 321 (May 1974).

Marcello, David A. "Freedom of the Press: The Journalist's Right to Maintain the Secrecy of His Confidential Sources," 45 *Tulane Law Review* 605 (1971).

Meiklejohn, Alexander. "The First Amendment Is an Absolute," in Phillip B. Kurland (ed.), *The Supreme Court Review* 245 (1961).

Mitchell, John N. "Free Press and Fair Trial: The Subpoena Controversy," 59 *Illinois Bar Journal* 282 (1970).

Mollenhoff, Clark. "Let's Take a Closer Look at 'Shield' Laws," *Human Events*, (February 24, 1973).

Moore, James William, and Helen I. Bendix. "Congress, Evidence and Rulemaking," 84 *The Yale Law Journal* 9 (1974).

Mulvihill, Dennis J. "Caldwell v. United States: The Newsman's Constitutional Privilege," 32 *University of Pittsburgh Law Review* 406 (1971).

Murphy, George H. "The Rights of Newsmen to Protect Their Sources of Information Under California Law," *Legislative Counsel's Opinion* (June 16, 1971).

Nejelski, Paul, and Lindsey Miller Lerman. "A Researcher-Subject Testimonial Privilege: What to Do Before the Subpoena Arrives," 1971 *Wisconsin Law Review* 1085 (1971).

Nelson, Harold L. "The Newsmen's Privilege Against Disclosure of Confidential Sources and Information," 24 *Vanderbilt Law Review* 667 (1971).

Nisely, Robert L. "Evidence: New York Shield Law Applies Only When Confidential Relationship Exists Between a Newsman and His Source," 23 *Buffalo Law Review* 529 (1974).

Norton, Nathan, Jr. "Privileges," 27 *Arkansas Law Review* 200 (1973).

Ortwein, Bernard M. "Evidence—Privileged Communication—In re Pappas," 6 *Suffolk University Law Review* 184 (1971).

Peifer, Stephen F. "State Newsman's Privilege Statutes: A Critical Analysis," 49 *Notre Dame Lawyer* 150 (1973).

Pike, Chan Poyner. "Constitutional Law—Evidence—No Testimonial Privilege for Newsmen," 51 *North Carolina Law Review* 562 (1973).

Rosen, Sanford Jay. "What's Wrong with Grand Juries?" 283–99 *Civil Liberties* 1 (May 1972).

Rupp, Carla Marie. "Investigative Reporters Reveal How They Do It," 108 *Editor and Publisher* 12 (January 11, 1975).

Ruvolo, Ignazio J. "Newsman's Immunity Statute—a Comparison to Statutory Form," 8 *San Diego Law Review* 110 (1971).

S. P. M. "Reporter's Privilege Under the First Amendment," 36 *Albany Law Review* 404 (1972).

Schaeffer, James S., and Joe A. Moore. "Federal Rules of Evidence," 9 *Trial* 39 (November/December 1973).

Schmidt, Benno C., Jr. "Beyond the Caldwell Decision: 11 'The Decision Is Tentative,' " 11 *Columbia Journalism Review* 25 (1972).

Sebastian, Raymond F. "Obscenity and the Supreme Court: Nine Years of Confusion," 19 *Stanford Law Review* 167 (1966).

Sharpe, Richard O. "The Newsman's Qualified Privilege Under the First Amendment," 16 *South Dakota Law Review* 328 (1971).

Sher, Susan Steiner. "Constitutional Law—Requiring Newsmen to Appear and Testify Before Federal and State Grand Juries Does Not Abridge Freedom of Speech or Freedom of Press Guaranteed by First Amendment," 4 *Loyola University Law Journal* 227 (1973).

Sherman, Jeffrey G. "Constitutional Protection for the Newsman's Work Product," 6 *Harvard Civil Rights/Civil Liberties Law Review* 119 (1970).

Sherwood, Margaret. "The Newsman's Privilege: Government Investigations, Criminal Prosecutions and Private Litigation," 58 *California Law Review* 1198 (1970).

Shuford, Bill, Jr. "Newsman's Source Privilege: A Foundation in Policy for Recognition at Common Law," 26 *University of Florida Law Review* 462 (1974).

Smith, Judith A. "The Reporter's Right to Shield His 'Reliable' Source," 11 *Publishing, Entertainment, Advertising, and Allied Fields Law Quarterly* 499 (1973).

Snider, Clyde H. "Public's Stake in Shield Laws," 29 *Missouri Bar Journal* 154 (1973).

Steigleman, Walter A. "Newspaper Confidence Laws," 20 *Journalism Quarterly* 230 (1943).

Stewart, William F. "The Newsman's Source Privilege—a Balancing of Interests," 2 *University of San Fernando Valley Law Review* 95 (1973).

Sytsma, Curl L. "The Newsman's Privilege After Branzburg v. Hayes: Whither Now?" 64 *Journal of Criminal Law and Criminology* 218 (1973).

Teplitzky, Sanford V., and Kenneth A. Weiss. "Newsmen's Privilege Two Years After Branzburg v. Hayes: The First Amendment in Jeopardy," 49 *Tulane Law Review* 417 (1975).

Tinling, Nicholas G. "Newsman's Privilege: A Survey of the Law in California," 4 *Pacific Law Journal* 880 (1973).

Tobin, Richard L. "Reporters, Subpoenas, Immunity and the Court," 54 *Saturday Review* 63 (December 11, 1971).

Tyler, Robert M., and Doris Kaufman. "The Public Scholar and the First Amendment: A Compelling Need for Compelling Testimony?" 40 *George Washington Law Review* (1971/72).

Velvel, Lawrence R. "The Supreme Court Stops the Presses," 22 *Catholic University Law Review* 324 (1972).

Warta, Darrell L. "The Newsmen's Privilege: A Need for Constitutional Protection," 10 *Washburn Law Journal* 387 (1971).

Ways, Max. "What's Wrong with News? It Isn't Enough," 80 *Fortune* 110 (October, 1969).

Weingrad, Ronald Carl. "Constitutional Law—First Amendment Right of Newsmen Not to Reveal Confidential Sources of Information to Grand Jury," 11 *Duquesne University Law Review* 657 (1973).

Weisman, Peter, and Andrew D. Postal. "The First Amendment as Restraint on the Grand Jury Process," 10 *American Criminal Law Review* 671 (1972).

Wright, Skelly J. "Defamation, Privacy, and the Public's Right to Know: A National Problem and a New Approach," 46 *Texas Law Review* 630 (1968).

Zafren, Daniel Hill. "Testimonial Privilege for Representatives of the News Media: A Summary of Recent Court Decisions, Proposed Federal Legislation and Compilation of State Laws," *Congressional Research Service: Library of Congress* (November 14, 1972).

LAW REVIEW NOTES AND COMMENTS

"A Bill of Rights for Grand Juries," 9 *Trial* 55 (1973).

"Assertion of a Journalist's Privilege in Conflict with the Final Judgment Rule in Civil Litigation: Gialde v. Time, Inc.," 1973 *Duke Law Journal* 1063 (1973).

"Bills to Protect Newsmen from Compulsory Disclosures," *American Enterprise Institute for Public Policy Research* (August 17, 1971).

"Branzburg v. Hayes: A Need for Statutory Protection of News Sources," 61 *Kentucky Law Journal* 551 (1972).

"Caldwell v. United States—Journalistic Privilege: A New Dimension to Freedom of the Press," 37 *Brooklyn Law Review* 502 (1971).

"Caldwell v. United States: The Newsman's Constitutional Privilege," 32 *University of Pittsburgh Law Review* 406 (1971).

"A California Privilege Not Covered by the Uniform Rules—Newsmen's Privilege," *California Law Revision Commission,* State Printing Office, vol. 6, p. 481 (1964).

"Chicago Court Defers Contempt Ruling," 64 *Editor and Publisher* 3 (August 4, 1934).

"Compulsory Disclosure of a Newsman's Source: A Compromise Proposal," 54 *Northwestern University Law Review* 243 (1959).

"Confidentiality of News Sources: Emerging Constitutional Protection," 60 *Georgia Law Journal* 867 (1972).

"Confidentiality of News Sources Under the First Amendment," 11 *Stanford Law Review* 541 (1959).

"Constitutional Law—*Branzburg* v. *Hayes*—Must Newsmen Reveal Their Confidential Sources to Grand Juries," 8 *Wake Forest Law Review* 567 (1972).

"Constitutional Law—Conditional Privilege Under the First Amendment—Denial of the Privilege to Credit Reports—*Hood* v. *Dun and Bradstreet, Inc.*" 18 *Harvard Law Journal* 238 (1973).

"Constitutional Law—Evidence—No Testimonial Privilege for the Newsmen," 51 *North Carolina Law Review* 562 (1973).

"Constitutional Law—the First Amendment Does Not Relieve a Newspaper Reporter of the Obligation That All Citizens Have to Respond to a Grand Jury Subpoena and Answer Questions Relevant to a Criminal Investigaion," 2 *Texas Southern University Law Review* 369 (1973).

"Constitutional Law—First and Fifth Amendments—Grand Jury Witnesses May Assert First Amendment Rights of Press and Association as a Basis for Refusing to Answer Questions—Immunity Extends Only to Subjects Specifically Mentioned in a Grant of Immunity—*Bursey* v. *United States*" 48 *New York University Law Review* 171 (1973).

"Constitutional Law—First Amendment—Privilege Not to Appear and Testify Before Grand Jury Granted to Reporter Seeking to Protect Sensitive Source When Government Fails to Establish Compelling Need—*Caldwell* v. *United States,*" 46 *New York University Law Review* 617 (1971).

"Constitutional Law—Freedom of the Press—First Amendment Right of a Newsman Not to Reveal Confidential Information," 9 *Duquesne University Law Review* 506 (1971).

"Constitutional Law—Freedom of the Press—Newsmen Held to Possess No Testimonial Privilege with Respect to Confidential Communications," 41 *Fordham Law Review* 1024 (1973).

"Constitutional Law—Freedom of the Press—Obligation of Reporters as Citizens to Respond to a Grand Jury Subpoena and Answer Questions Relevant to a Criminal Investigation" 50 *Journal of Urban Law* 291 (1972).

"Constitutional Law—Journalist's Privilege Under the First Amendment Guarantee of Freedom of the Press—*Caldwell* v. *United States,*" 2 *Cumberland-Samford Law Review* 223 (1971).

"Constitutional Law—Requiring Newsmen to Appear and Testify Before Federal and State Grand Juries Does Not Abridge Freedom of Speech or Freedom of Press Guaranteed by First Amendment," 4 *Loyola University Law Journal* (Chicago) 227 (1973).

"Constitutional Law—Right to Conceal Identity of News Sources—Difficulties in Formulating and Applying the Right to Actual Situations—*State* v. *Knops,*" 1971 *Wisconsin Law Review* 951 (1971).

"Constitutional Law: Testimonial Privilege of Newsmen," 55 *Marquette Law Review* 184 (1972).

"The Constitutional Right to Anonymity: Free Speech, Disclosure and the Devil," 70 *The Yale Law Journal* 1084 (1961).

"Defense Access to Grand Jury Testimony: A Right in Search of a Standard," 1968 *Duke Law Journal* 566 (1968).

"Fifty-seven Percent Don't Want Newsmen to Name Their Sources," 105 *Editor and Publisher,* 13 (December 9, 1972).

"Fight Over Freedom and Privilege," 101 *Time* 64 (March 5, 1973).

"The First Amendment Overbreadth Doctrine," 83 *Harvard Law Review* 844 (1970).

"First Amendment Protection of the News Media: *Caldwell* v. *United States,*" 3 *Rutgers Camden Law Journal* 46 (1971).

"Flexible Guidelines," 76 *Newsweek* 71 (August 24, 1970).

"Freedom of the Press—Reporter Has No Constitutional Right to Preserve Anonymity of an Informer If Court Orders Disclosure," 82 *Harvard Law Review* 1384 (1969).

"Freedoms of the Press," 83 *Newsweek* 77 (July 8, 1974).

"Gag Orders on the Press," 108 *Editor and Publisher* 1 (January 25, 1975).

"The Grand Jury as an Investigatory Body," 74 *Harvard Law Review* 590 (1961).

"Has Branzburg Buried the Underground Press?," 8 *Harvard Civil Rights/Civil Liberties Law Review* 181 (1973).

"Jailed Newsmen Plead for Confidence Law," 81 *Editor and Publisher* 7 (March 6, 1948).

"The Journalist and His Confidential Source: Should a Testimonial Privilege Be Allowed?" 35 *Nebraska Law Review* 562 (1956).

"The Journalist's Privilege to Withhold the Source of His News," *New York Law Revision Commission* Albany, pp. 33–168 (1949).

"Journalist's Testimonial Privilege," 6 *Michigan Law Review* 184 (1962).

"Judicial Relief for the Newsman's Plight: A Time for Secrecy?" 45 *St. John's Law Review* 484 (1971).

"The Newsman's Privilege After *Branzburg* v. *Hayes;* Whither Now?" 64 *Journal of Criminal Law and Criminology* 218 (1973).

"The Newsman's Privilege: Protection of Confidential Associations and Private Communications," 4 *Journal of Law Reform* 85 (1970).

"A Newsman's Privilege—the First Amendment," 25 *University of Miami Law Review* 521 (1971).

"Newsman's Privilege: The First Amendment Grants None," 25 *University of Florida Law Review* 381 (1973).

"Newsman's Shield Is Not Included in Judicial Rules," 105 *Editor and Publisher* 13 (December 9, 1972).

"Newsmen Have No Privilege Against Compulsory Disclosure of Sources in Civil Suits—Toward an Absolute Privilege?" 45 *University of Colorado Law Review* 173 (1973).

"Newsmen's Privilege—Where to from Here?" 11 *Publishing, Entertaining Advertising and Allied Fields Law Quarterly* 479 (1973).

"Note, The Constitutional Guarantee of Freedom of the Press—Does It Cover the Right to Gather News?," 8 *Journal of Public Law* 596 (1959).

"Note, The Listener's Right to Hear in Broadcasting," 22 *Stanford Law Review* 863 (1970).

"Partial Shield OK'd by House Subcommittee," 106 *Editor and Publisher* 13 (June 23, 1973).

"Press Protection: Why Shield Laws?" 9 *Trial* 30 (May/June 1973).

Privileged Communications: A Case by Case Approach," 23 *Maine Law Review* 443 (1971).

"Privileged Communications—News Media—a Shield Statute for Oregon?" 46 *Oregon Law Review* 99 (1966).

"Public and Press Rights of Access to Prisoners After Branzburg and Mandel," 82 *The Yale Law Journal* 1337 (1973).

"The Public Scholar and the First Amendment: A Compelling Need for Compelling Testimony," 40 *George Washington Law Review* 995 (1972).

"Reporter Has Unique Experience on Jury," 102 *Editor and Publisher* 34 (September 6, 1969).

"The Reporter's Privilege: A New Urgency," 1971 *Washington University Law Quarterly* 478 (1971).

"The Reporter's Privilege: Perspectives on the Constitutional Argument," 32 *Ohio State Law Journal* 340 (1971).

"The Right of Newsman to Refrain from Divulging the Source of His Information," 36 *Virginia Law Review* 61 (1950).

"The Right of Privacy: Normative-Descriptive Confusion in the Defense of Newsworthiness," 30 *University of Chicago Law Review* 722 (1963).

"The Right of the Press to Gather Information," 71 *Columbia Law Review* 838 (1971).

"The Rights of a Witness Before a Grand Jury," 1967 *Duke Law Journal* 97 (1967).

"Senators Stop Quiz into Reporter's Source," 85 *Editor and Publisher* 8 (May 10, 1952).

"Shield Legislation," 24 *RTNDA Bulletin* 4 (May 1970).

"Shield Legislation in the United States," *Freedom of Information Center Report* 3 (1968).

"The Shield Statute: Solution to the Newsman's Dilemma?" 7 *Valparaiso University Law Review* 235 (1973).

"Strong Newsmen's Shield Law Supported by Common Cause," *Common Cause Report from Washington.'*

"Symposium: The Question of Federal News Shield Legislation," 52 *Congressional Digest* 129 (May 1973).

"Television—the Art of 'Cut and Paste,' " 97 *Time* 56 (April 12, 1971).

"Testimonial Privilege for Representatives of the News Media: A Summary of Recent

Court Decisions, Proposed Federal Legislation and Compilation of State Laws,'' *Congressional Research* (November 14, 1972).

''Tinkering with the First,'' 9 *Trial* 34 (1973).

''Virginia Editor Jailed for Contempt,'' 65 *Editor and Publisher* 7 (January 9, 1932).

''Who's Hobbling the Press?'' 167 *The New Republic* 6 (December 16, 1972).

Index

About the Author

Maurice Van Gerpen is Professor of Political Science at Reedley College in Reedley, California. He is a specialist in public law.